PASSION, PROFIT, & POWER

Reprogram Your Subconscious Mind to Create the Relationships, Wealth, and Well-Being That You Deserve

Marshall Sylver

SIMON & SCHUSTER

New York London Toronto Sydney Tokyo Singapore

SIMON & SCHUSTER
Rockefeller Center
1230 Avenue of the Americas
New York, NY 10020

Copyright © 1995 by Marshall Sylver
All rights reserved,
including the right of reproduction
in whole or in part in any form.

SIMON & SCHUSTER and colophon are registered trademarks
of Simon & Schuster Inc.

Designed by Irving Perkins Associates, Inc.

Manufactured in the United States of America

1 2 3 4 5 6 7 8 9 10

Library of Congress Cataloging-in-Publication Data

ISBN 0-684-80178-7

Acknowledgments

On a project like this it is never easy to give enough credit where credit is due.

First and without a doubt I would like to thank my editor, Dominick Anfuso, for his belief against all odds that this book would be completed and for his late-night and weekend sessions that allowed this book to be finished on time. I know this is the first of many together and I would love to help put Giancarlo through college.

Second I would like to say thank you to all of the seminar attendees and people who trusted in my audio and video programs to increase the quality of their lives. It is because of you that this book was written. Your feedback and requests are what keep me going.

I thank Fern Lee for her faith in my lessons and for helping me get my message to everyone through my infomercial.

I thank Chris Petiprin for believing in me when no one else did. Aren't you glad you did? You deserve all the success you are now enjoying.

Thank you to Rich Carll, MacGyver, who can and does fix anything. You kept the computer purring when it shouldn't have been able to.

A big "You are totally loved" to my staff at Sylver Enterprises for knowing my ways and supporting me. You are the best team a person could have and it is with our collective hands that this book was written.

I thank all of my brothers and sisters for the lessons they taught me while I was growing up about the differences in human beings and the uniqueness of how we experience things. Each and every one of you is an example of what being family is supposed to be. I love all of you unconditionally and forever.

I thank my mother, Virginia, whose lessons make up the foundation of what I know to be true. Through your gentle love, patience, and guidance you have shaped the lives of not only your ten children, but also the lives of your sixteen-plus grandkids and all the people we come in contact with. The gift that you are to this planet is priceless and I vow to love you and care for you in the abundance that you deserve for as long as the universe exists.

I am eternally grateful to my brother Michel, who has been my right hand and confidant for the past eight years in particular. Thanks for wearing the spandex jumpsuit in my early magic shows. It was just a test of your loyalty. I am proud of your growth and focus and honored to be sharing this adventure with you. May you enjoy the life of a millionaire as much as I do.

Thanks to Cheryl Maxfield, my best friend, for your love, support, and faith. You are a goddess and the most special treat that I have ever had the pleasure of enjoying. The energy that you contribute to my life and the lives of all you touch is a testimony to the perfection of life. May you receive back the gifts that you give out a thousandfold.

Finally I acknowledge the God force in my life for the gifts and blessings that I have been given. May I continue to be guided in the ways of sharing my blessing in such a way as to multiply them for the use of all I meet on this planet and beyond . . .

To my family: my mother, Virginia; my brothers and sisters, Diana, Tim, Eileen, Robin, Fawn, Fred, Stacey, Marc, Mike; and all nephews and nieces present and future.

Contents

PROFIT

POWER

A Personal Letter from Marshall Sylver

Dear Friend,

Once upon a time two people were on the same path through the terrible black forest. One person had no idea where the path was going and was just hoping it ended up someplace he wanted to go. The other person knew for certain that this path led to the castle of outrageous fortune, satisfying relationships, and phenomenal emotional and physical health.

Both encountered many challenges, hardships, real and imagined demons along the way. Even though they both were on the same path they ended up in vastly different places. The one that didn't know where the path was going got frustrated, angry, and many times had doubts about whether he was on the right path. Because he had so many doubts he fought his battles with little enthusiasm or joy. Every setback seemed more severe, every challenge made him lose more belief in himself and what was possible.

The other person had a friend who had already been down the path and lived in the castle. The friend had told him that even though the path was filled with challenges it was worth the journey because the rewards were so great. The friend also gave him insights to learn from the journey and strategies to deal with the challenges as they arose. His friend also taught him how to enjoy the castle when he arrived so that he could live happily ever after.

The first person finally gave up and quit moving on the path. He became afraid of what might lie up ahead. He built a little hut to protect himself as best as possible from the beasts of the forest. After a time he began to believe that it was his destiny to stay in the forest and very soon he lost all ambitions other than those needed to merely survive. He always wondered what would have happened if he had gone just a little further down the path. He wondered if he would have found what he was searching for.

The second person kept meeting the challenges head-on. Each victory made him stronger. Each step on the path excited him more because he knew he was one step closer to his castle. Sure enough, the day arrived when the challenges became simple and he knew no matter what happened he could handle it. He reached the castle, he married the princess, he possessed all the gold, and he lived happily ever after.

Don't you wish you had a friend who could tell you what was at the end of the path? Wouldn't it also be more fun if you knew how to deal with the challenges that came up no matter how large they appeared to be? You do and it will be. Since I was and am just like you I am committed to helping you get more. I started my own journey down the path without the knowledge that there is indeed a castle. I had to learn the hard way what to do when the real and imagined demons arose. Since I have already been down the path and took special notes of the lessons I learned, I will now help you make your journey easier and much more fun.

Even though I know the path leads to a better place I cannot carry you, I can only teach and inspire you. You must take the first step. It is possible to have it all. You are in this very moment, by reading these words, taking the first step. It is with great joy and honor that I share with you these lessons, tools, and insights that will make your journey financially abundant, passionately satisfying, powerfully useful, and spiritually enlightening. The first steps on any path can be the toughest. When you start to experience your victories it will get easier and easier. I am certain that this book will impact your life positively and forever. Like a rocketship that changes its launch angle ever so slightly, you will now end up at a totally different destination.

Since thoughts are things, even just reading this book for fun will program you for success on your path. The language patterns, and the way that this book is formulated, will have massive impact on you *forever when you just read it now. Thank you for letting me be the man who helped you get everything that you deserve.*

Respectfully powerful,

Introduction

Imagine being able to face your greatest fears and move through them. Imagine being able to overcome your limitations, to believe in newfound powers and abilities, and to use those skills to create the life of your dreams. Imagine being able to duplicate the mind and thoughts, the body and physiology, and the emotional intensity of the ultrawealthy to produce wealth and financial abundance in your life. The process of Subconscious Reprogramming will allow you to keep your mind focused on your desires in life. You will not only learn this material, you will become it.

I believe that most people's challenges are from one of three areas. I call them: PASSION, PROFIT, & POWER! This book is divided into three sections.

The PASSION section teaches strategies for increasing the quality of your professional and intimate relationships with others. By learning how to magnetically draw others into your life you will find all the things you want in your life becoming more easily and readily available to you. Your connections and encounters with others will be more joyous and fulfilling.

The PROFIT section teaches the skills of the ultrawealthy. How to accumulate abundance and how to maximize material wealth. You will discover methods and practices to turn yourself into a money magnet and make more personal income than you ever thought possible. Money and the universal laws that govern its flow are principles that will spill over into the other areas of your life.

The POWER section will teach you to maximize your own personal force to obtain your desires. You will learn strategies to increase your physical energy, your personal happiness, and your appreciation of the wonderful, worthwhile, and impactive human being you really are! As you read this book you will learn to relax and enable your life to happen on purpose. You'll develop a calm and powerful presence and learn that power is for use.

I have designed the book in a series of easy-to-read chapters that will inspire you and guide you through the wonderful adventure called life. It is written to give you answers to the questions that stop most people from enjoying every moment of their lives. In essence, this is a handbook for living that allows you to get more enjoyment right now from the gifts you already have in your possession and how to create the gifts that you desire. It will enrich your personal life as well as your professional life.

Passion, Profit, & Power is unique because it both teaches you powerful life-enhancing skills, and it gives you instructions on the valuable process of Subconscious Reprogramming.

S.R. is easy to use. It not only educates you, it literally reprograms you on a subconscious level to have an overwhelming desire to take action on your new skills, to use them on a day-to-day basis, to create a life of abundance in the areas of relationships, money, and personal well-being. Part of the process of Subconscious Reprogramming is an extraordinary state of mental, physical, and psychological relaxation. In this relaxed state, you are most responsive to suggestions. At the end of this book I will give you specific steps to create your own Subconscious Reprogramming audiotapes to further reinforce your new skills and habits.

Your limitations, both physical and mental, are based on the programs that you and the outside world give to your subconscious mind. When you take charge and decide what will and will not affect you, you'll regain your power and you'll begin to tap in to your true potential.

In this book you will examine your current core belief systems and find what works and what doesn't work in your life. You will learn how to develop a new core belief system in yourself, and through my S.R. process you will be able to reprogram your new belief system into your subconscious mind to get the results you want out of your life immediately.

S.R. is the fastest way to get directly to your subconscious mind and change what you think. When you change what you think, you'll change what you do. Change wasn't meant to take a long time. You don't have to wait weeks to take charge of your life. In fact, ultimately, change will occur in the twinkling of an eye. In a single moment you'll decide you have had enough and you want more.

Don't you wish you could give yourself a suggestion to automatically do the things you desire most in life? Don't you wish you could give yourself a suggestion to automatically go to the gym, to stop smoking, to lose weight, to overcome any personal fear? Thousands of people just like you have already used S.R. to create a life of adventure rather than a life of maintenance. The dynamic tools and strategies that comprise this book are on the cutting edge of mind technologies and are the culmination of many years of the study of human psychology. Won't it be exciting to know exactly what to do to get what you want and have the burning motivation to begin doing it immediately? That's what this book has to offer you.

"Your life wasn't meant to be a struggle; it was meant to be an adventure. Start living the adventure now!"

Chapter 1

Choosing Reality

"Who said that every wish would be heard and answered when wished on a morning star? Somebody thought of that, someone believed it, look what it's done so far."

—From the song *"Rainbow Connection"* by Paul Williams, made famous by Kermit the Frog

"Everything begins in thought and what is reality is really only our interpretation."

—MARSHALL SYLVER

"Based on a True Story"

ACT ONE, SCENE ONE: The year is 1967. The scene opens on a poor family in the backwoods of rural Michigan. The old broken-down farmhouse has no running water, no phone, and no electricity. The mother and her ten children aged two to twenty-two are huddled around the dinner table. It's noticeable that no father figure is there. By candlelight we can see that the meal is a simple one. A makeshift apple cobbler made from the fruit of a single tree in the yard appears to be all the food this family will have at this meal.

CUT TO: Close-up on the faces gathered around the table. The older children appear to be sad and gloomy. Three of the children are far too young to understand the situation or show much emotion other than hunger. A close-up shot of the mother's face reveals that she is not sobbing and yet tears are leaking from her eyes despite her strong front. A final close-up on one young son who appears to be taking all of this in almost as if he were an outside observer. One of the sons starts to help himself and is stopped abruptly by the mother.

MOTHER: "Tim, don't take any food yet, we haven't said grace. Dear Father, we are grateful for the blessing that you have bestowed on this family. Even though there is no more food in this house we know that you will provide for us. We know that the challenges that we are encountering will make us stronger as a family. Protect us and guide us. Amen."

CUT TO: The kids scramble to dig into the small amount of food on the table. The mother sits back and watches, making sure that everything is shared and that everyone except maybe herself gets something to eat. When it becomes evident that there isn't enough, a close-up of the mother's face lets us hear her mutter something under her breath.

MOTHER: "Heavenly father, I know you will provide."

CUT TO: Suddenly there is a knock at the door. Who could it be at this time of the night? It's not like the house is a holiday destination. The oldest son rises to answer the door. When he does we see a neighbor with his arms filled with groceries. Behind him another neighbor, and another, and another, and another, until twenty bags of groceries have been delivered. The neighbors, knowing the family's challenges, have brought an abundance of food.

NEIGHBOR: "We thought you could use a little help and so we brought you a few things!"

CUT TO: The mother with tears of joy. The children laughing, dancing, and hugging and ripping open loaves of bread and other packages of food.

MOTHER: "God bless you! Thank you so much! Oh thank you, Lord!"

CUT TO: One young son looks up and absorbs the occurrences almost as if he were an outside observer.

Twenty-seven Years Later

ACT TWO, SCENE ONE: A montage of shots that look like an episode of *Lifestyles of the Rich and Famous,* all of them with the same central character. A man who bears a strong resemblance to the boy at the dinner table who watched as if he were an outside observer. We see him in a house on the ocean sitting in a hot tub on the roof. We see him getting out of a Rolls-Royce with a stunningly beautiful model-actress on his arm. We see him teaching thousands of people life-empowering knowledge and receiving standing ovations at sold-out events. There are shots of him teaching reprogramming skills to professional athletes, businesspeople, students, families, and others. We see him starring in a nationally aired television show as well as in a live stage show with dancers, multimedia video and lights, magical illusions, and more. Mostly we see him happy and healthy. A self-made multimillionaire with close relationships with his family and friends and a deep love and respect for his universe.

What you have just read is true. All of it. I wouldn't believe it either if I hadn't had the lead role. You see, the above script is my life. This book is how I rewrote my character and transformed it into a part that is a whole lot more fun to play. It's also about how you can do the same. My desire is that you will have as much fun with your life as I'm having with mine. If I can do it anybody can.

It wasn't until many years later that I realized the impact that day on the farm in Almont, Michigan, had. On that day I learned two things. The power of focused thought and the power of faith. This book is nondenominational. It is for anybody who wants more in their lives, no matter what their religious, spiritual, or political persuasion. It is the synopsis of many years of trial and error. Of severe heartache and mistakes. It is the culmination of paying attention to a confusing and oftentimes unforgiving universe and realizing that there is a way to win when you understand the game.

After studying most major religions and most transformational processes and techniques, I discovered the one common thread that ran through all of them: *thought*. It's thought that determines our faith. It's thought that interprets our life experience. It's thought that allows us to see some things and ignore others, and it's thought that decides how our bodies will respond.

The old farmhouse that was my first home didn't have electricity. What we did have was an oil-burning stove that in the winter all of us kids used to curl up beside to keep warm. We would sleep on the living room floor all snuggled up. The stove would get very hot and if you were to touch it you would get burned.

One night I was so cold that I accidentally brushed my arm against the hot stove in an attempt to get as close to it as possible. I needed to go to the hospital but my mother told me that I would be all right. My mom told me to rub the burn every day and believe it would heal. As I rubbed, I was to tell the burn that it would heal properly. She said if I did that, and if I believed in the power of healing, that my burn would heal and the skin would be clear. She was right. The third-degree burn that went from my elbow to my wrist is now just a little scar about the size of a quarter. It's my personal reminder of miracles.

I seldom get sick. To me when we get sick it's because we are off balance either physically, mentally, or emotionally. Any one of the three can make us very sick. Getting sick or bored or tired are all what are called **Non-Confronts**. It's the mind's way of creating a distraction so we don't have to deal with the issues that are going on in our lives. Other more subtle Non-Confronts are going to the bathroom, being forgetful, not hearing, or, in an extreme case, dying. I'm sure you're thinking, yeah right, and yet think of this: have you ever had a time when you realized you were so involved in what you were doing or was going on that you hadn't gone to the bathroom for hours? Have you ever heard of someone whose life mate died and a few months later they just gave up and died too? Everything begins in thought. A friend of mine recently created a cold in his system. When I saw him I asked him how he was doing. He told me that he needed a break from work. (Since he would never take the break unless he was sick, he made himself sick.) He also told me that he had talked to a few friends and that they had told him he should be prepared to be sick for the next four weeks. I told him that if he talked to someone who said he should be prepared to be sick for the next week he would get better faster.

How often do you hear someone say, "I think I can feel a cold coming on"? Think about that statement. You are giving signals to your body that you are getting a cold. As soon as you believe it, you will get the cold. I know a family that used to say every year, "We get sick every March," and sure enough every March they'd get sick.

After my burn experience I realized the value of faith in healing. Every time I feel a cold coming on and I begin to have the thought of sickness, I stop the thought and I immediately turn it around and focus on health. When you expect your body to heal itself, it will.

Let's take this one step further. Have you ever had this happen? You are walking along. You feel great physically but emotionally you are a wreck over some challenge in your life. Suddenly you turn around or you stoop to pick something up and you pull a muscle. You get upset, saying you didn't want this to happen, and yet your mind is already processing the fact that it happened and the pain grows worse by the minute and you become even more emotionally stressed out. The reason you pulled your muscle is that your body was feeling your emotional pain and it immediately developed its own pain too. This type of pain is another example of Non-Confronts. Since your mind was emotionally tense it created a tension in your body, and because your body was tense it put your muscles in a position to be injured.

The next time you go to a chiropractor or have a massage and they are working on a painful area, go into a relaxed mental state and see if any pictures and thoughts come up with the pain as they rub it out. For me, I have practiced this method so often I can usually tell you what the emotional or mental connection is. Do it and see what happens.

The only way faith can be relevant is by preparing the mind to receive it. Faith requires a firm and unquestioning belief in something for which there is little or no proof. How do we do that? By first being honest with ourselves and fulfilling our obligations to others. All we have is our word. When we don't fulfill agreements, we lose a little amount of faith. Do you know that statistics say we are the last generation that will do better economically than our parents? That's a statement for concern, especially for our children. How are they supposed to adopt a strong faith system? It's not going to come from the world; it is going to come from us. The greatest gift you can give to your children is to be a good example and help them to form a strong belief system in themselves so they will be able to handle the challenges in their life. (Also tell them not to believe in statistics.)

We can lose our faith by the actual words that we declare. Speak it and so it is. How often have your fears turned into reality? You fear something happening and it happens? We gain this belief when we're young. We either observed it in our parents or we adopted it ourselves and accepted it as truth. Children who are told that they are stupid, slow, and clumsy certainly learn to process information differently than children who are told they are geniuses who will grow up to be happy and rich. The same is true of adults. When you possess a belief or program that limits you, then it is easy to give up and say, "Hey, it's not my fault. I was born stupid." Until you decide what you will believe, you will continue to make the same mistakes over and over again. How many people do you know who have said, "I can't believe I did it again, I should know better by now"? With that type of thinking they *are* going to do it again. Until they take the "should" out of the statement and truly believe that they will *never* do it again, they will. Should implies something that we think would be good for us to do. **Should is what isn't, and we have to deal with what is.** What should have been is not necessarily what would have been, nor might it have been what was best for us.

Another important fundamental practice for me is to periodically analyze my beliefs. When I discover I am consistently responding in a way that doesn't serve me I relax myself and go back in time to the first instance I can remember responding that way. When I remember the reason I responded that way then, I can take action immediately and reprogram my thinking.

Here's a simple example of how one day I realized one of my own beliefs. Every morning I take a shower and I do a little two-step process. One, I tell myself that the shower is washing off all the dirt and burden from yesterday so that I can start anew. Two, I sing in the shower. I don't sing because I'm happy, I'm happy because I sing. One day while singing in the shower it occurred to me that I never take a bath. I know that there is no such thing as random thought. Even creative thought is stimulated by something. I closed my eyes and went back in time to see if I could discover the reason that I never took a bath. My journey took me to the back of the farmhouse that we used to live in. We had no running water and we had to get all our water from a sympathetic farmer down the road. I remember me and my siblings carrying five-gallon milk cans back home for the ten of us. We used this water for everything, including bathing. We always bathed in descending order. The oldest child would bathe first and then the next, then the next, and so on. I was seventh in line! I suddenly remembered how I hated to slide into that dirty water. I remember my mom or my sisters holding me while they tried to scrub me. I realized why I only took showers. After experimenting with a romantic bath in clean water, I realized my old programming was just that—old programming. Once I realized that, I understood why I never liked baths and by breaking the subconscious feeling I had programmed, I was able to reprogram my belief system to enjoy taking baths.

Do you have any emotional response that you would rather not have? This is an example of how I formed a belief about baths. The process is the same for any challenge that you have in life. Realizing these old belief systems and turning them into a positive experience, you establish a new belief system. The more knowledge that I take action on, the more my belief system keeps changing for the better.

EXERCISE: Take the time right now to think about something you respond to emotionally in a way that seems more than is appropriate. Maybe you get angry when someone is driving in a way you don't respect. Maybe you get frustrated and emotional when someone is late coming home. It might be that you get frightened by intimacy. Take the time right now and close your eyes. Let your body relax and go back in time to when you were a child. Since most programming occurred before the age of eight, chances are that the initial sensitizing event occurred before then. Once you have noted the situation that caused you to form the belief, say these words to yourself: "There is no reason for me to still respond as a child, I am safe now." Smile to yourself, open your eyes, and by the simple act of smiling you will begin to create a connection between the physical act of smiling and the emotional experience of feeling safe. So the next time you feel unsafe and you smile, you will again release the feelings of safety to your conscious mind. (This is the foundation of a process called a mind trigger which is explained more fully later in this book.)

One of my most vivid memories was the time that my mom decided to pack up everything we had in a car and a little trailer and move to California. The truth was we were moving because we couldn't afford to stay.

My mom took her last paychecks and bought an old run-down trailer. I thought it was a mistake at the time, yet my mother had the habit of just facing her challenges head-on. When she made up her mind she stuck to it. She made decisive, determined, decisions. This time it was moving to California.

On the road to California I learned many things. My first lesson came as I gazed in the back seat at my two younger brothers and my little sister sleeping one on top of the other. That's when we had our first of fifteen flat tires and I had another major spiritual shift in my life.

Mom pulled the car safely to the side. No one was hurt. I volunteered to go for help since I was the oldest child making the move to California. I was scared. We were a long way from home and I knew that someone had to be the strong one. I thought, how does my mother do it? As I ran to a clearing in the woods I came upon a farmer. Since the rim on the tire had split apart and was now wrapped around the axle I needed to borrow something that would cut through the metal. Well, everything worked out fine and the farmer was a real godsend. My mother was so grateful she gave him the last of the home-baked cookies. I said to myself, "She didn't have to give them all to him, did she?" Sharing. My mother explained to me that life is give-and-take. The farmer was nice enough to help us so we must give something back or nature won't provide for us in the future.

Suddenly, I knew what she meant. It was true. We didn't have much and still my mom always appreciated what she did have and was always thankful. In this moment I understood the expression "The Rich Get Richer." I contemplated the meaning of all this as I got back into the car. I must say I was quite proud that I had handled the first crisis that came up as head of the household.

Toward the end of our trip and certainly toward the end of our funds we came upon a car that was pulled over. The hood was up. My mother immediately stopped. I couldn't believe it. How are we going to help anyone? A man, his wife, and four kids were stuck. He had run out of gas. My mother offered to take him to the gas station and get gas. We unhooked the trailer and all the kids played as the three of us went for gas.

When we got to the gas station mom noticed that the man only put in seventy-five cents' worth of gas into a five-gallon can. When she asked what he was doing, he embarrassingly said that was all the money he had. My mother reached into her wallet and pulled out some money to fill up the can. The man looked at her as tears welled up in his eyes.

We took him back to his car and before we left my mother pulled out a little more money and told me to give it to the man. I knew we didn't have the money to give but my mother gave me this look that said don't argue. That moment, of my mother's blind faith that God and the universe would provide and the feeling of contributing to the well-being of others in need, had a profound and lifelong impact on me. My mother taught me how to take fear and turn it into faith. The power behind those actions has made all the difference in my life.

My mom taught me what to do without complaining. She taught me that all you really can do is deal with whatever comes up and make the best of it. She also taught all of us that we were responsible for our lives. She always let us make our own mistakes and silently stood by if we needed her support. She loved and continues to love us without judgment or conditions. All of her children know that we don't have to do anything special to warrant her love.

I'm sure that there have been many times that it has been a stretch for her to give that love unconditionally and yet somehow she still does. Regarding my father, she taught me that it is possible to not like someone's actions and still love the person. Her faith and her teaching me to always have faith have been the foundation for all that I teach today.

The ability to turn my fears and concerns into faith was an important moment in my life. I remember a client who was wrapped up in his fears so tightly that I had my doubts I could help him. He had lots of rationalized reasons for being so depressed. He found out that he had cancer, his wife left him for a younger man, and he lost his job all in the period of six months. He was stressed out and felt that he had lost all control over his life. He had degenerated from a very positive person with an excellent job into a negative and bitter man. After weeks of listening to his pain, I had a gut feeling to change the environment and we started taking walks while we talked. I usually take action on my gut feelings because they are more often right than wrong, even when I'm not sure why. I was acting on faith that the universe would show us the answers.

My gut feeling turned out to be the right move. During one of our walks in the park, my client started to notice people who were less fortunate than he but he still continued to complain about his bitter and lonely life. One day on our walk we ran into a young crippled child who was begging for money. My client looked at this young helpless boy and suddenly had a breakthrough. He had been stuck in his own situation and this little boy snapped him out of his own misery for a moment.

"I once was sad because I had no shoes until I met a man who had no feet."

—Old Saying

My client experienced sympathy for the young boy. He reached into his pocket and gave the kid twenty bucks. He was having the same spiritual shift I had when my mother and I were helping the man who ran out of gas. Do you see the similarities? What he was discovering in that very moment was there are many people worse off than himself. He suddenly stopped dwelling on his problems and began living his life by focusing on someone else. He realized that he had been thinking only of himself. He was stuck in his situation and so wrapped up in himself that he was blind to his own solutions. When this man started creating solutions in his life he discovered a new reality for himself and a better life. Now he says he can hardly imagine how bad off he was back then. He also learned that while we are in service to others we learn our greatest lessons.

Chapter 2

Subconscious Reprogramming and the Mind

Just how far can the mind go in its ability to enhance your life? My greatest challenge in helping people with their lives is getting them to take that first step in the right direction. Maybe you've gone through tough times and it feels like your life is beating you up. Maybe you never thought you really could have the things that you wanted. Then it gets harder to take that first step.

Everything begins in thought. When you take on the thoughts of a winner, you'll know how to win. When you turn up those thoughts loud enough, you will be motivated to take those actions. By pinpointing the mental, physical, and emotional habits of people that are creating what you want to create and then duplicating it, you can create passionate personal relationships, megawealth, and total self-empowerment.

If it's really that simple, what has stopped you until now from creating your life exactly the way that you want it? If you don't have what you want right now or if you want more, it's going to require some new action from you. In order for things to change, *you* must change them, because things aren't going to magically change in your life; it requires that you take a new and sometimes slightly scary action.

"Nothing has any power except the power that you give it."

There is a story about a man who was rowing upstream in a rowboat. As he was working hard to row against the current another man coming downstream ran into him and knocked him onto the shore. He cursed at the man coming downstream: "Why don't you watch where you're going!" he screamed. As he angrily began rowing upstream again another man coming downstream ran into him and threw him off course. Again he cursed: "You idiot, can't you see how hard it is for me to row upstream?" Once again he began rowing and once again another boat coming downstream ran into him. Except this time the offending boat was empty. Just as the man was about to curse the pilot of the other boat he noticed it was empty and didn't yell because after all who would waste their time getting angry at an empty boat. He simply put his boat back on course and continued his journey.

What if all the boats had been empty? What if he had just pretended that the other boats had been empty and instead of getting angry he just kept putting his boat back on course and kept moving toward his destination? How about you, are you getting angry or just putting your boat back on course and surrendering more quickly? Which do you think gets you to your destination more quickly and uses the least amount of energy?

No one can make you happy or sad or excited or angry unless you give them that power over your life. Decide right now to only give your power to those things, circumstances, and people that support you in getting what you want.

Even though you may not realize it, your subconscious is being programmed every day. The media and many forms of advertising have been subconsciously programming your mind and thoughts for years. People are paid millions of dollars to come up with ways of entering the consumer's mind for profit. Most people don't realize that they are responding to suggestions imposed on them by others every day of their lives. The people you come in contact with, the media, and the ways that you represent or interpret your circumstances and the occurrences of your life all affect the programs that you operate on. You might even use subconscious suggestions occasionally with a friend to inspire them to give you what you want, or if you are a parent you use it with your children.

Here is one example of how an ineffective program can impact your life. Many people have a hard time getting up in the morning. If you're that kind of person you actually have to give yourself a suggestion to make this difficult. I mean, how difficult is it to hoist yourself up, swing your legs over the side of the bed, and stand up? To make it difficult, you've got to convince yourself mentally that getting out of bed is laborious or you wouldn't stop yourself from doing so. How many of us hit that snooze button a few times to get more sleep?

When you've convinced yourself that it's hard to get up, or that it's difficult to stop smoking, or lose weight, or whatever your challenges are, you've responded to exactly what subconscious programs are, only in an ineffective way. All your life you've learned to noncritically accept suggestions. We all have. If you can teach your mind to make it difficult to get up in the morning, if you can train your mind to forget names the moment you hear them, if you can program your mind to need a cigarette, then you can also do the opposite. You can now train your mind to generate energy in your body. You can program your mind for instant and permanent memory. You can train your subconscious to want to work out or to stop smoking. You can train the mind to do anything you want it to.

To understand this process you need to realize that you have two distinct ways of processing information. You have a conscious mind and a subconscious mind. Your conscious mind is what I call the critical factor. It's the mind that's reading this material right now and determining whether the information I'm giving you is appropriate for you or not. It decides what is true or untrue, what's good or bad. Once the critical factor has decided how the information is to be interpreted, it allows it to pass through to the subconscious mind accordingly.

Your subconscious mind, on the other hand, is just a computer. It's noncritical. It isn't able to make judgments. When you learn to set aside your conscious mind and noncritically accept suggestions, change will become simple.

If you have ever used a computer you know that it takes a command literally. If you hit delete it deletes. If you hit save it saves. Even if you type in a command that is different from what you really want, it doesn't second-guess you, it just does as you have commanded or as it's been programmed to do. The sole job of your conscious mind is to determine critically what to believe and accept or what not to. It's the programmer that determines how the subconscious operates.

It's just as important to learn how to bypass or set aside your con-

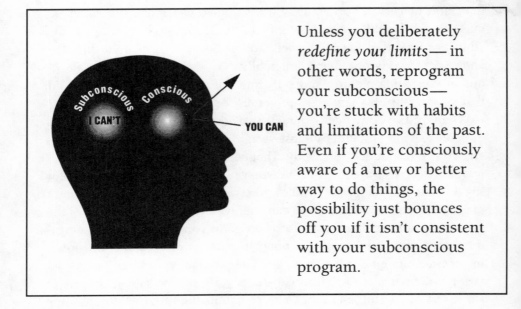

Unless you deliberately *redefine your limits*— in other words, reprogram your subconscious— you're stuck with habits and limitations of the past. Even if you're consciously aware of a new or better way to do things, the possibility just bounces off you if it isn't consistent with your subconscious program.

scious mind to those thoughts, beliefs, and programs that can serve you. Most people believe that there is no way to choose what to believe. Whether it seems like it or not, you are the only one who chooses what you think. After all, if you aren't, who is? You can decide in any moment what truths you will hold and how those truths affect you. Let's begin by examining how the mind works.

> **Experience–Thought–Belief–Habit–Life: "An experience creates a thought; when reenforced (through other similar validation) or repeated it becomes a belief/program. Our beliefs (programs) create our habits and our habits become our life."**

Every thought you think creates a psychosomatic or physiological response. It is impossible to think a thought and not have your body respond to it on some physical level. When you think something and act upon it as if it were true, what you believe to be true becomes true for you. You absolutely must change what you think to change your life. It is your representations of life and not what is actually happening to you that determine the quality of your life. Any thought held firmly in the subconscious mind will reveal itself in a very real and physical form.

"It is impossible to think something and not have it affect your physical world in some way."

Here's an exercise for you. As you proceed, open your mind up and create a positive mental expectancy of what the results are going to be. Find yourself a piece of string or yarn between twelve and eighteen inches long. Once you've done that, tie that piece of string or yarn to a weight such as a finger ring or a set of keys or something similar.

Place one hand beneath your homemade pendulum so it's about an inch away. Look directly at the weight on the end of the string and visualize. Imagine in your mind's eye that the pendulum begins to move back and forth. See the motion back and forth, back and forth. Let your eyes trace the path you want the pendulum to travel. The more you visualize it, the more you use your imagination, the more the pendulum will move. Allow your mind and eyes to trace that path that you desire the pendulum to move. As you concentrate, the pendulum will indeed begin to move back and forth. In fact, the more you concentrate the more it swings back and forth.

Stop reading now and do this exercise. One of the values of this exercise is to learn concentration. Your mind should be completely focused on moving the pendulum. Once you have the pendulum moving back and forth, I want you to begin concentrating on moving the pendulum in a circle. Again, look directly at the pendulum and see it, visualize it moving in a circle. Concentrate. Imagine, again let your eyes trace the path you want the pendulum to travel. See the circle getting larger and larger and larger. The more you concentrate, the more the pendulum will move. Stop the pendulum now with your hand. What caused the pendulum to move?

What you expect, you tend to realize. What you believe, is true. As long as you believe the pendulum will move and you concentrate on the movement and visualize the direction you want it to move you will cause the most minor movement in your arm. We call that psychosomatic movement. The pendulum moves psychosomatically.

"Psychosomatically" is derived from "psycho," the mind, and "soma," the body. Actually, it's your mind causing your body to move slightly. Your mind will cause your arm to move just enough to produce that movement in the pendulum. Your mind always moves in the direction of its dominant thoughts, and as long as you truly believe the pendulum will move, it will. Practice this again when you are finished reading. Master the art of causing the pendulum to move and take note of how well you concentrate.

This process is valuable to help you focus your mind and to completely concentrate on one thing only. This type of concentration is necessary when learning how to completely relax the body, which is the first process you need to learn in my Subconscious Reprogramming system. You go through a similar highly suggestive state twice a day, once as you awaken and once as you go to sleep. It's that point right before you sleep and right before you awaken when your mind, body, and spirit are still relaxed. In this relaxed state you are most responsive to suggestions.

"Trance or Subconscious Reprogramming is the noncritical acceptance of ideas or concepts on a subconscious level."

When you receive information from an outside source (other people, the media, and so forth) and you accept it as truth, that's programming. At the same time, when you say things to yourself, in your own head, that's self-programming.

You are being programmed on a daily basis. Thousands and thousands of bits of data are being processed by your mind both consciously and unconsciously. Begin now to recognize that any information you receive through your sensory-input mechanisms (eyes, ears, etc.) is a potential program. The moment you believe, and accept it as truth, you have been programmed. Conversely, anytime you communicate information to another person that they accept to be true you have programmed them. If someone were to say to you, "Do you ever notice how you always forget someone's name the moment you hear it?" and you agree with that person, you have programmed the software of your subconscious computer and told it that you want it to "forget names the moment you hear them."

Subconscious programs are any information that is noncritically accepted to be true. Particularly any "I" or "I am" statements said to ourselves or any "you" or "you are" statements said by others to us that we accept as truth. As you read this book you will learn to break down your belief system and decide what you want to reprogram about yourself. Whatever the ineffective habit is, you will learn how to reprogram that thought and change the habit to an effective one. Throughout this book you will learn the elements of Subconscious Reprogramming.

Chapter 3

Mastering the Rules of the Mind

To gain more power in your life you need to know how your mind operates and how to get it to operate the way that you want it to consistently. I know that you probably have, at some time in your life, read other books, listened to tapes, or attended seminars that were supposed to get you rich, make you a super-lover, heal your life, teach you enlightenment, or do something else that you greatly desire. While many of them probably had some ideas and concepts that could help you, they probably didn't. I know that you know how to stop smoking—quit putting that thing in your mouth. I know that you know how to lose weight—eat less and move more. I know that you know how to make more money—inspire others . . . etc., etc., etc. It's not that you don't know how. It's just that until now you haven't been able to get yourself to take consistent action toward what you want. Until now.

Let's imagine you want to get from point A to point B. Also imagine that the road is straight and long and you could walk it. You have seen others use a car before, only you yourself have never driven one. You know that the car is a useful tool to speed up your journey, so you make an attempt to teach yourself how to drive. You get in the car. The first thing you do is start pushing pedals, turning the steering wheel, pressing buttons and so forth. Since you don't know the first thing about driving a car, most likely you probably are either going to get frustrated or lucky. If you get frustrated, it is going to take you twice as long to get to point B since you have already wasted time trying to get the car moving.

You might even get completely annoyed and decide that contrary to what you have seen others do with a car that it's just a trick and cars don't really work the way they appear to.

On the other hand, maybe you fumble around and accidentally turn the key. Maybe it stalls as you try to get it in gear. Then after much trial and error you finally figure out what the steering wheel does, what the gas pedals and gear shifts do, and what the brakes are for.

Once you have learned how the car operates, all of your journeys from this point on will be more enjoyable and stress-free. In fact, learning how to drive the car will allow you to go more places than you ever imagined. You will be able to see and do much more than those who never learned to drive. Now that you learned how to drive it will be easier to navigate the road and to go further faster.

Most people learned how to drive from others—people who had already mastered the process and figured out the controls. Your mind is the car. The place you want to go, the habit or discipline you want to create, the outcome you want to achieve, they are the road. Knowing the road you want to go down is not enough—you must learn how to drive the car. The same applies to life. If you want to lose ten pounds and you keep eating fatty foods, then it will take you a longer time to get to your destination. Although you could create the success habits that you want through sheer mental force, you would probably be too exhausted to enjoy your destination once you arrived.

When you now begin to understand how your mind operates you will be able to quickly and easily change your actions on a consistent basis and get what you want. It will astound you how fast you get the results that you are looking for. When you can transform your habits with a snap of your fingers you will always be operating on all cylinders. Much like driver education, I've created some rules of the mind. Understanding these rules will allow you to use your mind as the powerful tool it really is.

RULES OF THE MIND

RULE NO. 1: **What you expect tends to happen.**

Those things you think about most tend to happen. What you focus on expands. Have you ever noticed that as you were thinking about purchasing a certain new car that everywhere you looked it appeared as if everybody else was driving that vehicle? Your mind will move in the direction of its dominant thought, and what you expect, you tend to realize. You will notice what you are thinking about. If I asked you to count the number of ducks at a lake you would probably not pay much attention to the number of geese.

RULE NO. 2: **Imagination is more powerful than knowledge.**

I wish I could take credit for that, only it was Albert Einstein who said it. What he meant was if a person believes something, it supersedes reality. It's true for them and they will operate in their "believed reality" as if it were true. If a woman believes that her man is cheating on her she will treat him as if he is and probably drive him to do so. Some people live as if the thing they are imagining has already happened. In any case it may as well have happened since they are living their life that way.

RULE NO. 3: **Every thought or emotion has a physical reaction.**

Have you ever gotten scared and felt the hairs on your neck stand up? I am sure you have known someone—maybe yourself—who caused such stress in their life that they created stomach ulcers. When you're angry it could stimulate your adrenal glands and cause your pupils to dilate or give you goose bumps. It's just the same as when you get a hug from someone you love. It can make you feel warm on the inside and actually release endorphins into your system, which help heal physical ailments.

Rule No. 4: A belief programmed into the subconscious mind will remain until it's replaced by another idea.

I have already told you that your subconscious mind operates like a computer; without judgment. Unlike a computer, though, it is made of organic material, so the impressions made on the "hard disc" have a more lasting impression. When it runs a particular program over an extended period of time it grows to hold that program more securely. Like someone who stoops all the time will find it difficult to stand up straight, the longer an idea is set in the subconscious mind, the tougher it is for the critical or conscious mind to replace it. When you begin to use any muscle differently it may resist at first until it is accustomed to the new range of motion. This doesn't mean it's impossible, it just means you need to be aware of what you are dealing with.

We have mental and physical habits. To perform a physical habit, we must first form the mental habit. In other words, we must think before we can act. If we wish to change a physical habit or action we must first change the mental habit or thought. Some people believe that cigarettes calm them down. This is totally incorrect. Since nicotine is a stimulant it couldn't possibly relax the nervous system and yet since most people associate smoking with pleasurable situations such as dancing or social-izing or dining, the cigarette has become the post-hypnotic suggestion or a mind trigger to positive psychosomatic reactions within the body. The body overrides the power of the nicotine to relax the nervous system.

Rule No. 5: The less the conscious effort, the more the subconscious mind will respond.

When you are forcing yourself to do something that is unnatural to who you believe you are, it is difficult to maintain the new habit. There's really nothing such as pure will power. If you've ever tried to go to sleep at night and you focused on sleeping you realized that falling asleep became impossible. In fact, the more you focused on sleeping, the less you could sleep. The more you thought about going to sleep the more you tossed and turned. The key in getting yourself to sleep at night is to allow yourself to focus on one thing, such as the incredible outcomes you want in your life. I promise you that you'll easily and readily drift into sleep when you focus on the positive things that you want.

If you have ever tried to lose weight or quit smoking you've realized that forcing yourself to do something makes it harder to do it. To reduce conscious effort you must program your mind to believe the new action or attitude is natural. In other words, a program about who you are instead of what you do is more powerful. (Examples: "I am a non-smoker" versus "I don't smoke." "I am a multimillionaire whose money has not been deposited in my bank account" versus "I can make money.")

RULE NO. 6: Each new program makes later programs easier to accept.

Minor victories lead to major victories. Small commitments lead to large commitments. An object in motion tends to stay in motion, whether it's a speeding car, an emotion, a habit, or a belief. Success breeds success. When you begin to accept your own ability to change this new program, you cause all future programs to be implemented more easily. Just by believing that changing habits is easy you begin to make it so. Also as you begin using Subconscious Reprogramming to create new habits and disciplines, you will find that the creation and implementation of these new beliefs will become literally instantaneous. When programming your mind, any win is a move in a positive direction. Ask yourself right now: "What's positive, powerful, and productive and moves me in the direction I want to go?" Do something now.

RULE NO. 7: Your body will produce what your mind believes.

Since every single function of your body is controlled by your thought process, an extended emotional belief can actually cause organic changes. The more you focus on something the more likely it is to show up in your body. That's what we call "dis-ease" or disease. Mental anguish can cause physical dis-ease. I had a client in who kept talking about what a pain in the neck his family and his job were. Five years later, it was discovered that he had cancer in his neck. That's how powerful your mind really is.

RULE NO. 8: Your mind seeks validation for previous beliefs.

Since your mind moves in the direction of its dominant thoughts your mind can only respond to the things that you think about, and it responds most quickly and openly to suggestions that are similar to preceding suggestions or beliefs. That which we seek we do find. If you look for the bad in an individual or a situation your perceptions of that quality will be heightened. When you look for the bad, that's what you'll find. When you find the bad, it reinforces that previous thought structure and will move you further in that direction of those negative feelings about that person or that situation.

The same is true in the positive sense. When you look for what's working in your life it expands. When you expect the best in others and look to what they are doing right, you will hardly notice what they are doing that isn't what you want and everybody ends up winning.

Chapter 4

In a Perfect World

"Determine where you are going and how you get there will become obvious."

—Marshall Sylver

Thoughts are things. They have form. They can motivate people to move mountains. They can confine people tighter than chains or prisons. They can inspire us to create miracles, and the newspapers are full of stories about the demons thought has created. Thoughts are things. Thoughts are chosen. You weren't born with issues and problems. You created them. When I was a child and we didn't have running water or much food I didn't know that it could be otherwise. A fish never knows it's in water. On the day we were eating apple cobbler because there was no other food in the house I was happy. It's not every day you get to eat dessert for dinner. I didn't know it was all we had.

Many people stay in fear because it's all they know. It's how they've been programmed from childhood. As children many people feared the dark, feared being hurt, feared the unknown, nuclear war, crime, sickness, and especially feared God. When you live in a world of fear you are blinded to the light. You will not have the courage or the desire to find the passion for life that you deserve. Society does its best to program you to hold on to fear. Yes, it's possible to see life as a helpless situation. In fact it is easier to believe that you might as well not even make an attempt since it's not likely that you will get what you want. You might even say to yourself, "Even if I had my life in order what does it matter? Some outside force could easily wipe me and the world out tomorrow.

What's the use?" I know that it is possible to see life that way, and yet is it effective? You have the power to control how you think and you must use that power.

Programming is partly understanding that the mind doesn't interpret unless it has a pre-established basis of comparison. Like a computer it can only run the software that was put there. No software means an inability to open that file. Since most of your foundational programming was put in place before the age of eight it was most likely put there by someone else. Your first programmers were your parents, your siblings, or any other person you held as an authority figure. Anyone who you believed laid down beliefs that you have accepted most of your life to be true. Many books teach that you must "heal the child within." I've got news for you. Unless you're pregnant there ain't no child inside you. What is inside you are the programs that were created when you were a child. Since it's impossible to go back, the question has to be, "How can I use what happened to me as a child to benefit me now?" As a child on that cold winter night when there was no food and I saw my mother's tears, I made a decision never to see my mother's tears again if there was any way I could help it. I know that one of the reasons I have been driven to create wealth in my life is so that she would never want again.

"Even if you could never *fix* what's wrong with your life, what stops you from creating everything that you want?"

Years ago, I had a friend who called and told me that he was in financial difficulties. He asked if I could lend him some money. I make it a habit never to lend money that I wouldn't plan to give away. I'd rather not lose friendship over money. So to assist him I lent him the money he requested and made the mental note to surrender if I never got it back and to be joyous if I did. Anyway, a few months after I lent this friend money he called again with another hard-luck story. It was then that I realized that lending him money (actually giving him money) wasn't supporting *my* desire to help mankind *or his* desire to be self-sufficient. My friend had put into his belief system that everyone would help him out of his difficulties. Lending him the money was not helping him. It was impeding his learning process. I chose not to lend him the money and when he got angry, I explained my analysis and I was able to get him to own up to his problem. Later in this book I will share with you the clues of success and you'll learn that projection is one of the most effective ways to determine if you are supporting or inhibiting yourself and others through the programs and beliefs that you hold to be true.

Programming is also understanding that the mind has a tendency to go toward pleasure and to run away from pain. Throughout this book I am going to give strategies to not only get what you want, I am also going to challenge you to make the price of not getting what you want very painful. It's kind of like putting salt in your own wounds. People reach a point of readiness for change when they reach their own personal bottom. When things get as bad as it seems they can get, only then do most people do anything about it. For myself I have found that it can be very useful to "crash myself" or speed up the downward cycle. This doesn't mean if your problem is overeating that you should gorge yourself, or if you are a workaholic you should destroy your marriage. (Although you'd probably pay attention then, wouldn't you?) What this means is that you let your mind take you down the path your current actions would take you and then decide if that's where you want to be.

I have something very personal to share with you that I've never talked about in public before. It's something that I'm not proud of and yet it's my belief that by sharing this with you that you will know my level of commitment in teaching you how to take charge of your life. When my family moved from Michigan to California I was fourteen and in the ninth grade. The move was a considerable culture shock to me and the first year we lived in California all I could think about was getting back to Michigan. I went from being the coolest guy in school to being one of the biggest geeks. I didn't change and yet I just had no clue how to fit into the Southern California lifestyle without compromising myself. My clothes weren't right, my hairstyle wasn't hip, and I guess the kids at the city school just kind of viewed me as a country bumpkin.

In an effort to fit in I succumbed to peer pressure and began experimenting with drugs. It was tough on kids then and I know from my sixteen nephews and nieces that it's even tougher today. I wanted to be accepted by the kids at my new school so bad that I leaned on the drugs to let me fit in socially. The desire to be in with the in crowd got me into a lifestyle that never served me and never serves anyone. Even though consciously I knew it was bad for me, I, like most young people, thought I was indestructible. For about six years until my early twenties

I used drugs on a fairly regular basis. By then I wanted to stop but didn't know how. Whether it's cigarettes, overeating, alcohol, being a workaholic, or drugs, if it doesn't help you it hurts you.

One day I was up early in the morning watching a sunrise. This was just before I made a full-time commitment to serving others. I had been studying hypnosis and Subconscious Reprogramming for six years. I told myself that if Subconscious Reprogramming really worked now was the time to use it. I knew if I could change my habit I could teach anyone else to do the same.

I closed my eyes and went into my relaxed state. First I went back and experienced fully all of the times that drugs had held me back from accomplishing the things that I had wanted. I focused on remembering all the details clearly, particularly the very painful ones. I wanted to remember. Next I let my mind travel forward into the future to experience what one year, five years, ten years of the same behavior would mean in the course of my life. I noticed how my skin and body had aged prematurely. I saw myself trying to explain to my children not to do what their dad was doing. I saw them grow up and use drugs and their children use them too. I took note of the fact that my finances were drained, that the people I hung out with were all underachievers like me because they just didn't have the energy to excel. I made the experience as bad and as painful as possible. I let myself feel the emotions. Sitting on the beach I began to sob and cry. I didn't care who saw me—I was doing this for me!

Just when I knew I had turned up the pain as far as I could I jumped up and spoke these words, "It's easy for me to change!" I asked myself, if you could change at any moment which one would it be? The answer was a resounding NOW! Then I snapped the fingers of both hands to give myself a mind trigger. A signal to my brain to begin the change process. I then said out loud, "I am free at last!" I opened my eyes for a few moments and looked at my world as the new person that I knew I now was. I moved and smiled and stood in my now healthier body the way someone who had just made a massive shift would. I sat back down and took a deep breath. This time I let my face smile with the radiant joy of someone who has made a major breakthrough. I closed my eyes and went back into my relaxed state.

This time I went into the future knowing it would be without drugs. I saw that I had more energy, that I was more creative and able to get more of the things that mattered to me done. I saw that my bank account was huge because of the money I saved and because I was more effective every day. I saw that my friends were active, healthy, motivated people who got high on life and were genuine. I experienced for the first time since I was a child a sense of wonder and playfulness that created an endorphin rush that stimulated my mind and body greater than any drug ever could. I then fired off my mind trigger again. I snapped both of my fingers simultaneously and said, "Yes, it was easy for me to change."

The next few weeks had their share of new learning experiences. First I learned that quite a number of my friends and I had nothing in common once I had changed my lifestyle. Second, I found out that when you tell someone that if they ever sell you drugs again you will turn them over to the police they don't ever sell you drugs again. (Talk about burning the ship you went to war in!) Now that I wasn't numbing myself anymore I realized that I had a lot of extra time on my hands that I could use to focus on the things that mattered to me. I had always hypnotized myself to believe that the drugs were a way to relax. (Remember, whatever you train your mind to believe to be true , the process of hypnosis.) Little did I know that because they were draining me physically, financially, and emotionally, they were actually the source of much of my stress. When I became free over a decade ago I realized that any habit or belief could be changed or created using this same process.

I call this method of change E.S.P. It stands for Ebenezer Scrooge Process. Did you ever read *A Christmas Carol* by Charles Dickens? Do you remember when the Ghost of Christmas Future showed Scrooge where his life was going and it inspired him to change it? This strategy works the same way. I also named it the E.S.P. because it causes you to predict the future. Predicting the future is really quite simple when you know the past. Remember, an object in motion tends to stay in motion, whether it's a baseball, a relationship, or a life.

Here's how you use E.S.P.:

1. Define the habit or belief you want to change. Remember to define it in what you want instead of what you don't want. ("I eat only when I'm physiologically hungry," instead of, "I don't eat when I'm bored.")
2. Make a list on paper of times that the old habit or belief stopped

you from getting what you wanted and enjoying your life fully. (Putting these on paper first will make it easier to recall later when you are in your relaxed state.)

3. List the areas of your life that would positively be impacted by the change. (Examples: "Losing weight will save me money, attract more relationships or improve the quality of existing ones, improve my self-esteem, give me more energy for work and play, let me live longer.")

4. Say the words "It's going to be easy for me to change." This creates a positive mental expectancy and creates a program for your subconscious mind to follow. Go into a relaxed state by closing your eyes and focusing your attention on each of your body parts, starting with your feet and progressing upward. The more relaxed you are the more effective this will be. (For a free copy of a fractional relaxation script to aid you in this process, contact my office at 1-800-92-POWER.)

5. Turn up the pain by reliving moments from your past when the old belief or behavior stole happiness and joy from you. Let yourself remember in vivid detail the occurrences. Let it depress you and let your self get emotional. *The purpose is to feel bad.*

6. Let yourself mind-travel into the future on this path and experience how five years, ten years, twenty years on this path would feel. Again, let yourself feel the emotions. Go through the pain. Make it feel bad, get depressed, get angry, make it as bad as you are willing to take it.

7. At the peak of the pain stand up and say, "It's easy for me to change!" "It's easy for me to change" is actually a master program since once it is accepted by the subconscious mind all other programs will be accepted with greater ease. Simultaneously, fire off a mind trigger. Mine is a double-snap. Yours could be a hand clap, a tug on your ear, or anything that you determine you will always respond to when you fire it off. Open your eyes and act as if the change has already occurred. Smile and be proud of the new you.

8. Take a deep breath and close your eyes again. Go into your relaxed state and let your mind project forward in time on your new path. Let your mind see how this one distinction so completely enhanced so many areas of your life. Let yourself feel the

emotion of joy and celebration. While you are visualizing this, let yourself laugh out loud, grin from ear to ear, and feel the passion for life and living that you deserve. When you are at your peak state of pleasure, fire off your mind trigger again and again.

9. Open your eyes and smile. Say out loud, "It was easy for me to change!" By speaking in the past tense you are letting your subconscious mind know that you have already accepted that the change is permanent.

In retrospect I realized that even though I was considered to be successfully meeting many people's standards, a part of me was a scared, sad man. I was one of the top-rated young magicians in the country, I was a radio personality, I had my own business, and yet I was still afraid that I would never amount to anything. Since my vision was so big I was afraid that even if I got some of my dreams I would never get them all and I would feel like a failure. As long as I had an excuse of why I hadn't succeeded no one could blame me for not getting what I wanted. That day on the beach shifted me in many ways.

One of the residual effects was that I started to realize that people who don't get what they want either really don't want it or are afraid to get the thing that they want. Here's an example. Let's say someone comes to me and says, "I want to stop smoking." I say, "Quit putting cigarettes in your mouth and lighting them." They say, "Hey, it's not that easy." I say, "Sure it is. It's a lot more work to put a cigarette in your mouth than it is not to." When a person really wants to stop smoking they just stop. They lose interest in smoking. It's easy to make yourself do something or not do something. It's only difficult to make yourself do something long-term unless you have actually become the person you want to become. In other words, if you were to program your mind to believe you have quit smoking you can always start again. Quitting something doesn't preclude the possibility of starting. On the other hand, when you program your mind that you have become a nonsmoker you have changed yourself instead of the action of smoking. One is a change of your habit; the other is a change of you. You have cured the cause instead of bandaging the effect. You are a product of all your habits.

A man was sitting in his home one day when he noticed the roof was leaking. He placed a pan under the leak and then suddenly noticed another leak. He grabbed another pan and then noticed two more leaks. Soon he was running around frantically trying to catch the water so as not to ruin his rug. If he had only looked outside he would have seen it wasn't raining at all. The truth was that his sprinkler had gotten turned around and it was soaking his roof. Rather than catching the water he could have just turned off the sprinkler. Cause and effect. Every action you do either consciously or subconsciously is motivated by thought. Every one of them. Thought is the cause, the action is the effect. Even thinking something is caused by thinking something else first. You want to change your life? Change the thought or program.

"When you change your habits you change who you are. Better still, when you change who you believe you are you will automatically change your habits."

Since what you believe is true for you, I want you to close your eyes and say out loud, "My mind is open and responsive to new ideas and concepts." Go ahead and say it now . . . You see it's not enough to learn. Knowledge is not power: **the ability to take action on knowledge is power.** Say it three times: "My mind is open and responsive to new ideas and concepts."

I also ask you to start being honest with yourself and ask yourself some soul-searching questions. What has stopped you until now from creating your life exactly the way that you want it?

There have only been two reasons that someone would want something in their life and not get it. First, they really don't know what to do. Second, they know what to do but can't get themselves to do it consistently if at all. With the knowledge in this book and through S.R. you will be able to accomplish both. You will gain the specific strategies and characteristics of people who have massive success in their lives and it will teach you the mental, physical, and emotional balance necessary for a healthy existence. At the end of each section, I have included words and phrases that will inspire you on a subconscious level to break old programming habits and obtain a more proactive way of life. The S.R. scripts can be recorded on cassette and played back for even greater impact. This book will also teach you how to create your own custom programs specific to your desires and plans.

Our belief system gets planted early in life. Our belief system is measured by how we interpret the situations in life from childhood. Your belief system can make you a hero or a villain. I don't feel that it's our environment that creates belief systems, it's how we view life and interpret situations in our life that establishes our belief system. If it was the environment, then all children would be more alike, whereas in real life, one family member might live a happy and fulfilled life and the other member might be frustrated and unfulfilled. It's also not occurrences. People have similar occurrences all of the time and have different perceptions of what actually happened. It all comes down to how they allowed the circumstances and their environment to program them. What they chose to believe to be true and what they denied.

When you analyze the past you will discover that often beliefs are unfounded, ineffective, and untrue. If someone said that you were stupid all the time, and you gave power to that belief, you will go through life thinking and believing that you are stupid. You've accepted that belief system as a reality. This belief system would actually impede your ability to think and to process information.

So what's real for one person might be completely different for someone else. For example, when I was a teenager I used to do volunteer work part-time after school. I used to stop at one house where two elderly sisters in their seventies lived. Both widows and living a comfortable lifestyle, these two sisters had shared their whole lives together and yet their views of life were completely different.

The older sister, by two years, had found her second youth. She rode a bike, she belonged to a bridge club, she was active in church and other social events. She loved to travel. She was happy doing everything that she could. She didn't have enough time to do everything she wanted. Her younger sister constantly complained that she was never at home and if she knew what was good for her she would slow down.

The younger sister was just the opposite. She seldom left home. She walked and acted like an old lady. For her, life was winding down. She was tired and she really was waiting to die. Her positive belief system in herself was nonexistent. Why did her older sister have such a healthy outlook on life and she didn't? I believe it was their belief systems that they individually adopted when they were young. It is up to you to create your own happiness in life. In order to do that you must have a strong belief system in yourself and a spiritual appreciation and understanding for God and trust in the universe to provide, and it will come to pass.

What I found out to be true for myself is that the opposite of fear is faith. Find faith in yourself. Learn to believe in yourself. Discover what makes you passionate about life. Explore what you love. Discover what gives you the ability to wake up in the morning and feel like seizing the day. "**To thine own self be true.**" Faith is creating a belief system in your personal life that will carry over into your intimate, professional, and spiritual life so you will have the passion for life that leads to success in all areas of your life.

Be like the sister who created a life of adventure rather than a life of maintenance. My proven methods, characteristics, techniques, strategies, and skills will help you achieve all your desires in life.

It is time to analyze your belief system. What old belief habits are holding you back in your life today? What belief habits have been holding you back all your life?

EXERCISE: Fill in the Blanks

Rule #1: What we expect _____ __ _____.

Rule #2: Imagination is more powerful than _____.

Rule #3: Every thought or emotion has
a _____ _____.

Rule #4: A belief will remain until it's replaced
by _____.

Rule #5: The less the conscious effort
the _____ __ _____ _____ will respond.

Rule #6: Each new program makes later
programs _____ __ _____.

Rule #7: Your body will produce
what _____ __ _____.

Rule #8: Your mind seeks _____ for previous beliefs.

Chapter 5

Creating Your Destiny

"Who were you on the day you were born?"

—MARSHALL SYLVER

Years ago when I first made a commitment to serving others I also made a decision that regardless of where I was now I would create my life exactly as I wanted it. Elvis Presley has always been a hero of mine. He was one of the greatest entertainers the world has ever known. He was a Cinderella kid who went from rags to riches doing what he loved. On the day he was born did he know he was Elvis? What I'm wanting you to ask yourself is at what moment did these beings such as Elvis realize who they were? And didn't the realization determine their existence from that point onward?

I believe that David Copperfield is one of the most phenomenal magicians of all time. Did he know that he would become a megastar or did it just happen? I think that at some point a long time ago he knew without a doubt who he was. Many years ago I woke up in the morning with a rush of adrenaline. I realized that I was the greatest hypnotist of all time. My critical mind kept trying to interject, "You're just being egotistical," it told me. I said to myself, "Hey, someone has to be the greatest hypnotist of all time, how about me!" I started to really ask myself that if I was the greatest hypnotist of all time, if that was my destiny, would I do things any differently than I was doing them now? Many things popped into my head. I knew in that moment that as long as I carried the thought of who I really was I could never go back to my old self. I got really excited. I knew in that moment that I could lead an outrageous life. Not one of moderate love, passion, wealth, and fulfillment. I could create a life of total pleasure and service. For years I had been setting goals that were obtainable from where I was and yet not exciting. I wondered if I were in a higher place, would I be setting higher goals for myself. I thought it might be exciting to take a peek into the future of the greatest hypnotist of all time and see what exciting things I had in store. How hard would you work if you knew absolutely for certain what would happen? How motivated would you be if you knew positively that daily exercise for three weeks would get you on the path to create the body you've always wanted? If you knew that you were going to eventually get everything you wanted, wouldn't that remove any stress from today? Certainly you would let your life happen on purpose and realize that all of those little things don't really matter. I'm going to tell you a secret. Be sure not to share this with everyone you come in contact with. *Everything is going to turn out perfect.* There is nothing you can do to change it. You may think at some other time you are messing things up and yet **everything happens for a reason and it serves you.**

Not only is everything going to be perfect but thinking that things won't be creates them that way. Since reality is created through validation, and validation is created by the things you put your attention on, then the belief that things aren't unfolding perfectly makes you less effective and takes away from your personal enjoyment of the moment. What you think and do today determines how tomorrow is going to be. When you have already determined how tomorrow is going to be, it makes today more fun.

When I first decided to do a national infomercial I encountered huge challenges. In the beginning everyone told me that no one would want to buy the product that I was selling. Finally I found someone who wanted to do the program but they wanted everything. They wanted most of the profits, they wanted to own me for five years, and they wanted to control all of the creative aspects too. This wasn't what I wanted. I decided that the only way it was going to get done was to do it myself.

This started a whole new series of challenges because now I was the one who was on the line financially. I was the one who was totally responsible for the success of the show. Many times throughout the process of creating the product and self-producing the television show I heard my own mind say, "Maybe they were right. Maybe no one is interested in what you have to offer. Maybe all the time, effort, and money you are putting into this is going to go to waste." Every time I felt the anxiety coming on I would close my eyes and feel the feeling of what it was going to be like when the show was a grand-slam home run. I also decided to enjoy the process as much as the result. I also kept focusing on the feelings that it was going to win. I'm glad I did. The show went on to be one of the biggest shows of 1994. It has helped hundreds of thousands of people and is still going strong.

Everything that has happened to me in my life has been a part of the process of me becoming who I am now. Being poor through my life, becoming interested in magic, becoming a disc jockey, and even my challenges have created me exactly the way that I am. I love my life and every day thank God for my blessings. I do know that my most challenging times were made easier by keeping my vision on where I was going. Right now you are going to do the most important exercise you have ever done. What I am about to direct you to do will have more impact on where your life is going from this moment on than anything ever has. If you choose to do only one exercise from the many powerful ones detailed in this book, DO THIS ONE! I call it Expansion Thinking.

One day when I was in my early twenties, I was searching through my couch for Kraft Macaroni & Cheese money. At the time, Kraft Macaroni & Cheese was fifteen cents a box. I wasn't searching for the money to buy the butter or the milk needed, all I wanted was enough to buy the box of Kraft Macaroni & Cheese. I sat down as I was searching for the Kraft Macaroni & Cheese money and said, "Enough! There's got to be more. This isn't fun, I don't like it. If other people can get what they want, how can I get what I want?" I realized my life had come to a place where my dreams had died. So I sat down and did the exercise you are about to do.

Eight years ago I envisioned that I would wake up in the morning as the sun was rising over the mountains and as the sun rose it would awaken me from my slumber. I'd go and put on my running clothes and go outside to my private lake where I would run around the one-mile circumference five times. Exercising, energizing, getting my body more healthy. I'd come back to my home and step into my environmental shower, which misted me from all sides. As I got out of my shower, I put on the double-breasted suit that my maid had laid out with a fine silk tie, monogrammed custom shirts, all tailored perfectly to me. As I looked at myself in the mirror, I'd pat myself on the chin and I'd say, "Damn, you look good," knowing it was a glorious day for fools when modesty became a virtue.

As I went downstairs I could see that my chef had prepared for me a breakfast of fresh fruits, teas, muffins, a healthy start on my awesome day. As I looked out on to my backyard I'd see my private aviary, with the birds, all waking up to the day. The cockatoos, the macaws, the tropical birds greeting me with a hello. At that moment there'd be a knock on the door. And the knock on the door is my driver, and he says, "Good morning, Mr. Sylver, your limousine is ready." I'd get into my limousine now and I'd drive toward my office building.

As I arrive at my office building I'd see across the black onyx of the multi-story building in large chrome letters the word SYLVER. As I walk past the doorman he says, "Good morning, Mr. Sylver. It's so great to see you." As I get on the elevator, I take it to the penthouse suite. The penthouse elevator opens and inside is my reception area. As I look on to the reception floor it's covered in marble, imported from Italy. Inlaid into the walls are built-in saltwater fish tanks. As I walk past my receptionist, she says, "Good morning, Mr. Sylver. The people from the Pentagon are waiting for you in the conference room. I say, "Let them wait. The government has always made me wait." And as I passed by my receptionist she says, "Marshall, it's great to be a part of your team." I go to my office and take care of a couple of details. Then I go to my conference room where I meet with the members from the Pentagon.

As I do my presentation, my conference room is fully outfitted with video, visual aids, and special electronic processors that allow me to make a killer presentation. After which I close the deal with the Pentagon officials on putting stress-reduction centers on military bases across the world, literally putting an end to war. I go back to my office and I make a few phone calls when suddenly my administrative assistant buzzes me and says, "Marshall, the people from the network are here to interview you for their show." I do a national television interview. Moments later, my administrative assistant tells me we need to prepare for my first speaking engagement of the day. I get ready for the presentation, and as I get into the limousine we drive up to the hotel for a presentation to one thousand members of IBM. It's a one-hour keynote. Motivating them, inspiring them to sell more. At the end of the presentation, a standing ovation.

I get back in the limousine and go back to my office, and of the many notes on my desk, one is a call from my sweetheart. She says, "Honey, I'd like to meet you for lunch." I call her back and I say, "I'll meet you on the roof." We go up to the roof at noon, get into the private helicopter, and speed off to a distant mountain. On the mountaintop the pilot lays out a picnic lunch for us, of fish, chicken, fruits, and vegetables. As we enjoy the lunch, the pilot takes off and leaves us alone for a while so we can enjoy dessert. After dessert the pilot comes back and picks us up and takes us back to the building and drops us both off on the roof. I kiss my sweetheart goodbye and tell her I'll see her later that day.

I go back to my office and my administrative assistant tells me it's time to go on to our next meeting. My next presentation is for the people of Kodak. We go off to the multimedia image presentation, with dancers and video, which not only inspires people, but trains them for the skills of success that they need. Another standing ovation for another fantastic presentation. My driver takes me back to the office where I wrap up my business for the day and then he finally takes me home.

When I get home, I change again into my workout clothes, and I go into my private gym, where I exercise my body for optimum fitness and vitality. After my workout, I clean myself up in time to enjoy dinner on my back patio, as I watch the sun set over the mountains. As it does I get into my sports car and drive to a nearby hotel.

As I approach the hotel, the marquee out front says, ULTIMATE POWER, STARRING THE GREATEST HYPNOTIST OF ALL TIME, MARSHALL SYLVER (that's me!). I go into the hotel and to my dressing room. As I go to my dressing room, the general manager of the hotel peeks his head in and says, "Marshall, we've got two sold-out shows again tonight. We're not paying you enough!" I agree with him and I go out to do my first performance of the evening. It's a rock-and-roll hypnotic show, filled with pyrotechnics, lasers, video, and dancers. I invite sixty people from the audience to be hypnotized at once. I give them suggestions to sing like Madonna, dance like Chippendale dancers, travel to a past life, walk on broken glass, and expand their potential in a fun and entertaining way.

After the show I come back to my dressing room and there's a bouquet of flowers sitting there that has a card attached. I pull the card out and it says, "We're from HBO and we'd like to do the story of your life." My second performance of the evening earns another standing ovation, another fun-filled performance, helping people be entertained as well as reach their true potential. I go back to my dressing room exhausted and satisfied. There's another card on the dressing room table. I pick this one up and it has the faint smell of a familiar perfume. I open the card up and it says, "Sweetheart, I went home early. The wine is chilled, and the sheets are warm." I get into my sports car and I drive home. (Quickly!) At the door, I'm met by a beautiful woman who loves me and supports me. And as we go to sleep in each other's arms, I look down at the foot of the bed and I see a fire burning in the fireplace.

I look up above me and I can see the stars clearly, because my bedroom has a retractable ceiling. I look up and I wonder, where is that kid who was searching for Kraft Macaroni & Cheese money in his couch, so long ago. And I wonder what kind of decisions did he make, what things did he do, and where did his path take him? I hope he figured out what to aim for, because without aiming he could never have hit it.

When I sat down some years ago to write out my perfect day of work, I had to do the Expansion Thinking first because, in the words of the author, Zig Ziglar, I'd fallen into what's called "stinkin' thinkin'." The whole key to expanding yourself and having something to aim for is to make dreams, goals, and plans as exciting as possible.

In my ideal workday, where was I then? Back then, I had a car that was barely running. I was on the verge of being kicked out of my apartment because of nonpayment of the rent and I was the manager. All I paid was a hundred dollars a month. I also had very little food in the house, and I had no friends to speak of. The only people who still associated with me were the people I owed money to. Sounds pretty incredible, doesn't it? What you just read is what I wrote eight years ago.

Eight years later my own show has appeared on the main stage of the Riviera in Las Vegas, and at Caesars in Lake Tahoe. I've had the great fortune to speak in front of a thousand IBMers and work with corporations like Kodak and Ford. In addition we have done numerous programs all across the country for many individuals and have helped them get what they wanted in the areas of their relationships, wealth, and emotional and physical well-being. Two years ago when I designed my professional offices we designed marble into the floors, and built-in fish tanks into the walls.

In addition, my current home is in Las Vegas, and even though the roof doesn't retract there is a spa up there, so I can watch the sunset every evening and relax. I'm driving the car of my dreams and my relationships have never been more passionate. Everything that I wrote down back then has either already happened or is happening now. Your path starts now. Just by writing it down, you have already begun.

Be imaginative, dream the impossible dream. As you are creating what you want in your life right now it is important to realize there is nothing better than here now. I want you to do your own Expansion Thinking worksheet right now.

> *"A mind once expanded can never contract to its original size."*
> —RALPH WALDO EMERSON

EXERCISE: Take a clean sheet of paper and write the words "Expansion Thinking" across the top in double-size letters. Underneath that in smaller letters write the words "People, places, things, awards, experiences." Then for at least five minutes write down everything that you have ever wanted. This will come out more as a shopping list than as a story. The only thing you must do is focus on your paper for at least five minutes. That means keep your face on the paper. When you look up at the ceiling or at the wall it will distract you. Keep your face on your paper, write for at least five minutes, have fun—and do it now!

Exercise Part II: Take two new sheets of paper. Across the top of one, write the words IDEAL DAY AT WORK. Across the top of the other, write IDEAL DAY AT PLAY. Since you have already done your Expansion Thinking worksheet, your subconscious mind has opened up to the possibility of creating your life exactly the way you want it. Now you will write out your Ideal Days at Work and Play as if they were happening right now. These will be written more as stories than as a shopping list. Make both days exciting, fun, and sensory-explicit so that your imagination can begin working on the accomplishment of your plans. Creating your Ideal Days exactly as you want them allows Providence to take over.

PASSION

Chapter 6

How Never to Be Lonely

"When you learn to be happy being alone, you can always find a way to be happy."

—MARSHALL SYLVER

Think about that statement for a moment. This statement is vital for establishing your core belief system. You will never need the approval of another human being when you are totally content with being alone. When you learn to enjoy being alone, not just tolerating it, actually enjoying the experience of being alone—you can never be lonely. No matter what your current circumstances you can ultimately decide to be alone. You can walk out on your family, your job, your friends and you really can be alone anytime you want to. I'm certainly not suggesting you do any of the above things, and yet just knowing you have the complete freedom to do that will take away all of your self-imposed pressure. When you know you can have something anytime you want it the obsessive desires will go away. When you learn to enjoy being alone a funny thing also happens—other people will feel the loss of pressure from you to get together and will actually want to get together with you more often. Since you don't need them, you only will want them. Wanting is needing without the projected guilt attached.

One of the best ways to start enjoying the state of being alone is to change the words you use when you are talking to yourself and others about this time. For example, which feels better to you: "I guess I have to be alone today" or "I get to spend the day in my own company." How about telling someone you are going to spend the day with your best friend and when they ask who that is you cheerfully respond, "Me!"

> *"He is his own best friend who takes delight in privacy; whereas the*
> *man of no virtue is his own worst enemy and is afraid of solitude."*
>
> —ARISTOTLE

Let's take it one step further: let's pretend that you put as much energy into your time alone as you do when you are planning time with others. Do you clean your house only when you know that someone you want to impress is coming over? Do you use the good china only when someone worthwhile is going to be eating at your house? Who could be more worthwhile than the person reading this book right now? Have you ever dressed up just to impress someone? Do you remember how you felt when you looked in the mirror? It felt fantastic to look at yourself and say, "I look wonderful!" I guarantee you that you act differently when you think you look good than when you feel like you have just thrown something on to get through the day.

The fastest way to begin to enjoy the time you get to spend with your "best friend" is to immediately change the vocabulary around those alone times and make them real celebrations.

Whatever it is you are doing, do it as if it were the last time you would ever get to do that. As I am writing this I am sitting on my back patio in the middle of a beautiful afternoon. The golf course is right beside me and the ducks are quacking merrily along the pond. I have set a glass of fresh juice for myself and the sounds of jazz are wafting from the house. I could have been writing this in my office, and it did take quite a bit more energy to do all the preparations to set up the table and the chairs and the computer outside and yet even though it did I have been inspired since I sat down. In addition, even if no one else ever read these words, I'm having a perfect day! As I learn to treat myself with the same love, respect, and pampering that I would give to any of my other best friends, it becomes increasingly easier, even enjoyable, to spend time with myself.

How do we get better at treating others by being by yourself? Simple, when I am cooking for myself as if I were about to entertain royalty then I get better at cooking when I have other guests. When I am in the habit of dressing impeccably for myself, then that surprise guest will always get me dressed to impress. When I am in the habit of treating myself with love and respect I will learn even more completely how to treat others with love and respect. Have you ever known people that would give to others before they would take for themselves? Are you one of those people? Can you imagine if you treated yourself like visiting royalty and you treated your friends and family even better how wonderful that would be?

I'm sure you can now understand that how you feel about being alone is a direct reflection on your own self-esteem. If you don't really love your own company how in the world can you expect others to love it? If being with yourself is something you just tolerate (on at least a subconscious level), you will project that energy to those people around you and they will just tolerate being with you. When you begin to treat yourself with the love and respect that you deserve, then it will come easy to you to do the same for others. The loss of tension in yourself as you work to make yourself more attractive to others will also make you calmer and more lovable and more desirable.

Begin today to plan a special time you can spend with your "best friend" and make it fabulous. Plan a special meal for just you, dress up even when you know that no one else will see you, leave yourself a love note or even call yourself and leave a message on your answering machine so you have a great message to hear when you get home. If this sounds crazy, great! Maybe being crazy is just what you need to get yourself to enjoy the wonderful times you can have anytime you want to be with your best friend—you.

Another good exercise to practice in learning to love yourself is to spend one whole day on your wants. For just one day dare to be selfish. Do things for others and when they thank you tell them they're welcome and yet the reason you did it is because it felt good to you. Not only will you get a funny look from them it just may make them think about being selfish later on and taking pleasure from giving to someone else. Part of the basis of this exercise is understanding that the more joy you can get out of the things that are going on in your life the more everyone wins. Learn to love yourself for you and the rest of the world will appreciate you more fully.

Some people have a hard time loving themselves since they believe there is little to love. Even highly successful people go through challenges sometimes. I have worked with thousands of individuals on a private basis in one-on-one therapy. Although I really enjoy helping people in this intimate setting I now have so many demands that the best possible use of my time is to work with as many people at once as possible or to work with people that have a substantial impact on a great number of people. That's the reason that my current clients pay thousands of dollars for a single session and tend to be movie personalities, professional athletes, and political and social leaders. My belief is that by giving these people a greater understanding they will in turn pass it along. For the general public I do have a telephone service that gives guidance to individuals. What this means is that you can talk one-on-one to one of my success coaches and they will get right to the heart of the matter and help you. Should you want information about this program be sure to call my office (see address and telephone number at the end of the book).

> *"It doesn't matter who you are, the number of people who show up at your funeral will be largely dependent on the weather."*
>
> —WILL ROGERS

Years ago I was working with a well-known public figure who revealed to me that he wanted to commit suicide. He said that with all his agents, managers, attorneys, and accountants he felt out of control. He said that he was just tired of it all and didn't think anybody was noticing how sad he was. He had talked to the suicide hotline many times and decided it was time. I said I understood and that suicide is one way to pretend like we are in control. It's also one decision that we can make that no one can stop us from making. The only challenge is once we have acted on that decision our whole life is even more out of our control. I told the client to close his eyes and go forward in time to the time of his funeral. I asked him to notice who showed up and what each person who was there had to say. I told him to notice the emotions of the people who were there. I also had him let any person of his choice get up and talk to the gathering about his accomplishments.

When the client came back to full awareness he had a lot to say. He realized that there were plenty of people who cared about him. He also realized that even though he had accomplished much there were many things he still wanted to do. He also realized that he had lacked the balance in life, such as family and recreation, that he needed. He told me that he now knew that instead of taking away from his work his family actually energized him and made him more effective.

I did this same exercise and had a similar response. I noticed a few things. One was that many people showed up (thank God it was sunny!). Another was that sometimes I got so caught up in the daily challenges that I didn't notice that I really was getting somewhere. Also that there were lots of things that I still wanted to do and had better get moving on them just in case I did die before I expected to. And two, that I had many, many people who loved and supported me. Do this exercise now to help you understand where you are and where you are going. Even without doing this exercise you must ask yourself: "What will it say in my obituary? Will I have lived a life of contribution and excellence?" If you don't think that your funeral notice would be something that you would be proud of if it happened in the near future, then start living today as if it were your last. Start something right now that they will talk about after you're gone. Get moving, it may be closer than you think.

"Death is such a wonderful thing that it should be saved for last."
—Comedian DAVID BRENNER

One final note about regrets in life. To worry about death is to already be dead. To worry about the inevitable is to speed up the process. My father passed away this year. He was stubborn and set in his ways. Our lifetime relationship had been rocky at best. He didn't like to call me, so if there was any contact between us it was up to me. I hadn't seen him for sixteen years because he moved to a rural town in Michigan called Ontonagon. For some reason I believed that it would take a long time to get to where he was since I believed he was so far "back in the woods." When he died I made my first trip ever to Ontonagon when I went for his funeral. The plane ride lasted seven hours, the car ride another three. When I got to the town two things occurred to me. One was that I was angry with myself for being so selfish that I had never really thought about how long it would take to get to him. Ten hours seemed like the blink of an eye since I would never see him again. Second, that life is timing. Here I was finally in his town and I was two days too late. It taught me a tremendous lesson about letting go of unimportant things. It has put me in the habit of connecting more completely and instantaneously with the people I love.

I cried many tears of sorrow for my father's passing and I cried many tears of joy for the lessons he taught me. Life is for the living. Since you are reading this book I'd have to believe you are physically alive. Pick up the phone right now and call someone that you have been meaning to call for a while. Heal that relationship right now or just let them know you were thinking about them. The key is do it now. Don't be three days late, it's very painful.

EXERCISE: Is there anyone in your life you have an existing challenge with? No matter how angry you are, no matter who was *right,* is there anyone who you need to reconnect with before it's too late? Take a moment to close your eyes and in your imagination do a mental inventory of who matters to you. It could be a family member, an old friend that you had a falling out with, or just someone you haven't called for a while. Take the time to reconnect now.

Chapter 7

Becoming a Passion Magnet

"You must become what you want to attract."

—Marshall Sylver

In life and especially in the area of relating to others we get back what we send out. In the section on profit I am going to teach you some techniques and strategies for becoming more persuasive and influential. One of the things you will learn is that getting what you want from others, whether it be attention, affection, or some material object, is largely dependent on what you send out. If you ask questions and make requests that are fun or easy (or both) to say no to, that's probably what you'll hear. In relationships the same is true. When you are loud and abrasive the only people that will tolerate you are probably loud and abrasive themselves. They are the ones that don't notice your actions.

A man was walking down the road between two cities. He came across an old farmer sitting on a fence. "What kind of people are in the town up ahead?" he asked.

"What kind of people are in the town where you're from?" the farmer replied.

"Where I come from the people are liars and cheats—that's why I left!" the young man stated.

"That's what you'll find in the town up ahead," was the farmer's reply.

A second young man on the same road passed the same old farmer and asked the same question. "What kind of people are in the town up ahead?" he asked.

"What kind of people are in the town where you're from?" the farmer replied.

"Where I come from the people are loving and kind and would give you the shirt off their backs," the young man said with a smile.

"That's what you'll find in the town up ahead," was the farmer's reply.

The process of karma is not such a tough thing to figure out. When you are putting out supportive, loving energy into your universe you will surround yourself with supportive, loving individuals. The more you help to align your circumstances the more the planet's circumstances are aligned, therefore the more joy you will experience. This reflective process of getting back what we send out also has to do with perceptions. When we operate under a certain set of principles we begin to believe that everyone is operating the same way. People who have marital affairs think everyone else is having marital affairs. People who are honest and trustworthy usually believe that others are the same way. Since we notice what we focus on, we find what we believe exists and we don't even notice what we believe doesn't. Karma is the belief that everyone is like us, so if we are doing "good" things we begin to view the occurrences of our life as "good." When we do "bad" things, we begin to view the occurrences of our life as "bad."

We notice the things that we think about. When your focus is on a healthy lifestyle you will notice the people who take care of themselves. When you are career-minded you will notice those who are motivated in their career. It's the same with your personal life. When you're searching for a person or persons to have a relationship with, remember to stay true to your path. Be who you are. Now that you are analyzing and changing your present belief system, rather than conforming and adjusting yourself to be something you're not, be who you really are. You don't need to do anything to be loved. Just be who you know you are. It's the only way to experience real love.

When you're doing what you really love, and creating the life that you want, it will be easier to create a relationship that will be supportive of what you want. When you stay true to your path you will look around and someone on a similar path will become extremely attractive to you. Instead of looking for love, let it happen by being the best you that you can be. If you are prepared and know what you want in a mate, you find out soon enough if he or she is the right one or someone to practice being loving with.

Relationships are mirrors of ourselves. They reflect our inner selves outward and we see the things that we like and don't like about ourselves in our mates. We notice the things that we focus on. When you reflect back to what you're looking for it's imperative that you become who you want to be. If you don't like the kind of people that you're attracting, examine what you don't like about them and notice if it's something that you don't like in yourself. If it's true that we mirror reflections of ourselves, then you can evaluate what you don't like and see how that connects with who you really are. If you have a quality in yourself that you don't like, you can choose to change it immediately and start attracting those people you really want in your life.

Become the person that you want to attract. Even though you want to stay on your own path, it's essential to realize that to attract the person of your dreams you are more likely to find them on common ground. If you want to attract an athletic, healthy, career-minded individual, you must now start down the path of becoming an athletic, healthy, career-minded individual.

Release your wants to the universe and trust in yourself that sometime, while you're at the gym, the health food store, or at the motivational tape store, you will bump into a potential mate who's involved in the same things you are. Become the person that you want to attract.

In every area we get back what we send out. In the late nineteenth century, a member of the English Parliament went to Scotland to make a speech. En route his carriage became stuck in the mud. A Scottish farm boy came to the rescue and with a team of horses pulled the carriage out of the mud. The boy was so awed by the man he would accept no reward. The statesman asked, "Is there nothing you want to be when you grow up?"

The boy replied, "I want to be a doctor."

The man said, "Then I will help."

True to his word he made it possible for the Scottish lad to become a doctor. More than fifty years later on another continent another statesman lay dying of pneumonia. Winston Churchill had been stricken and lay in despair when a wonder drug called penicillin was given to him.

The drug had been discovered by Alexander Fleming. Fleming was the Scottish boy and the man who had helped sponsor the boy's education was Randolph Churchill, Winston's father.

Finding love requires perseverance. You are truly worthy of love exactly the way you are. If finding that special someone is a priority in your life, you've got to set down an action plan just as you would do in any area of your life. Then enjoy the journey as much as the destination, or more specifically:

"Savor the wanting as much as the having."

My mother used to say, "Waste not, want not." I've taken that little gem of a saying and adapted it into a formula for when you want to get to know someone. It's the thirty-minute formula. I make sure that all of my first dates are no more than thirty minutes. I think it's respectful for both parties. Why waste each other's time if you are uncomfortable together? Instead of asking your potential partner out on a long date, meet him or her for coffee or tea or just to chat. When I mention I have only thirty minutes of time, that gives us both a fail-safe way to cut the meeting short if that's what one of us wants.

If when you get together with someone you find out he or she's not a person you really want to spend time with, then after that thirty minutes you always have the explanation that you need to get back to work. However, if you end up really liking the person and he or she is the kind of person you'd like to spend more time with, you can suggest changing your plans and extending the date if the other person would want you to. This gives your date the option to get out of the circumstances if he or she isn't comfortable.

Something else I'm pretty specific about when I'm looking for a partner to spend some time with or a primary relationship, is that I know exactly what I want in a person. I know exactly what their spiritual, emotional, physical, and mental characteristics are. In fact, I know so much what I want in a mate, I can cover most of the questions in thirty minutes. I think some people are afraid to get specific about what they want in another person because they feel lucky just to have a date. I also know it is attractive for a person to tell you what they want because it makes them seem like they aren't desperate. It makes them seem like they have the luxury and the confidence of getting exactly what they want.

If your priority is finding the perfect girl- or boyfriend, then you must know exactly what you want in that person. Ponder and get specific about their physical, mental, emotional, and spiritual attributes. In fact, if you write it down and know it, it's pretty easy to cover all the questions in stimulating conversation within a short period of time. When you know exactly what you want, then you will also appreciate it more when you experience it. As you grow, so will your desires. As your self-love and self-respect grows, your belief of what you deserve will also expand. Start now to grow and expand your own desirability. Make yourself available by putting out into the universe that you are looking to make someone lucky and give them the chance to spend a lifetime with you. The universe will provide when the time is right. Have faith and don't settle for anything less than what you want. Definitely know what you want. By refusing to settle for less, you can have it all. It is possible to get everything you want in a relationship.

Years ago when I was single and frustrated about where my relationships were taking me, I decided that the best way to get the kind of relationship I wanted was first, be very specific, and second, tell as many potential candidates what I wanted. I said to myself, "How can I find someone in San Diego that fulfills my needs? I know! I'll advertise!" At first I thought I was going to embarrass myself, then I finally decided I would rather be embarrassed than alone. I also figured that if people could run those little personal ads and be satisfied with the process, I could run a full-page spread. Remember that sometimes you've got to be outrageous to get what you want! What follows is the ad that I wrote defining exactly the kind of woman that I wanted. Yes, the ad was written to be placed in a paper, and yes, everything in the ad is what I wanted in a woman. It was also written in a truly effective style of marketing since I was on a mission!

GENEROUS POSITIVE BUSINESSMAN SEEKING SEXY ADVENTUROUS INTELLIGENT WOMAN

Intention: *Paradise!*

Are you a special lady who is tired of bars and the single scene and looking for adventure with a man who really cares about what you want?

Then read on!

My name is Mr. E. That's because for now my name will be a Mr. E to you. I am a fairly high profile individual and because of my two professions I know that many people will recognize me from my picture. I don't mind if you do, I just want to maintain a little mystery for now. I'm looking for one special lady that's really ready to get everything she wants and knows that she is woman enough to deserve it. Are you that woman? Maybe, maybe not. The first thing it depends on is who I am so allow me to bare my soul in all its naked vulnerability. I know that the right woman will appreciate the honesty. I also know that my idea of a perfect life and yours may be different so here goes.

I am not writing this ad because I have to. I'm writing this because I know the caliber of lady I'm looking for is as tired of the lies, frustrations and BS as I am. I have no challenge in meeting women and asking them out. In fact asking women out is a whole lot easier than putting my heart on the line in print for who knows how many people to see in this ad. I'm just tired of meeting someone who I thought was a wonderful woman on the first date, only to find out on the second that she is a drug addict, alcoholic, anorexic with a fatal attraction to me and an ex-boyfriend who is in the mafia who wants her back. Don't think this is so far off. I know we have all had our dates from hell. I'm writing to be honest from the start and give the right lady the chance to make the right decision.

Now what about me. I thought you'd never ask. I'm 28 years old. I am 6', 178 lbs. I don't think of myself as a hunk although some people say I'm attractive and I believe them. There is a picture in this ad so you be the judge. I really believe my physical body is a temple and do my best to take care of it. Almost no red meat, very little dairy products, and lots of exercise. I love the entertainment field and particularly live theatre and movies. Dining out is one of my favorite hedonistic delights.

continued

In addition I like: Skiing, Sushi (yum, yum), Tropical Vacations, Running on the Beach, Fireplaces, Hot baths & Candles, Dancing, Old Pinball Machines, Risk Taking (ski diving, paragliding, African safaris, . . .), Erotic art, Giving and Receiving Massages, Outrageous Wealth, Champagne, Long Talks, Flowers, and Committed People.

I know that's a lot. My downside is that I can be very intense. I want everything now. I don't believe you have to wait for anything and some people find that my pace is just too much. I have also been very demanding in my relationships and have now found greater joy in preferring that things be one way and enjoying however they are for the moment. I can also get very impatient with people who can't make up their minds and have been known to lose interest quickly if things don't appear like they are going anywhere. My past romances have been with three absolute angels. Each one of them enriched my life in ways that I will always cherish. I have had my share of one night stands (in my younger years of course) and been in the company of some of the finest ladies on the face of this earth. The ladies I have had long relationships with will surely back me up on my level of commitment to going for the good and sticking with them when they needed me. As long as a person is actively going for the good I will be there.

I also am a workaholic, and a playaholic. I will cop to the fact that my life credo is "Work Hard and Play Hard!" My intention is to live every day as if it is my last. I am an entertainer and I have a company that leads motivational and persuasion seminars. My show is a highly produced variety show with pyrotechnics, rock and roll music and a thousand laughs. My seminar is done for major corporations like IBM, Kodak, Kentucky Fried Chicken and a host of others. I am generally travelling at least two or three days a week so you would have lots of time for yourself or your friends.

I love to exercise and will get some kind of masochistic delight every day by running 3 to 5 miles or maybe an hour or two of pushing metal at the gym. I'll love it when you tell me this is important to you as well.

What I am looking for in a woman is specific although I am willing to open my mind to lots of options. There are some very specific things I don't want.

What Mr. E Doesn't Want:

1. Promiscuity—In this day of health risks I want it to be known that I am not one. I am looking for a lady with a background that is

continued

sans the same. If you know more than 200 professional athletes by their first name and you are not a sports reporter—I am not interested. What I mean is if you are or have been promiscuous let's just be friends.

2. Drugs or addictions—No drugs, Nada, Nope, None, not even cigarettes or occasional pot. If the pot in your life is used for making split pea soup on a cold rainy day this may be love. If you enjoy Dom or Moet we'll have a great time. I love an evening out dancing, and getting loose with a few brews. I just want it to be choice and not habit.

3. Major Issues—I love personal growth seminars. I teach them. I really support my partner in her peaceful growth. If you are still angry at your parents or think your last boyfriend scarred you for life, see ya! If you have an equal blend of learning about living and then living I think you are just the kind of spiritual person I'm looking for. I love to play. Bike riding, kite flying and communication can be wonderful learning experiences.

4. Prudes—If you think foreplay is 1½ hours of begging don't call. If you think oral sex is talking about making love stay away. If you think sex is a control device you won't experience the real power of Love. Making Love is an act of Love. I promise that you will never be denied any hug, kiss, or cuddle you request. Not even your teddy likes affection as much as I do.

5. Sexual Fiends—If you and your collie are real close or if you want to bring by your portable trapeze to my house, no thanks. I love passion and variety all in the name of love and respect. As I said I am reasonably normal (reasonably) and totally monogamous.

6. Fear of Emotional or Material Wealth—Don't laugh! Some people will throw a wrench in the gears just when things start to get really good. Most people don't do this on purpose it's just that to create excitement in our lives we have to have some kind of challenge. If the challenge you want is correcting what's wrong instead of going for what's right—the two of us will butt heads big time. I'm into the struggle as long as there is a reward. You will have to love playing this game of life to its fullest and constantly going for more or I will drive you crazy.

7. Ownership—I don't want to own anyone nor do I want to be owned. I do want a monogamous relationship that could lead to deeper and deeper levels of commitment. I am not looking to get married immediately. Someday yes—just not today.

continued

That's what I don't want. In fact that's what I won't stand for even if I find it out later. This is the really hard part, what I do want. If you are still with me, we will have a chance, after years of love, to blow the dust out of each other's wrinkles. I am really nervous in saying what I do want at the risk of seeming like an insensitive schmuck who thinks he can custom build a woman. Well maybe I am and maybe I do. If what I want makes you mad you are definitely not the one I'm interested in. I know that my higher power will bring this ad to the attention of my goddess so right now I'm going to describe you to yourself. I know if I don't set out some guidelines that this ad may be answered by some women that I'm not compatible with so please give me a break. As with most people the difficult part for me is asking for exactly what I want.

You are between 21 and 31. You are healthy, slender and attractive. What this means is that your diet is similar to the one I described earlier and your figure reflects it. You take my breath away when I see you in a swim suit. I like an athletic woman who has a firm bottom and slender legs. I'm really not too concerned about what's on the chest, I'm more interested in what's in it. I really appreciate a woman who takes care of herself. Your skin, teeth, and hair are healthy and clean. I'll give you the same, there is something about a clean body and a fresh scent that is a real turn on.

You are intelligent. You enjoy learning and asking yourself questions like "Do fish cry?" and "How would you describe blue to a blind person?" You love to stretch your mind as much as your body.

You are positive. You look for the good and you find it. You are spiritual. What this means to me is that you have a place inside of you that recognizes you are not alone. You are secure and have already "found yourself." In other words NO NEGGIES!

You like the same things I do. It really is more fun that way. (Is this guy a genius or what!?)

That's it. If you have looks, brains and attitude you seem like a slice of heaven to me. If after all this you are still interested then you might want to know what you could expect from a romance with me.

Romance with a capital R. I love women, especially my woman. Whoever she is at the time. I believe that this life is precious and with me you can expect lots of travel. In the past year my romantic travel included London, the Bahamas, Orlando FL, Lake Tahoe, Kansas City, and numerous long weekend trips to Las Vegas, San Fran-

continued

cisco, Murrieta Hot Springs and La Costa. You can expect much more of the same.

I love buying things for my lady and think that a woman is supposed to wear jewelry and beautiful clothes. Please read loud and clear—I am not a chump. I know when someone is gold digging and when they have a genuine heart. I will help you experience all the wonderful things that life has to offer as you let me know your heart is true. If things work out I would certainly consider elevating your life style and reducing your need to produce income.

I love the romantic touches. You can be certain that you will have more flowers then you have ever had in your life. It would also make me feel great to give you a full massage and hot bubble bath. If you're really nice I might even shave your legs!

Does this feel good to you? I hope so. It was written in complete sincerity and every word is true. Even though I made an attempt to make it entertaining you should also know that I am being sincere.

I know that it may be a little awkward to answer a personal ad. Please know that I felt strange writing this. It will be really fun when you now take a chance and give me a call on my voice mail. Please forgive me for using voice mail. It's the only way I could think of to protect myself from midnight calls. I would also love a recent full length photo and a letter telling me about yourself and how to get ahold of you.

Who knows, maybe we'll be right for each other and maybe we won't. I know for a fact whatever happens it will be fun. And just maybe I might be your dream man and you my dream lady, won't that be nice.

Just write to: Mr. E
2670 Del Mar Heights Rd. #277
Del Mar, CA 92014

Or Call: (619) 599-3323

When I went to place the ad, I started talking to the advertising rep of the newspaper. She was young, attractive, and, I was soon to find out, single. While she was doing the paperwork for my ad, she read it. I sat beside her while she was reading what I had written and felt a little foolish. When she finished she said, "I know I'm not supposed to do this and yet I really want to. I think I can save you the money this ad is going to cost you. I'd like to apply for the position!"

Boy, was this a lesson in learning to ask for what I wanted! I figured I didn't have anything to lose. If this woman and I didn't work out, I could always run the ad later! As it turned out, the romance didn't last and yet the experience reinforced the need to know exactly what I wanted and be fearless in requesting it. Let as many people as possible know what you are looking for.

ASSIGNMENT: Write your own "love ad." Make it fun, make it real, and make it sell as if you were actually going to run it in the newspaper. You can use mine as an example. If you are currently looking for a relationship, then this exercise is essential. If you are dissatisfied with your current relationship and can't put your finger on the exact reason, this will help you to clarify what's wrong.

Postscript: I am currently enjoying a wonderful relationship with a goddess of a woman who adds value to every area of my life. While I was working on the above material she asked to read my love ad. After she got done reading it, she came over to me and gave me a great big hug and a passionately wet kiss. She said smugly, "I fit every element of your ad." Yes you do, sweetheart, yes you do!

If you are single right now, remember to savor the wanting as much as the having. I have married friends who wish they were single and single friends who wish they were married. Both experiences can be joyful when you let them be and live in the moment. Both can be hell if you constantly wish you were somewhere else. Enjoy being single while you're looking for the ideal mate. Only when you can be gloriously single can you be happily married. Remember to stay in practice. If you ever played sports, chess, or anything similar, you had to play and practice to be good. Relationships are no different. You must stay in shape for communicating and relating at all times.

So if you walk into a party and scan the room and don't think you see that special someone, have fun, enjoy yourself, and practice relating to other people. Call it warm-up, practice, whatever, just do it.

I once had dated a woman who after I went out with her a couple of times told me the only reason she went out with me is that I was very nice to a friend who wasn't attractive. She figured if I was nice to her friend then I'd be nice to her. Practice being loving to all people and you'll be ready when it really matters.

Chapter 8

The Seven Strategies of Passionate Relationships

What's the difference between healthy, passionate relationships and ones that just get by? There are some very specific foundational characteristics that will allow your current relationships to grow and flourish. Even if you're single you'll want to learn these now so you can build a masterpiece of love. What follows are the elements that I have found to exist in all truly passionate relationships.

1. BE IN LOVE WITH YOURSELF FIRST

"In a relationship, two halves don't make a whole, they make two halves."

Even when you are working on yourself it is possible to love the person you are. Unless you love yourself it's difficult to respect anyone else who holds that high an opinion of you. Remember the words of Groucho Marx, "I refuse to join any club that would have me as a member"? How do people form low self-esteem? In addition to the programs of our subconscious minds most of us as children were taught to put others first. Although in principle it works for children it doesn't work for adults. The reason it doesn't work for adults is that when you focus on others before making certain you yourself are healthy, then you are not able to give at your full capacity to others. Relationships are like teeter-totter scales. They come together because each side balances the other. Whether it's business or whether it's pleasure, you relate to other people because they fill a desire or need in you and you fill a need or desire in them. Maybe the need between two people is someone to talk to. Maybe it's a mutual desire for a lover. Maybe one person needs encouragement and the other loves to encourage. Maybe they're in the same places in their careers. It might be that they're both athletic. In a less-than-healthy relationship, maybe one person needs to be controlled and the other needs to control. Whatever the circumstances are that bring a couple together, they balance each other's needs.

If the relationship gets out of balance mentally, physically, or emotionally, harmony will be disrupted. When one outgrows the other in one of these areas that person has a choice to make. You can either grow to balance out the scale, or you can pull the other side down. Let's imagine a heavyset couple that form a relationship. If one of the partners starts to lose weight, then the other has a choice to make. Since the other partner may be worried that he or she will lose their now more healthy mate they will have to decide between losing weight themselves or to tempt their partner who is losing weight to eat one more piece of pie. Some relationship partners sabotage each other just to make sure that they stay together. Maybe one of the balancing elements is career. Maybe one starts to grow professionally and the other doesn't. Both must have the confidence to grow, or one side gets insecure, and then he or she will often sabotage their partner's success. By doing this, the balance needed to perpetuate the relationship is maintained. Sabotaging your partner's success is a common trait in unhealthy relationships because it is one method of control. The mentality is, "As long as you're not too successful you won't outgrow me." A person who is in a healthy relationship views the other person as an inspiration and challenges himself to grow with that person.

"Relationships are like a book, in that they are for learning."

Some books are short books, which you read quickly just for distraction and fun. Some are read only for the content, and what you learn to help your life. Others are novels that you read slowly, hoping the story goes on forever. Funny thing about books though, no matter how many times you pick up the same book, when you read it the ending is always the same. Sometimes you'll notice something you didn't notice the first time like in a relationship that breaks up and gets back together. When you read a book you will also learn things that will allow you to enjoy the next book more, just like relationships.

I have many friends who keep repeating the same mistakes over and over again. Do you do that? Since we need to learn certain relationship lessons we will inevitably be attracted to the kind of person that can best teach us that lesson. When we understand ourselves, then we can change our needs into wants and attract other types for a more fulfilling relationship. I know you will have learned lessons in your last relationship that will allow you greater understanding and enjoyment in your next. Otherwise the next will be a lot like the last.

Finally, just like books, when you set one down after reading it, you must set it down with respect, dust it off, unfold the corners so that it's attractive to the next reader. If you are in a relationship that is ending, do your best to remember the valuable lessons you learned rather than resenting the ending.

As I said above, one reason people quite often will attract the same type of person is so they can learn a specific lesson. There often will be another phenomenon occurring. I have friends who ask me, "How come I keep attracting the same types of people?" I always ask them, "What makes you think they were that way when you met them? Maybe you trained them that way." In one of my high-end intensive seminars I teach something called the Training Cycle.™ What this is is a way to teach people how you want to be treated. Many people have the mistaken belief that if you give someone everything they want all the time then you are guaranteed a great relationship. They have the mistaken belief that if they make the other person's life so great that their mate would be foolish to go anywhere else. Their inner battle cry is, "You'll never find anyone who will treat you better than me!" Maybe they are right. The only challenge is that it's very hard to respect someone you can walk all over. Doormats are for stepping on. A better strategy is to learn the Training Cycle. This process works in all relationships, whether it is lovers or parent and child or employer and employee. I know that the thought that humans can be trained as easily as animals may be harsh to some people and yet it still is true. Whether you believe it or not it is still happening.

Years ago when I was first out on my own I used to buy unwanted parrots for sale in the newspaper. These would usually be birds that were wild or misbehaved or for some other reason undesirable. I mean, after all, who would give up a well-behaved and affectionate bird? I would buy these birds cheap, tame them, teach them a trick or two such as roller skating or basketball, and then resell them for a profit. I still love parrots. In fact I still have two named Magic and Passion that I have had for many years. Training parrots gave me a tremendous insight into how humans train each other to treat one another. I also noticed that the principles work whether the "trainee" wants them to or not. I know you may be thinking that it sounds a lot like manipulation, training someone else how to act. But the fact is, you are going to train them either accidentally or on purpose. You may as well decide how you want to be treated. Let me explain it first in the terms of training a bird and then I will teach you how to apply it to people.

Here's the basic strategy for the Training Cycle™:

1. Decide what you want the new habit or action to be.
2. Reward the action or any part of the action when you catch it every time at first.
3. Create a signal or a mind trigger (like Pavlov's bell) that you can use when you notice the desired behavior so you can trigger it later.
4. Insist on greater response each time.
5. Reward it sometimes with an extra reward (a jackpot) and at other times not at all.
6. NEVER reward the undesired behavior.

Let's imagine I want to get my cockatoo to play basketball. A being will play a game as long as they know they can win. It's important to know in advance what you want the entire behavior to be before you start the training cycle. When I am teaching a bird any new behavior, chances are the bird has no clue as to what I really want. (Do you ever get the feeling that some of your relationships are the same way?) What I have to do is get the bird to do anything that is moving in the direction that I want it to go and reward that. In other words, catch the bird doing something right. Scolding a being for doing something "wrong" does not let it know what action you do want it to do.

In the basketball example, catching the bird doing something right could be even as minimal as touching the ball. What I do is hold the seed (the reward) over the ball so that the bird has to lean over the ball to get what it wants. When it does, it is naturally touching the ball. At that moment I give the bird the seed it was reaching for and one additional. I repeat this a couple of times. Then what I do is hold the seed way back and just sit quietly. What happens is because the bird has no idea what he needs to do to get the seed he will just begin doing anything and eventually the bird will touch his beak to the ball. This is what is called a natural behavior. Basically it is catching the bird doing something right. I immediately give it verbal praise and a few (jackpot) seeds.

Now I begin to plant a direct cue or command. I put the ball in front of the bird and say, "Basketball." The bird will reach forward and touch the ball with his beak. Now is the tricky part. You must wait for the bird not only to touch the ball, you must also wait until, in his frustration, he will actually pick it up. At that moment I give him a jackpot of seeds. Now that he has learned he has to pick up the ball to get a seed, you never give him a seed for just touching the ball. The next step is to get him to pick it up and place it through a hoop. What we do is start with the hoop very close to the ground and the ball right on the edge. When the bird picks up the ball I subtly guide it so that it falls through the hoop. Each time I reward the bird I move the ball a little further from the hoop and move the hoop a little higher. Each time I also give clear communication as to what I want and only reward the behavior when the bird completes the action. Eventually the bird can be trained to pick the ball up off the table, walk to the other end of the table, and drop the ball into the hoop. The bird doesn't know the first thing about basketball —it just knows what it needs to do to get its reward.

Does the bird feel manipulated into playing basketball? Of course not, it gets the seed, it could care less. Is giving someone what they want in exchange for something you want wrong? Of course not. And besides, who cares? Everybody is winning. Understand this undeniable truth: every interaction is a negotiation on some level. Even unconditional giving is given for something in return even if it's the great feeling you receive from unconditional giving. A few important notes on training any creature, whether it's your bird, your dog, your husband, your girl-friend, your child, or your student. (Again, if the thought that you are either intentionally or accidentally "training" another human being makes you feel like I am comparing human response to animals—I am.

Either recognize it or become the trainee.) Sometimes you must skip the reward even when the behavior was exactly what you wanted. If you reward the being every time, then what it will do is start to slack off and only do the minimum required to get the reward. When it knows that it is expected to not only do the behavior, it is expected to do it well, then it will. It's also important to randomly give the being a jackpot so that every time it will try harder in hope that this is the time it will receive the big payoff. This is a lot like the behavior of gamblers in Las Vegas. They put a coin in the slot machine and every so often they get a few back. The thing that keeps them going is that they know that there is the potential for the big payoff. Sometimes you will go through a period where the being doesn't seem to respond at all. Sometimes you will have to take a step backward to go forward or find a reward that the being wants more.

How does the Training Cycle apply to humans? Exactly the same way. My current girlfriend used to date a man who was extremely jealous. My girlfriend is not only stunningly beautiful (on a scale of one to ten she's ten squared!), she's very intelligent and has a great attitude. When she and her then boyfriend would go out, if she so much as smiled at the waiter or another man he would get angry. After he got angry she would try to smooth over the situation by ceasing to smile at the waiter and she would also turn up her loving attention on the boyfriend. It doesn't take a genius to see that she was actually training him to be jealous. Being jealous got to be a very effective way for him to get everything he wanted. Whenever he got jealous she would stop paying attention to other people and turn her total attention toward him. What reason would he have to be any other way? She also started reacting the same way to him, whereas before she had never been jealous.

This created a massive challenge for us since I have a job that puts me in close contact with many beautiful women. When my girlfriend and I first met she had a hard time with this. With my work she was tolerant and yet in social circumstances she would become very cold if she thought I was giving another woman too much attention. If I had just diverted my attention from the other women every time she got angry it would have gotten her what she wanted at the moment, but it would have compromised our relationship by making me unhappy. In the long run it would have built up resentment in me rather than the healthy action of building up self-esteem and confidence in her.

The great thing about the Training Cycle is that both parties win. So instead of letting the tension escalate I retrained her response to my giving attention to other women by not responding when she got angry. One time when I was talking to another woman she came over to "spray her territory" and gave me a kiss on my neck. I stopped my conversation with the other woman and said to her, "You are by far the most beautiful, loving, sensuous, intelligent woman I have ever met." She gave me another hug and held my arm while I continued to talk to the other woman. This happened on other occasions. She would see me talking to another woman and if she got mad or angry or gave me the cold shoulder treatment I would ignore it. If she came to me with a loving gesture I would return it tenfold and give her the attention she was asking for. Before long every time she got jealous she would give me loving attention rather than get angry or cold.

But she told me that often she wouldn't even notice when she was getting angry or cold since she would just be responding emotionally. Since most people don't notice what they are doing when they are reacting we created a method to keep us in a loving place. One night after we came home from a party she made a comment about the fact that she was jealous when I talked so long to a well-known movie actress. I told her I noticed that she got cold and short with me and that she had made a rather cutting remark toward the actress. I quickly added that it felt really good when she stopped herself halfway through the remark and apologized. She said that she noticed that she was falling into the old jealousy habit and didn't realize it. Since I always say a fish doesn't know it's in water I asked her if she wanted to create a secret code that would silently communicate that one of us was uncomfortable and wanted to get back to love. She did, so now when we are out and either I notice she is getting jealous or she just wants me to give her more attention one of us gives the other the nonverbal signal. When I signal her she stops and notices what she's doing and she decides whether she wants to continue down that path or not. When I see her signal me that she wants more attention, then I decide whether I want to fulfill her request for attention or if I want to sleep on the couch that night. What we have done is effectively created a signal or a "command" for the behavior.

The Training Cycle described above can be used with your kids, your peers at work, and your friends. It is important to realize that since you don't have a right to be treated a specific way you have to create it. The sooner you take responsibility for the fact that others treat you the way you have trained them or the way that they were trained previously, the sooner you have the opportunity to interpret their actions any way you want and the happier you will be.

THROAT-SLASHING ORDER

NOTE TO THE ROMANTIC: The above example is my own. Paying attention to women other than the one I'm in a relationship with is something I like to do. I would rather be with someone that realizes this. While I do appreciate and respect all women (and men too), I have noticed something that has made my life more fun. It's what I call the throat-slashing order. Jealousy is definitely a sign of insecurity. While we must work on our own self-image I have also noticed that some people are in relationships in which one or the other seems to intentionally make the other person jealous. Not only is this unhealthy, it's unnecessary. Most people don't become jealous because they notice their mate is paying attention to someone else, they become jealous because they fear that their mate will like the other person more. What the throat-slashing order concept does is set the parameters. Imagine you are in a room with your loved one and a number of others. Imagine a terrorist bursts in and says he is going to slit the throat of everyone except you and one other person and you must choose who will survive or everyone will be killed. Whom would you choose? Heavy-duty question, huh? The other people in the room might not be romantic interests. They might be family members, friends, a job. The need to know who or what comes first is what drives some people to jealousy. Just letting them know they come first quite often is enough to ease the tension. Think about your life. Do you let your primary relationship know they come first? Maybe you should. In fact, maybe you should right now.

The number-one inner quality I've encountered in people who have successful relationships is that they don't need relationships. They only want relationships. They are whole all by themselves and the reason they desire to relate is not to make themselves whole but rather to get more in their life. Say these words out loud: "**I don't need a relationship. I am whole as a person right now.**" Remember that when you love yourself you are a greater gift to someone else. When you love yourself it is joyful to be alone.

Creating a passionate relationship is possible no matter how long you've been together and it only takes one to ignite the spark. If you are in a relationship an important strategy to remember is:

"You don't have to fix anything to go for more."

You don't have to fix anything to go for more in your relationships no matter what level the relationships are at this moment. It's better to have a relationship than to talk about a relationship. If you're spending a great deal of time talking about what's wrong, you hardly have time to appreciate what's right about the relationship. In a relationship you're always going for more or going for less. In every moment you're either getting closer or further away from the person you're relating to.

One of the ways I use to determine whether my relating is healthy or not is to ask myself, "**Am I getting more in my life because of this relationship or less?**" Years ago I was in a relationship that had an abundance of learning. There was much more pain than joy. Since I believe more is learned in pain than pleasure this was probably the most educational relationship I have ever had. More than eighty percent of our time together was spent talking about how to relate rather than relating.

One very important lesson I learned toward the end of that relationship was something that I still use today with my current love. That is: **If you are the first one to notice the relationship is off track, then it is your responsibility to make the first move to get it back on.** It's important to believe that if you notice that it's off track at all you were the first to notice.

One day my current girlfriend and I were sitting in my car. I said something to her that I often use to diffuse the energy of disagreements in my romances. I said:

"Would you like to get back to love?"

This is a request that in a healthy relationship is next to impossible to say no to since it puts full responsibility on the shoulders of the one saying no to make the next move. In all of the times I have asked that question only once has someone said no. Even then I felt a certain amount of relief. I knew I had done all that I could. In that particular instance she said, "I don't want to get back to love until you decide to stop treating me like you're treating me." Now, I had believed that I was treating her appropriately. Since she had a different opinion I figured no need to argue—I just wanted to get back to love. I said, "Please forgive me if I hurt your feelings. I realize you don't want to get back to love, and still I was wondering if you would mind if I put my hand on your leg?" What can you say when someone is being this honest and letting you do whatever you want to do and still loving you? She half-heartedly shook her head. "No, I don't mind." Since I was having fun I continued, "Would you mind if I stroked the back of your head even if it feels good to me?" She looked at me with a look that said, "You are such a jerk!" but said, "No, I don't care if you touch me."

A moment later I was caressing her hair and she said, "You know sometimes it's so hard to be mad at you, especially when you are being so loving and having so much fun." I realized that I was having fun and feeling good about myself because I knew that I was being loving and had made the first move to get back to love.

People in great relationships see the other person for what they are right now and they never fall in love with someone's potential.

"Never fall in love with someone's potential."

You might be attracted to someone's potential but you should realize who he or she is today and fall in love with that person. If you're in love with a person who says maybe someday I'll change, or you're in love with how your mate used to be, you're in love with someone who isn't there right now. If you're waiting for your lover to change and they never do, it's only going to build up frustration and resentment in you.

"You can't build a reputation on what you're going to do."
—HENRY FORD

Although Henry was talking about business it is just as true in personal relationships. You must fall in love with who the person is right now because right now is all you have. If someone tells me she'll love me forever, I know what she means is she'll love me forever—today. You can never know what anyone is going to feel tomorrow, and neither can I.

Great relationships have no demands, they have desires. You must be willing to totally release all expectations, since expectations set you up to be let down. You must be willing to surrender and learn to deal with what emerges. Experience all your relationships as they are instead of what they should be. What they should be is what isn't. You must deal with what is.

If you're having a tough time with this, ask yourself these questions: Do you feel your needs aren't met a lot of the time? Do you think you get treated unfairly more than other people do? If you said yes to either of those questions, open the window of opportunity and release your need for a relationship, and start desiring a relationship instead. This mental shift in thinking will change your whole outlook on your relationship, marriage, or partnership.

When you learn to like your own company you'll really be able to love that someone special in your life and discover a well-balanced relationship.

2. I SAID, "DO YOU SPEAKA MY LANGUAGE?": COMMUNICATION

"Words have no meaning, people have meaning."

One of the first important steps to a healthy and passionate relationship is the art of communicating. Effective communicators take responsibility for both sides of the communication. They take responsibility for both the sending and the receiving. They make sure that the other person understands what they are communicating and also give feedback to the other person so that they are sure of what they heard. Communication is one part speaking and two parts listening. That's why you have one mouth and two ears.

"Effective listening means you listen without interrupting, with genuine interest, and without owning what the other person is saying."

Also realize that no matter what the other person is saying, it is their opinion. It may not be what actually is. You don't have to believe what someone else says about you to be a good listener. Who you are is not who they think you are—it's who you think you are. When you are centered, other people's opinion of you will mean less than your opinion of you.

Have you ever noticed that the fastest way to make someone feel loved is to truly pay attention to them? When you're in a conversation, totally focus all your attention on what they are communicating. If you're distracted, tell your lover or friend and arrange for another time to talk. Be honest enough to tell your partner you can't give them your full attention in the present moment. Wouldn't you rather have someone tell you that they couldn't concentrate instead of having them pretend to be listening when they really weren't?

Years ago I was dating a woman and we were experiencing massive challenge. During the course of a seminar I was conducting in Mexico things came to a head. At one of the breaks she decided she needed to talk to me about her concerns. She talked for a bit and then I talked. When she started talking again I began to get concerned about the time since I had to go back and teach the seminar. She asked me why I kept looking at my watch when she was talking but I never looked at it when I was talking. I told her I couldn't talk to her and look at my watch at the same time. She said how can you pay attention to me and look at your watch at the same time. It was in that moment that I realized that if I am just pretending to listen to someone and I am really thinking about something else I am doing both of us a great disservice. I am wasting both of our time, since I probably will not remember what was said anyway. So what I do now is communicate honestly: "I am focused on something else right now. It doesn't appear as if we are getting anywhere. Can we either let this go or agree on a time to resume this conversation later?" It's amazing how effective this level of honesty and clear communication is.

"Why ask why?"

—Bud Dry Commercial

One simple strategy in effective communication is to ask "what questions" instead of "why questions." When you ask why you will get a subjective opinion. "Why did this happen?" is a different question than "What caused this to happen?" An even more effective question is, "What can we do to make sure this never happens again?" And finally an even more effective question: "What can we now do to get what we want?" Whew! What a mouthful!

Experiment with this simple exercise: Every time you are about to ask yourself or someone else a why question, find the what question and ask it instead.

Make sure you ask questions for an action that gets you what you or both of you want. You don't have to know the reason something happened to figure out what to do to get what you want. I have ended many disagreements with the simple phrase:

"What do you want?"

It makes your whole life easier. Now you can decide to either give them what they want, compromise, inspire them to want something different (and notice I said inspire, not browbeat), or surrender and accept that you cannot reach an agreement.

Oftentimes honest communication is inhibited when a person is concerned about being accepted. If you are worried about what people think of you, how can you possibly communicate what you really feel? Instead of spending so much energy trying to look good, how about learning communication skills that get you and the people you relate to more of what you both want.

3. HONESTY

"And the truth shall set you free."
—JOHN 8:32

"Why bother moving your lips if you're going to lie, and why bother listening if you think you are listening to a lie."

The next major strategy for passionate relationships is honesty. So often we hold on to our inner thoughts because we feel that others will not like us and they will want to leave if they know the real person. The only way *you* can be truly loved is to be truly *you*. If you are lying to someone they will fall in love with the lie and not you. What is a lie? Any untrue statement or action. Another form of lying is withholding information pertinent to the circumstances. "Well you never asked me," is the defense that most people use when they are caught in this kind of lie.

You must be honest and believe the other person is being honest with you. If you are afraid someone will not love you if they know who the real you is, then instead of lying, what would happen if you started working on you? Wouldn't your life be more joyful if you were with someone who supported you now instead of having to both hide who you really are and work on yourself at the same time?

An old Pink Floyd song has the lyrics, "You've got to be trusted by the people that you lie to." So true. You don't have to be trusted by the people that you are telling the truth to. It doesn't really matter does it? If you are telling the truth you will know that you are doing all that you can. On the other hand it has been my experience that the people that worry the most about other people lying are usually lying themselves. There is also a great satisfaction in both telling the truth and knowing the truth. When you tell the truth you have given as much as you can give so you become secure in the knowledge that you have done all that you can. When you know that what the other person is telling you is the truth, then you can make a judgment based on what is rather than trying to guess "Do they really mean that?" or "Are they just saying that so I won't feel bad?" or "Are they saying that so we won't get into a fight?"

"No need to lie to me, we hardly know each other."

Another phenomenon that I have noticed is that people seldom lie to strangers. When you don't care that much about a person you don't mind how the other person will respond. Have you ever started a new relationship and found it much easier to tell the truth because you felt there wasn't that much to lose? Did you also think that since you had no foundation of lies that you didn't have to build one on the other? In my most honest relationships (ones where both sides are telling the truth), I have noticed a higher level of telepathy. Since there is no camouflage or deceit it is much easier to know what the other person is thinking. When a relationship is open, strong, and healthy it is easy to know what the other person is thinking because you truly know the real person. It's when there are lies between you that it becomes cloudy and unclear as to what the other person wants, since at times you know the truth and at times you know the person is lying. When a person is always telling you the truth it becomes easier to know what they are thinking. This knowing what the other person is thinking often occurs in the beginning of a relationship. Think about it. You just met someone and maybe you've only dated a couple of times. If it doesn't work out you can handle it. So you are honest with them and they with you. Pretty soon though the challenge is to keep the relationship on track and a little white lie is told. Maybe you felt uncomfortable and yet you had to do it to save their feelings, right? Another white lie is told and soon it becomes the norm. If you are in a relationship right now that has many little white lies, then you are in a relationship that has or will soon have big lies.

What's so wonderful about this process of honesty in a relationship is that when you are open and honest and expect someone else to be the same, quite often you will create in them the qualities you admire. A couple of friends of mine were having challenges with their relationship. The man was having an affair and the woman didn't want to believe it. Since I knew both of them as well as the woman the husband was having an affair with, I knew that it was true. I don't place judgment on how others live their lives, I only offer guidance when it's requested.

One day the wife approached me for that very guidance. She loved her husband dearly and wanted the relationship to stay together. I knew that she had been told by many people that her husband was going against the agreements of their relationship and having an affair, so I knew it wouldn't do her any good to hear it again from me. She told me that she wanted to trust her husband. I told her to do so. She also wanted to bring him closer. I told her to work on herself instead of ways to hook him in; that way if things didn't work out she would be in a much better position to attract a healthier relationship. She did both. She began treating him with the same love that she had given him when she had no idea that he was playing around. She told her friends she didn't want to hear them talk about him in anything less than glowing terms. She found ways to genuinely compliment him on his honesty and truthfulness with her. Instead of getting angry she turned up the love. If she inquired about where he was and he lied she just smiled and turned up the love. She also started focusing on herself more. When he wasn't there, rather than sitting at home moping she went out by herself or with her girlfriends and had fun. She made sure that she enjoyed her times alone and made better use of them. She went to the gym and lost the ten pounds that she had been wanting to lose and she started dressing sexier, like she did when she and her husband first started going out.

What happened was quite a few things. First the husband started feeling guilty because she was treating him so well when even he had a hint that she knew. Every time she believed him when he lied he felt worse. Since she was treating him so well he felt more and more guilty about deceiving her. Also, since she was working on herself she started to become more attractive to him. The pretty young thing he had been dating on the side suddenly didn't seem so pretty. Also, since she was looking better and dressing sexier, he started getting nervous about the fact that maybe she was seeing someone else. (Remember: liars always think everybody else lies as much as they do!) Suddenly she was in the driver's seat and she was being pursued by him. The last I talked to her she told me that one day he broke down and confessed the entire affair. She said that she had made it so safe for him to be honest that he was. She told him that she knew all along and that she wasn't angry. She told him that the past was the past and yet if it happened again that she wouldn't put up with it and would leave. They cried, and as far as I know, they haven't had any challenges since.

Learn to trust and be trustworthy. When we get insecure with ourselves we start doubting the integrity of others. When you treat someone as if they are being dishonest you will actually train them to be. How often have you come home to be questioned by a mate as to where you have been? "Why didn't you call?" "How could you treat me like this?" You might be coming home to tell them great news and you end up getting all wrapped up in their insecurity. It robs you of your joy. This type of action will erode the relationship faster than anything else. When one stops trusting a partner the mind will start imagining all kinds of crazy things that will spiral the relationship into a nosedive, ending in a broken relationship. **If you accuse your partner of something, sooner** or later they will decide they might as well commit the crime they are being punished for.

If you are going to lie, why bother moving your mouth? You're just going to say something that has no value. If you are going to lie and lead the other person to believe that you're someone you're not, you'll never give them the opportunity to love who you really are.

On the other hand, a person will tell the truth when they believe that you really want to hear it. If you get angry when you hear things that aren't pleasant, do you really think that will inspire someone to tell you the truth? People will tell the truth when they think that it's the most fun thing to do. One way to get someone to tell the truth is to trust them. Tell them you trust them. Compliment them on their honesty. Let them know how important that is to you. They will want to tell you the truth because they know that's what you want to hear. Expect someone to tell the truth and they most likely will. No matter how unpleasant the truth, when you make a way someone can win they will tell the truth more often.

Have you ever lied? If you answered anything other than yes, you're lying.

"There really are only three kinds of people. People who lie and say they don't, people who lie and say they do, and people who really belong in the first group."

For me an important fact to remember is if someone lies to you, be quick to forgive and they'll be more apt to tell you the truth. Always be honest with yourself. Give others a chance to love you for who you really are instead of the facade you are putting on. Lying also undermines all the really wonderful qualities about you, since people will begin to doubt you even when you are telling the truth.

Many years ago I read an excellent book called *The Way of the Peaceful Warrior* by Dan Millman. If you haven't read this book, you must. It is one of the all-time classics of personal development. I was so impressed with the book I determined that I had to meet this great spiritual teacher. An actual meeting with someone who had impacted my life in the printed word would definitely impact me more in person. Around the time that I attended Dan's seminar I had been putting myself through huge emotional turmoil. I never realized how my trying so hard made me unattractive to others. I sent out the signal "Hey there's something wrong with this guy, that's why he has to tell you how great he is!" It was kind of like the magician who tells you, "I have here an ordinary empty paper bag." Your mind will immediately ask, "What's not ordinary about the bag and what's hidden in it?" I'll never forget Dan's subtle and loving remark when he asked me, "Marshall, what would happen if God called you tomorrow and told you to take the day off?" Subtle like a brick! Yet, he was right. Since I wasn't too impressed with my life it was difficult to project that into my world.

ON A LIGHTER NOTE: Without honesty karma has a funny way of catching up. Consider the cigar smoker who purchased several hundred expensive stogies and had them insured against fire. After he smoked them all, he filed a claim pointing out the cigars had been destroyed by fire.

The insurance company refused to pay, so the man sued. The judge ruled in the man's favor saying that the cigars had indeed been insured against and been destroyed by fire. So the insurance company paid the claim and when the man accepted the money promptly had him arrested for arson.

---

4. AGREEMENTS

"Relationships don't exist. Relating does."

Do relationships really exist? You can't put a relationship on the table. It has no weight, it takes up no space. Since we all know that the form of relationships can change in a heartbeat, did it exist in the other form at all? Is it possible to believe you have a relationship with someone who doesn't believe they have a relationship with you? If so, who's right?

Relationship as defined in the dictionary primarily means a connection or a way of relating. When people speak of their relationship being bad or good, what do they mean? What they mean is that the connection they have with the other being makes them feel good or bad. In other words, in a good relationship they like themselves when they are in the presence of the other person. **When you bring out the things in others that they like about themselves they will believe that your relationship is healthy. When they bring out the best in you, then you will think the relationship is healthy**. When this occurs a natural bonding takes place. You want to be with them because you like yourself more when you are. It's always more comfortable to know what to do to be accepted, loved, and appreciated than to have to guess. Your way of relating to another person is based on your spoken or unspoken agreements. Healthy relating is always based on clearly defined agreements. When you have clearly defined agreements your ability to relate to each other is a simpler, more natural process. Since both parties know what is expected, both know whether they are operating within the terms of the agreement or not, and both will be able to have a better idea of what kind of response a specific action will garner. When you know the basis of how you relate, you get to choose whether to relate or not.

Is it possible for two people to be in a relationship where one person feels the relationship is great and the other thinks it's terrible? Of course it is. Does this make the relationship good or bad? Neither, and both. Since we all have our own relationships even with the people that we believe we are sharing a relationship with, I guess we're the only ones who decide whether that relationship is good or bad. In any instance, it can either be a learning or a loving moment.

Relationships are built on agreements, agreements of how you will relate to each other. As long as the agreements are upheld, the relationship will be harmonious. When an agreement is broken, it must be amended, or eventually a major disruption will occur and the relationship will suddenly turn cold. Think of the agreements in a relationship as a written contract, just as sacred as any legal contract you've signed. Some couples even write down their agreements to solidify them. While not always necessary, this process can be effective when there has been an extended period of miscommunication.

Some people think that relationships should just flow, and if you have to talk about what you want there's something wrong with the relationship. In the beginning of a relationship that's part of the attraction, the mystique, the not knowing what the other person wants. While this may be fun in the short term, in the long run it's easier knowing what to do to win. Imagine trying to get someone to paint you a masterpiece if you didn't tell them what you wanted it to look like. They'd paint their idea of a masterpiece and it may not be anywhere near what you wanted.

I remember a couple not too long ago that came to me for consultation. They argued about everything—even taking out the garbage. They loved each other and yet there wasn't a day that went by that they didn't spend most of their time disagreeing about something. After several years of marriage, they no longer had any agreements between them. They came to me as a last resort before they decided to get a divorce. They really didn't want to separate but still they had decided it was their only alternative to find a happy life.

I asked them to write down everything that they loved about the other. Not to my surprise they both came back with a long list of many admirable qualities that they loved about the other. I then asked them to write down a list of all the things that each one would want in a perfect relationship. While some of the items were different, many of the items were in alignment. Simply by taking the time to determine what was important to each one they began to realize they had a basis for relating. On the items that they wanted that were dissimilar they were able to agree to compromise and trade-offs. She wanted an agreement to have him help keep the house clean, he offered to pay for a maid to come in once a week to clean the house. He wanted time with his friends, she agreed if one night per week would be devoted to romance with just the two of them. For these two everything worked out fine. For others, including myself, sometimes things aren't so rosy. I was once in a relationship where the agreements that I wanted were not something that my partner could give me no matter what I gave to her. Since these things were very important to me I knew I had no choice other than to transform the relationship and find someone who was more suited to my desires and me to them.

"The only way to be wronged is to have rights."

The surest way to have your rights violated is to have rights. You don't have any rights in relationships. So, losing the belief that you have rights is going to be a real fast way to deal with what is rather than with what you think your rights are. Statements like "It's my right to be treated this way!" or "I have a right to know where you've been!" are going to set you up for a confrontation. Unless you have an agreement with somebody, don't expect the person you are relating with to respond in any specific way. Once you've made an agreement with someone to respond in a given way, then the decision to either break or uphold the agreement, not the rights you believe you are entitled to, will determine the health of the relationship. Having expectations is just setting yourself up for a one-two punch. You are setting yourself up to lose by holding the belief of "Hey I expected someone to do this" or "I expect love to be this way" or "I know this is the way it's supposed to be when two people love each other" or "You should really respect me." You've got to deal with what is. You've got to deal with what is going on in your relationship right now.

Rather than get upset because someone you're relating with goes against what you thought was appropriate behavior, a more effective strategy is to ask, "Can we have an agreement about this in the future?" Then in the future if something comes up you can ask, "Do we have an agreement on this?" When you are aware enough to realize that you don't have an agreement (read this: clearly communicated agreement), rather than find your partner wrong, see the situation as an opportunity to bring you closer.

A few years ago when my girlfriend and I had just started dating we went out with her sister and her roommate to a dance club, the three gorgeously beautiful women and myself. After I paid the cover charge for all of us we walked in and I felt as if two hundred male eyes were magnetized, drawn right to the women and to my lady in particular. We stepped into the club, and not sixty seconds later, two men approached the woman I was with and started talking to her. The first man obviously pushed the other man aside and he left. That left the man talking to my date standing there with her. Now mind you, I just paid the cover charge and since I just brought the women in I was feeling a little bit indignant this guy monopolizing my date. A moment later my date turned to me and said, "Excuse me, I'm going to go dance." At that moment I thought, "Oh, this is great!" When I saw her go to the dance floor with this stranger, I immediately started looking around the nightclub to find the most beautiful woman I could find to dance with just to get even with her.

At that moment my date's sister caught my eye and I could see by the look on her face that she was wondering what my next move would be. I smiled, got a grip on myself, and said, "I'm going to be nice, would you like to dance with me?" The sister and I went to the dance floor and came back a few minutes later. Shortly after that my date returned from her dance with the stranger and asked me, "Uh oh, am I in trouble?" I replied, "No, we don't have an agreement on this. From now on though, I would like to have one should this come up in the future." She said, "Okay." I said, "How about this, from now on when we go on a date together, you give me first and last dance or the options on those two. In between you can dance with whoever you want to without even asking me." I told her how a male cat, when it walks into a room, will quite often spray the curtains just to mark its territory. I told her, "I want people to know who you came in with and I want them to definitely know who you are leaving with. Fair enough?" She said, "Fair enough." In addition, I said, "When you danced with that guy, I was insanely jealous." Now, just me saying I was jealous dissipated all the negative energy. It not only took away from all the energy of actually being jealous but it also allowed my date to either be sensitive about what I was feeling or not to be. Either way, it wasn't her responsibility to respond in a specific way for me, and it allowed me to release the truth and get to know her by watching her natural response.

Previously I had many instances in my life where I hadn't been so open and so honest and so communicative when my mate did something that didn't make me happy, and rather than telling them I was frustrated or I was angry or I was jealous I simply held the emotions inside. Well, what you resist persists and if I would have held the jealousy inside of me, I guarantee the rest of the evening wouldn't have been much fun with my date. Instead, she went overboard to show me affection and give me attention just to let me know I was the most important guy in her life at that moment. The rest of the night was awesome. We formed a new agreement and from that moment on whenever we went out dancing and guys approached her, she would politely say, "No, thank you. I'm with somebody. Maybe later," and both of us would win.

So, when you experience upset as an opportunity for learning and you ask yourself the question "What is there that is good about what is going on here that can bring us closer?" then you are going to create a closer relationship with that person and everybody wins.

What happens when someone breaks an agreement? When you want to keep a relationship healthy you offer an amendment to the agreement. If you are the one who broke an existing agreement (the offender), then it is your responsibility to make it up to the other person (the offended). Let's say I have an agreement to meet my girlfriend for dinner at seven P.M. and because I was working late at the office I don't show up until seven-thirty. When I do it's obvious that she's not happy. At this moment I am faced with the choice of either ignoring her or offering an amendment. Here's an example of how offering an amendment works:

SHE: "Marshall, why are you thirty minutes late?"
ME: "Am I?" (I know I'm late—just checking her memory!)
SHE: "Yes you are, didn't we have an agreement to meet at seven?"
ME: "Oh yeah, please forgive me. It's just that I got on the phone at the office and couldn't get off. Let me make it up to you, let me buy dinner."
SHE: "Buy dinner! This is the third time in a row this has happened. Besides, I thought you were buying dinner anyway."
ME: "Okay. How about I buy dinner tonight and again on Friday night?"
SHE: "No, Marshall, that's not enough. I'm getting really frustrated that you keep disrespecting my time over your clients. You need to offer a better amendment."
ME: "All right, how about dinner tonight, dinner Friday, and Friday night after dinner I give you a hot bubble bath and a full body massage?"
SHE: "Well, you're getting closer."
ME: "Okay, here's my final offer. Dinner tonight, dinner on Friday, bubble bath and full body massage and breakfast in bed on Saturday morning."
SHE: "How about dinner tonight, dinner on Friday night, the bubble bath and massage, breakfast in bed—and all of the last things happen up in San Francisco this weekend?" (We live in *Southern* California!)
ME: "I surrender. No more, you win, let's enjoy dinner before it gets too expensive."

In the above example, since I was the one who broke the agreement it was my responsibility to amend it. She pointed out to me that we had an agreement by asking me, "Didn't we have an agreement to meet at seven?" If someone breaks an agreement and fails to offer an amendment, then the way to point it out so they have the option of offering an agreement is to ask them if you had an agreement. If you find someone is constantly breaking agreements and then denying the agreements' existence, then to get them in practice you might consider writing the agreements down. When *you* break an agreement, *you* must offer the amendment first or it is meaningless.

In the above example I was willing to give her an amendment that she would accept. Let's imagine that she wanted more than I was willing to give. Let's imagine that I didn't think being late was that big a deal. Since the practice of amending agreements isn't a license to extort, let's imagine we couldn't reach an amendment. What would happen would be a dialogue similar to what is below:

> ME: "Well that sounds like too much to me for just being late. Is there any other way I can amend breaking our agreement?"
> SHE: "No, that's what I want."
> ME: Well, I'm not willing to give you that. I guess we have some choices. You can either accept the amendment I've offered and agree to forgive me and enjoy this meal now or we can agree to sit silently and you can look angrily at me for this whole meal, or we can agree to pass on dinner right now and get together at some other time when we both feel better. My own personal choice would be either the first or the last and yet I'll leave it up to you to choose."
>
> If she says she chooses the first option and then still stares at me angrily, then I would ask her if we had made an agreement for her to forgive me. If she admits she made that agreement, then it is up to her to offer me an amendment. (Heck, maybe I can get this dinner for free after all!)
>
> When you learn that all you have is your word, then the agreements that you make will become more specific and all of your relationships will be more fulfilling and fun. Agreements and amendments aren't just for intimate relationships, they are for all relationships. Your business and professional relationships will be positively affected as well.
>
> I had a supplier who constantly was late in shipping me

products. Finally I asked them if we could create an agreement for the on-time delivery of my materials. They said that they would. We created an agreement/amendment combination that said they would reduce my bill by 5 percent each day that they were over the promised delivery date. This did two things: it stopped them from making agreements that they couldn't keep, and it made them keep the ones that they did make.

ASSIGNMENT: Think about a current relationship that would be better served by making a more specific agreement. Approach the other party and let them know that you are having a challenge with the circumstances and ask them if they would be willing to create an agreement that would help both of you get more. Be sure that the request is made in a way that makes it seem as if you are taking responsibility for how you are feeling. Once you have created an agreement that both of you can feel good about explain to them the process of amendments. Let them know that from time to time people have the challenge of keeping their agreements and that you would also like the agreement that if something comes up that the offender will offer an amendment.

---

5. BE RESPONSIBLE FOR YOUR OWN FEELINGS

"I'd rather be happy than right."

The next strategy for maintaining extraordinary relationships is to take complete responsibility for how you feel. **Nothing has any power except the power that you give to it. No one can make you happy, sad, angry, or passionate unless you allow them to.** Arguments occur when we give up that power and usually take on the physical characteristic of what we learned as a child. When I hear the expressions "He keeps pulling my strings" or "She keeps pushing my buttons" I always ask the person to show me their strings or buttons. They always say, "Well there aren't any real strings," and I say, "Exactly."

Take responsibility for your blaming of the other. For instance, when you say, "You make me so mad when you do that!" take responsibility for your feelings. "I get so mad when you do that." Making someone else responsible for how you feel is giving away your power, taking responsibility for how you feel is getting it back.

Most marital arguments have blame dancing on the surface of the argument. We love to blame some outside force for stopping our own personal growth. Once you release the blame mentality from your mind, then your mind is free to take stock of who you really are . . . a responsible loving person. Someone who will own up to his own problems and issues and grow through the process with the help of your loved one.

Don't covet someone's position unless you are able to accept their responsibilities as well. When you take on responsibility for yourself it elevates you to a power of being trustworthy to your partner. It will help your mate feel secure and safe.

When your lover is talking about what's happening inside of them, be responsible to listen to what they are saying. Your partner can only change what goes on in his or her own heart and mind not yours. It's not your mate's responsibility to make you happy. If you make your mate responsible for your happiness you'll set yourself up for a great letdown by expecting them to take charge of your emotions. Since it is impossible for anyone to make anyone else feel something, you would be putting your partner in a no-win situation. Only you have the power to control how you feel.

In addition to being fully responsible for how you feel, take the time to train the people you surround yourself with to take responsibility for how they feel. Take charge of your own environment. When things get emotional, keep coming back to what and how questions instead of why questions. "What can we do to get back to love?" "How can we be sure this never happens again?" If something is happening that bothers you, take responsibility to address the issue in a loving way that would elevate the intimacy of your relationship. Act instead of react. Inspire your mate with honey instead of vinegar. Charm your partner to want to give you what you want rather than browbeat.

When I get into challenging situations I always ask myself, "What's good about this? What lesson about relating can I learn right now that will increase the quality of all my future relating?" No matter what challenges come up, can you think of things that are actually good about the situation and use them to go for more? Take charge of your own environment and be totally responsible for how you feel.

It is better to be happy than right. Having rights gives your partner the opportunity to wrong you. A passionate relationship has no rights. When you have rights in a relationship you set yourself up for being knocked off balance.

It's been my experience that highly successful relationships are created by people who communicate well with others, and they are quick to let the other be right. It's impossible to argue with a person who's always agreeing. Maybe you say, "I can't agree with someone who's totally wrong." Maybe they are and maybe they aren't. If you were them you'd feel the same way they do. If you had lived their life and had their experiences, then you would hold their feelings and opinions. My father once held up a Ping-Pong ball between his thumb and fingers. He asked me what color the ball was. I said it was white. He told me no, it's black. He asked me again, "What color is the ball?" Again I said, "The ball is clearly white." Again he said, "No, the ball is black." He did this until I thought he was an idiot and then finally he showed me the other side of the ball and sure enough it was painted black. The challenge was that since I was immobile from my position I couldn't see it from his angle at all. He told me, "Marshall, it is possible that two opposing views could both be right—walk a mile in the other man's moccasins before you call him a liar."

Learn to compromise. Maybe the way the your mate believes is more effective in the current circumstance. If you spend time arguing about what or who's right you don't get anything done. Be willing to surrender to the other person and go down their path. If you discover the path isn't exactly what you really want you can always change your mind later. The sooner you go down any path, the sooner you'll know what action to take.

6. KNOW HOW YOUR LOVER EXPERIENCES LOVE
"All They Wanted Was Chicken Soup?"

"When you love someone, what they want is the best that you can give them."

Have you ever had your mate get angry or sad over the stupidest things? Have they also ever acted like something you knew was important, wasn't? The number-one strategy for creating passionate relationships is to **know how you feel love and express that information in a way that inspires your mate to want to give it to you.** The reciprocal is also true. **Know how your mate experiences love and be willing to give it to them in the way that they want it.** This is the most important characteristic of all for being in a passionate, intimate relationship.

"What may be love to you may be meaningless to me."

Let's say for example that you experience love as chicken noodle soup, and when someone gives you chicken noodle soup you absolutely totally know that you're loved. On the other hand, unless they give you chicken noodle soup you really don't know that they love you at all. So you're in relationship and you say to your mate, "Sweetheart, please give me some love." Now let's imagine, in this instance, your mate experiences love not as chicken noodle soup but as tomato soup. So when you say, "Please give me love," because they genuinely love you they say, "Sure," but when they do, instead of giving you chicken noodle soup, they give you tomato soup, and they give it to you with the best intention. They say, "Here, honey, here's the love you're asking for." Now you look at the tomato soup and you kind of get a little sad and you say, "No, I want love, honey, please give me love." So in an effort to please you they say, "Sure, I'd love to give you love, I love you," and they give you another bowl of tomato soup. By now you're getting frustrated, and you say, "Please, all I'm asking for is a little love," and they give you yet another bowl of tomato soup. By now you're not only getting frustrated, you're getting angry. You say, "You know, all I'm asking for is love, all I want is love. Please give me love." Since they love you and they want to make you happy they give you all the tomato soup they've got. They give you all they could possibly find, they give you every ounce of tomato soup they could possibly give you. Then you say, "You know what, you don't love me. You just don't give me the love that I want, you don't love me." They say, "I've given you all the love I can. I don't have any more love to give. I'm totally drained, There's nothing left. I've got no more love." Then they start thinking, they just aren't good enough, and both of you start looking somewhere else for the love that you desire. Does this sound familiar to you? Maybe someone you know, maybe someone you know intimately? Has a relationship you've been in ever been like this?

Finally, you turn to your mate and in exhaustion you say, "You know what. All I wanted was a little love, and you just kept giving me this tomato soup. If you had just given me a teeny tiny bit of chicken noodle soup I would have been happy." And your mate says incredulously, "Chicken noodle soup? I thought you were asking for love. Everybody knows that chicken noodle soup isn't love. Whenever my mom gave love to my dad she always gave him tomato soup. Tomato soup is love." You can't believe what you are hearing, how could this person be so stupid? You say, "No, that's not love to me. All I wanted was a little chicken noodle soup, just like my mom used to give my dad."

Then your mate says, "You mean if I gave you chicken noodle soup you'd be happy?" You say, "Yes, that's what I've been asking you for, I said I wanted love." Then happily and eagerly, even though they don't understand it or believe it, they give you chicken noodle soup. When they give it to you, you feel totally loved and totally happy. Now your mate says, "I need some love too." You're so happy about being loved that you reach down and you are just about to give them some chicken noodle soup when it dawns on you that what they want is tomato soup.

People don't experience love in exactly the same way. So what your partner wants may be totally alien to you. You might not even understand how they could possibly feel love by getting this other thing from you that to you means so little. Yet if you really want your partner to feel loved and appreciated, then you need to be willing to give love to your mate in the way that is meaningful to them, and you need to be able to inspire your mate to give you love in a way that matters to you. Now of course tomato soup and chicken noodle soup are just metaphors. Well, maybe they are anyway.

One person might experience love as sex and another as someone to talk to. It may be that one person experiences love as someone buying them things, and another person as someone wanting to spend time with them. It doesn't matter what the equation is, know that if your mate is willing to give you what you want and you're willing to give them what they want, you're fortunate. If you arrive in that place even once in a lifetime you're among the chosen few.

7. OPERATE FROM A PLACE OF LOVE— SURRENDER AND FORGIVE

"There is no question to which love is not the answer."

The final element to creating an outrageously passionate relationship is to make sure you're operating out of a place of love instead of a place of vengeance and punishment. All relationships are challenged from time to time. If they weren't there would be no excitement. When I ask my seminars, "What's the worst possible situation that you could find yourself in within your relationship?" the answer is surprising. I would have thought that most people would say anger. Not so. Most people say the worst thing is when their mate is unaffected. They would rather their mate got angry than uninterested. At least when they're fighting they're paying attention. So if you are having challenge in your relationship, rejoice! You are way up from the bottom and moving back toward passion.

Are you doing what you're doing to get even or to get back to love? The way to know what your motives are for sure is to ask yourself this question: "Is what I'm doing going to make the other person feel better or worse?" If you're doing it to hurt them or to let them know how much you're hurting, you're probably operating out of a place of vengeance. Again, this may get you to being right, but it's not going to get you to being happy.

It only takes one person to get a relationship back on track. As I've told you before, if you're the one who notices when you're in the middle of a disagreement, then it's your responsibility to get it back on track the moment you notice it's off. The next time you sense the discussion is taking a turn for the worse and you are the first one to notice, stop and say, "Honey, you know what, I love you and I'm not sure how we got off track and I'd really like to get back to love if you're interested." Now isn't that going to blow them away? What do you think your lover's response would be? If the immediate response is, "No, I don't want to get back to love," there's your answer and you have choices to make. Are you wasting your time in this relationship?

Just how long do you think someone would continue to raise their voice if you said the above in a sincere voice and you really meant it? If the other party still wants to argue maybe that's all they want. Maybe all they really want is to argue and the content of the argument doesn't really mean anything. If that's the case, smile, enjoy the motion, and get through with the argument as quickly as possible or even put a time limit on it. "I'm willing to fight for the next ten minutes, then after that I want to have some fun, how about you?" Remember, the fastest way out of an argument is to agree and decide you'd rather be happy than right.

On the other hand if their response is, "Yes, honey, I'd love to get back to love," then you're well on the way to fun. With this type of loving communication don't you think the argument is going to calm down a bit and put you both in a place of ease? This will open up the opportunity to go for more instead of less.

Communicate how you feel love and express it in a way that inspires your mate to give, and also know how your mate experiences love and be willing to give it to them in a way that they want it. Unless you're willing to give your mate love in the way that they want, you can never expect to get the love that you need in your life in the way that *you* truly want. If you're taking from your mate without giving, eventually the well will run dry. If you're not willing to give your love what they want or give your mate love in a way that's meaningful to them, at least be honest with them.

Surrender and let them know it's not possible to get what they want from you. At least create an environment where they can get what they want somewhere else. It doesn't mean that you have to break the relationship up, it just means that you can transform it and add to it. If your mate likes to go camping and you don't, let them go with someone who does. If they like to watch old black-and-white romantic movies and you don't, let them develop a friendship with someone who does—regardless of the friend's gender. I guarantee you that by opening up and by being honest, by letting your mate know exactly what's important and loving to you, you'll free yourself to know whether or not you're going to get what you want in that current relationship. No matter what happens, let the truth set you free and be totally willing to experiment with your life and your relationships.

Now that you know the most common characteristics of people that have the ability to create incredibly passionate and successful relationships, it's time to move on. In the next chapter I'm going to share with you more relationship secrets. I'm going to help you develop skills to attract others. I'm going to help you with a mental shifting in thinking that will make all the difference in your life. I will provide you with the necessary tools to be more charismatic, magnetic, and attractive. To attract or reattract that special someone.

A relationship is supposed to enhance your life, not take energy and focus away from the things that matter to you. So if you're devoting the majority of your time to having a relationship instead of just experiencing a relationship and having it add to what your life is about, then you're probably in the wrong relationship. If you're in a relationship that makes your time at work and your time caring for yourself easier and more pleasurable, then chances are you're in a relationship that's good for you. I'm often asked by people what to do when their mate says, "I'm leaving and I need to go." The answer is: give them what they want. **The very best thing you can give someone is what they want.** It's impossible to give them something better. These people will complain, "They don't know how much I love them" or "They don't know how good I am for them and they don't know that their life is better because of me." Well, maybe it is and maybe it isn't. The truth is, unless it's what they want, you're not giving them love, you're wanting to control their emotions. Besides all that, do you really want to be with them? I mean, who wants to be with someone who doesn't want to be with them? If you force yourself on someone, nature's way is always going to come back to the true course and eventually you're going to have to deal with them wanting to leave. If you are trying to force someone to love you rather than make yourself more attractive to the universe, then you are playing a losing hand. The very best you can give someone is what they want. If someone wants to leave you, the very best thing you can do for them is to support them and encourage them in their decision. Pack their bags, hold open the door, and wish them luck.

If you're the one contemplating transforming the relationship and moving on, then before you go maybe you should be sure and ask yourself . . .

Chapter 9

Is There Any Way to Get What I Want Here?

"This is not an either/or world, it is an and world"

—MARSHALL SYLVER

When I reach a point where I seem to be challenged more than joyful in my relating to others it's usually because one or both of us aren't getting what we want. If someone is not giving you what you want, it is usually because you are not giving them what they want. I have created a chart that will let you know if there is a way for both of you to get what you want. Here's the chart:

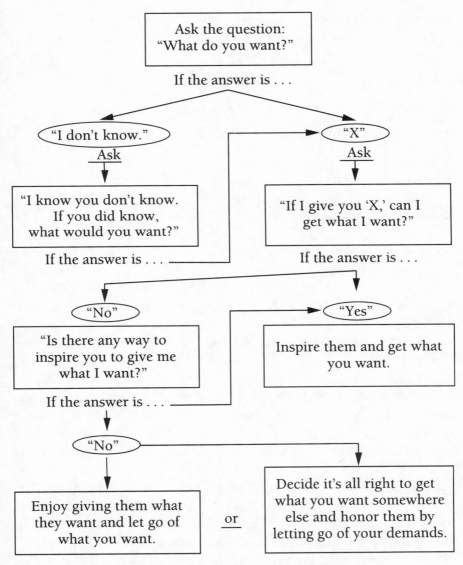

Transform your demands into desires.

The bee takes nectar from the flowers and in the act of pollination allows the flower to perpetuate and continue. If you pull all of the seeds from the tree, if you pluck all the fruit, all the apples and the oranges, and don't plant any of those seeds in the ground, then eventually you will have no apple trees or orange trees or places to receive the fruit nature has to offer. Nature is give-and-take. It is a barter system with nature.

Once I know what we both want, then it is really simple to ask myself a question: "How can I inspire my mate to give me what I want?" If my partner says, "No, there is no way for you to inspire me to give you what you want," then at least I know not to waste my energy, not to waste my emotion on asking this particular partner for what I want. While I'm on this train of thought, it is imperative, though, that you look at it from both sides. Are you truly willing to give your partner what they want? Is there a way for them to inspire you to give them what they want?

I was in a relationship a while back that was particularly challenging —many years of ups and downs of what I would call massive dramatic motion. During the period of the relationship, one of the things that I discovered was that if you are in a relationship where your partner flat out tells you, "There is no way to inspire me to give you what you want," you should believe them. When you hear those words, then the best you can do is heed them, and realize that this is the moment of truth in your relationship. It took me four years of hearing the same thing before I realized that I couldn't get what I wanted there because she didn't have it to give.

When going for more in your relationships always focus on win-win. There is a way for everybody to get everything they want in an abundant universe. In one of the exercises that I teach in my seminar, I have a person select one of two objects, either an apple or an orange. After they have selected, say, the orange, I ask them, "All right, you have the orange, I have the apple. What is it you need to give up to get the apple?" Invariably, the person will offer back the orange and I say, "No. What do you have to give up to get the apple?" The person will again say, "Well, the orange." After going back and forth numerous times, finally the person in frustration will quite often just reach out and say, "Please, I would love the apple. Could I have it?" and when they take the apple from me, they have won the game. Understand this simple truth: You don't always have to give up something to get what you want.

When creating a win-win situation, remember that this is not an either/or world. This is an *and* world. You can have everything you want and so can everybody else. You can have it all. There is a way to have a perfectly loving, satisfying primary relationship and still have relationships outside to fulfill your other needs. In fact, not only is it possible, it's healthy. I can't imagine ever thinking one person could fulfill all of my desires and all of my needs all at once. It's either ludicrous or I've got very, very simple needs. Now, if they are simple needs, that is healthy and appropriate. When you center your world around one other human being with no outside stimulation, then eventually you will have nothing to talk about. Eventually that relationship, no matter how fulfilling, would become stale and boring and the person would start looking outside of their primary relationship to get more stimulation and excitement.

When you truly love the person and want to spend time with them, it is quite possible that you can do just that and have permission—that is, have the opportunity to go outside that relationship to receive more love, to receive more attention, to receive more fulfillment.

Next, always experience upset as an opportunity for learning. Experience the challenges in your relationship as a way to bring you closer. Since relationships are for learning, anytime something comes up that isn't fun and doesn't appear to be the passion that you enrolled yourself in the relationship for, then it is nature's way of telling you, "Hey, there is something to learn here." If there is something to learn about relationships while you are in a relationship, certainly the information can be used to get you closer. When you are in a fight, close your eyes, take a deep breath, and ask yourself: "What goodness is here to bring me closer to this person that I love?"

When you experience upset as an opportunity for learning it becomes just another chapter in the book you are creating together. *Never* threaten the end of the relationship unless it really is over because once that is said it becomes a possible reality. You are going to learn in a future chapter how experiencing the upset fully instead of resisting it will make it disappear. Instead of getting upset with the challenges, you are now learning to deal with them as they come up. Forming mutually agreed upon strategies will enhance your relating and help your life in every way. When you learn to deal with your primary relationships in more effective ways you will deal with the other ones that way too.

Chapter 10

Bring on the Passion!: The Number-One Skill for Attracting (and Keeping) a Mate

"Self Confidence = Attractiveness"

—MARSHALL SYLVER

The number-one skill in creating any healthy, happy, mutually empowering relationship is to have high self-esteem and to be focused on your needs first. What causes self-confidence and self-esteem to make us so attractive? When you believe that you are worthy of a healthy, passionate, abundant relationship you will communicate that to other people. When people see you acting confident they will believe that there is some reason that you feel so good about yourself. Even if it isn't evident as to why you would feel so confident, what happens is that others will begin to believe they must be overlooking something about you that you know that they don't.

I have a friend who is a total pig. But he's also totally charismatic. I have no judgments about him or how he chooses to live, he's just a pig and he knows I think he's a pig. He's not a pig because he weighs three hundred pounds, which he does, nor do I call him a pig just because he eats a lot, which he also does. I think a person should weigh exactly what he or she wants to weigh. I think he's a pig because he dribbles food every time he eats, whether we are in private or public. His hair is always partly combed and he pays very little attention to how he looks or his manners. He's a pig. For the longest time I couldn't figure out what was so charismatic about him and he definitely is charismatic. Not only was I drawn to him when we first met, I also noticed that others were too. When we would go into a nightclub or to a party, invariably he would be the one who would end up with all the beautiful women talking to him. The thing I finally realized is that my friend makes no apologies for who he is. It's obvious when you meet him that he likes himself. It's also obvious that whether you like him or not that's fine with him. If you like him he's your friend, if you don't like him he doesn't get angry, he just smiles and lets you be. One other thing about my friend, he's worth way over $100 million. Even though he is extremely wealthy, I have never heard him talk about his money when we are out being social. I think the reason that he is charismatic is that he knows he is worth so much and doesn't really care what anyone else thinks. He likes himself and when you're around him you get a sense that in spite of the fact that he is a pig that there is something about him to like.

A few years back I was single and I was going to a party with a buddy of mine. The party was on a beach in San Diego, and as we were walking to the party I noticed another party also happening on the beach. An extremely beautiful woman was standing beside the fire at that other party and it was evident that I wasn't the only one who thought she was attractive, since she was surrounded by a large school of land sharks. In other words, men on the prowl. I told my buddy to wait just a few seconds—I was going to get that beautiful girl's phone number. And my friend just laughed and wished me luck. Now, I consider myself a good-looking man, and yet the guys surrounding this woman could have all been off the cover of *GQ* magazine. They were all dressed in swim trunks, since the party was on the beach, and they all looked like they lived in the gym. Muscles bulging, bodies gleaming, teeth glinting in the moonlight. As I walked up to the woman I whispered in her ear and thirty seconds later she gave me her phone number. I went back to my buddy and he was shaking his head in disbelief, and asked, "What on earth did you say to that girl to get her phone number?" I told him I simply walked up to her and said, "You're an extremely beautiful woman and if I had been invited to this party, I'd love to get to know you. Since I'm on my way to a different party, though, it might be better to get together over a cup of coffee or a cup of tea some other time. If you're single I'd love to take you out, and to do that I need your home phone number." She paused, then she smiled and reached into her purse, pulled out a pen and piece of paper, wrote out her number, and handed it to me. The other guys standing around her were staring at me in disbelief. I'm certain they all had been working on this project for at least half an hour. Days later when we went out for coffee I asked her, "What was it that made you want to get together with me?"

She said she was blown away by my self-confidence and by the way I walked directly up to her and told her exactly what I wanted. Anyone with that level of confidence must have a whole lot going for himself. Anyone who seemed that confident without being cocky must like himself. If he likes himself, there must be something there to like. Even though we only went out romantically a couple of times before we realized we wanted different things, it was a lesson that I've remembered since. From that moment on I decided to push past my own inhibitions and give others the gift of meeting me. Don't you think that you're enough of a gift to share with others?

In Chapter 6 of this book I taught you how to never be lonely, that is, how to enjoy being alone. If you want to build greater self-confidence you must change your current programs. Here are some other pointers on how to increase your self-confidence. Lack of self-confidence is created by poor subconscious programming. The messages that go through your mind that say things like, "They'll never like me because I'm too (short, plain, fat, poor, stupid . . .)." None of these things have to be true. First of all, maybe the thing you think is not appealing is the very thing that the world will like about you. Second, no matter what label you put on yourself that zaps your confidence I wonder what your basis of comparison is. One of the first ways to begin building your self-confidence is to focus on what's great about you. Begin by making a list of all your qualities that you like. Next, stretch the list to include the things that you could like about yourself if you worked at it.

A woman at one of my seminars named Doris once said she didn't like herself and that there was nothing to like. I asked her if she could list the things she didn't like. She told me she could go on forever. I asked her to list the things she liked about herself, and she said she couldn't think of any. I had noticed that she had made friends with one of the other attendees. I asked Doris to tell me all of the things about the other woman that she didn't like. She said, "I can't think of any." I said, "No, really think hard. I'm sure you can come up with some." She said, "Why would I try so hard to find things I don't like about her?" I said, "Exactly! So why would you search so hard in yourself?"

Remember that the things you say to yourself on a subconscious level determine how the outside world appears to you. Who controls what you think? You do of course! Nothing and no one forces you to think the things you think. If you are working on gaining greater self-confidence and creating a higher self-esteem, then the simple act of writing out the qualities in yourself that you like will begin the process. Here are a few examples of what I mean: "I am a worthy and desirable human being. I have many outstanding qualities to share with others. I know others are lucky to spend time with me. I only want to be with people who want to be with me. People dig me!"

Okay—stop reading this book right now and write out *your* list of qualities that make you a desirable person to be with.

Chapter 11

The Taking Touch

"What would happen if you took absolute selfish pleasure in giving to others?"

—MARSHALL SYLVER

I never do anything for other people. Everything I do I do for myself. If I give someone a massage I am doing it because it feels good to my hand. If I have a conversation with someone it is because it is stimulating to my ears. If I lend someone money it is because I get selfish joy from watching them feel good. I never do something for someone because I expect them to respond in a specific way because I know that this sets me up to be frustrated and resentful if they don't respond the way I want them to. I call this process of selfish giving the **Taking Touch**.™

I first thought about the Taking Touch when I was at a friend's house petting his cat. My friend has the most incredibly intelligent cats, not just trained, truly intelligent. I believe that these cats know exactly what you are saying to them and have knowledge of the English language. Something else I've noticed about his cats—and any cats for that matter —is that they will only allow you to pet them for as long as they want to be petted. When they've had enough they're gone. I've also noticed that most people like to pet cats long after the cat has been satisfied. The cat will be trying to get away and they'll be holding the cat down and petting the cat as if the cat were enjoying it, the whole time Little Whiskers is right on the edge of bolting. The moment the person loosens up their grip, kitty is are off and running. Sound familiar? All I can say is that if you are petting the cat for the cat's sake you are going to be disappointed. Regardless of how it turns out, the cat is sooner or later going to get up and leave and most likely not say thank you. When you pet the cat you had better be doing it because it feels good to your hand or you will lose.

Years ago I bought my mother a car. This was a big deal to me at the time since I really didn't have a lot then. I'll never forget the day that I gave my mother the keys. Since it was a workday for both of us, she got picked up from work and brought down to the car dealership by one of my sisters. I remember waiting for them to come down to the dealership thinking, "I'll bet she cries. I'll bet she jumps up and down and hugs me and kisses me and makes a big ol' scene."

I was really excited by the time she and my sister got to the car lot. When they arrived my mother got out of the car and said, "Which one is it?" I pointed to the vehicle. She said, "Do you have the keys?" I gave her the keys and she said, "Thanks honey, I've got to get back to work."

What! No crying, no slobbering tears of joy all over me, no big ol' scene? Come on! I paid a lot of money for that car. I deserve more than "Thanks honey"!

She jumped in the new car and left the parking lot with me standing in disbelief. As I stood there I contemplated what had just happened. I decided that I would feel joyful regardless of how her response had been. I decided to get joy from what I had done rather than from her response. If I hadn't decided to get joy from my actions I would have lost out on two levels. First, I would have missed out on being happy and second, I had already paid for the car.

After that day in the parking lot my mother has told me many times how much she appreciates the car and I know that she means it. We have even talked about what happened on that day and we have had many laughs about it. It seems that she was having a tough day at work and her boss wasn't going to give her the time to even go pick up the car. I think her boss was a little jealous that anyone's son would buy them a car. At any rate it was my decision to feel good about the selfish act of giving her the car, which allowed me to have fun either way.

If the only reason you give love or anything else is to get a response, then you'll lose. If you're in a relationship and they don't respond the way you want them to it's going to be frustrating and aggravating. When you do things for the selfish reason that it feels good to you, you win.

Here's another example. I was recently in my car and my girlfriend and I were having a tough day and things weren't going well. In the middle of the day I realized we hadn't talked to each other for probably ten minutes. Now in that moment thoughts were going through my brain, such as, "Forget it, I'm not going to say anything, you know, it's all her fault we got to this place." As I looked down into the passenger seat where my girlfriend was seated I saw that she was wearing a short skirt, and her beautiful long sexy smooth legs were draped across the edge of the seat. I thought to myself, "I'd love to touch her leg," and in the next instance I said to myself, "No! Forget it, she hasn't been very nice, I'm not going to give her that pleasure." Well, a moment later I thought, "That's stupid. You're going to make *yourself* lose because you don't want *her* to feel good." So in that moment I reached down and I touched her leg and I caressed her knee in a loving fashion. And do you know what? It felt fantastic to my hand. Funny thing is, after I touched her knee for my own totally selfish motives, just to get pleasure in my hand, she had the nerve to lean over and kiss my neck just because it felt good to her lips and because she was being selfish too.

Begin right now to practice the Taking Touch. Say I love you to someone else without expecting them to give anything back. Tell them how you feel just because it feels good to tell them. You can practice the Taking Touch in all areas of your life. If you're going to lend someone money, lend them money as if you were giving it to them. In other words, give it away because it feels good and not because you expect some favor or even the return of the money later on. Practicing the Taking Touch in all areas of your life will create more peace and well-being in all of your relationships.

Chapter 12

Unlocking Sensual Passion

"Sensuality is being in touch with all of your senses."
—MARSHALL SYLVER

Do you want to be more sensual? Do you want to project that sensuality to other people so that they want to spend time with you? Then get in touch with your senses, and I mean all of them. Some people think sensuality means dressing sexy and yet that's not the whole story.

> **"Sex appeal is being turned on to yourself. Sensuality is the ability to be in tune with and to stimulate the senses both in yourself and in others."**

All the senses—sight, smell, sound, touch, and taste.

In my seminars we practice different sensuality exercises. A good exercise to get in touch with your senses is to devote one whole day to practice using more of your senses. Spend the whole day experiencing things in a sensory channel different from what you normally would. Find sensuality in the smell of fresh-baked bread and everything else you come in contact with. Notice the sensuality of the water streaming across your face in the shower as it trickles down your body and tickles your skin. Feel the sound of the music and let yourself cry when you read a sad or compassionate article or book. Dare to run your fingertips down the windowpane to feel the sensation of the glass. Taste something that you have never tasted before, like raw pepper. Rub the towel across your body real hard after bathing to get your circulation going. Dance with yourself totally free of inhibitions. Act like you are the most sensual person in the universe. For just today let yourself be in touch with all your senses.

Our senses are often mind triggers for past experiences. Since most people only pay attention through sight and sound they don't realize that they are responding to subconscious triggers that are coming in through other sources. For example, the smell of fresh-cut grass takes me back to my childhood. A friend of mine who smokes has a Zippo lighter. He loves the smell of the fluid as he lights up his cancer stick because that smell reminds him of his father. Every time he lights up he thinks good thoughts of his father.

Sensuality is being able to positively stimulate all the senses of others. If you want to create sensuality with someone make sure you affect all of their senses, of sight, smell, sound, touch, and taste. If you are with your partner or out on a date, put on pleasurable music, build a fire, pay attention to the colors and textures of the clothing that your partner is wearing. Burn aromatic candles and notice the fresh smell of their body. Touch their smooth skin as you pass by. Part of the sensual feeling is how you go about stimulating the different senses. The more you use your imagination the more exciting the result will be.

Also pay attention to what is stimulating to the people you want to attract. Think about what will attract your partner or date. Are you wearing a particular perfume or cologne because you like it even though your mate doesn't? It's easy to let your ego get in the way and dress only for yourself. That's great if you always want to be alone. If you are wanting to spend an intimate evening with someone else you would be wise to *dress for them.* I know this seems contrary to much of what I've taught you. Remember I said that relationships don't exist, only relating does. When your dress or appearance pleases the other person and they feel better around you, then you can believe they will be more fun to be around and probably treat you better. On the other hand, if you really want to "dress to express," then you'll find out soon enough if the other person wants to hang out with the you that you are expressing.

If you know that they like a certain smell, flowers, or a certain type of dress that accommodates their needs, then practice the Taking Touch and feel joy by giving them that.

Chapter 13

Pain Is Pleasure Resisted

"Everything experienced fully vanishes."
—MARSHALL SYLVER

I believe any relationship is bound to have some things that might be experienced as pain. And yet the distinction is that pain is pleasure resisted. In other words, when you put your total attention on something and experience it fully, it will vanish.

When a person is in pain, their attention is heightened, and they pay attention to every little detail of their pain. Unfortunately we are more in touch with pain than pleasure. My method is to work through the pain to the pleasure as fast as you can. This method works on any kind of emotional, physical, or mental pain. We all experience pain, and yet the distinction here is that pain is pleasure resisted.

Take a piece of paper and draw a single line down the center of the paper (see example below). First on the left side of the chart name all of the common characteristics of pain. Make sure these are elements common to all forms of pain. Burning would be a characteristic of one kind of pain and not all, so burning wouldn't work; yet heat would, since many people experience a form of heat even when they've been cut. List these elements now before you read on.

Your list may look something like this one and may include some or all of the examples here. Now go to the right side of the T and see how many of the characteristics of pain could also be used to describe pleasure. All or at least most of them, right?

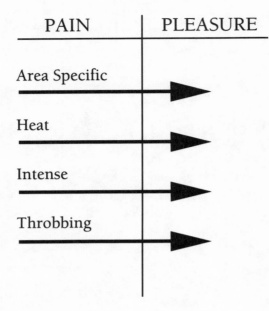

PAIN	PLEASURE
Area Specific	
Heat	
Intense	
Throbbing	

How is this knowledge useful? It's useful when you now realize that **experiencing pain fully makes it disappear.** What is revealed is that pain and pleasure have many of the same characteristics. You usually feel pleasure and pain in a specific area; it's intense, it throbs, it's exploding, and so forth. If this is so, what makes us treat pain and pleasure so differently?

The difference is people very seldom resist pleasure and quite often they'll resist pain. In other words if you were to feel a throbbing in your hand and instead of trying to make it stop simply experienced it for the throbbing that it is, you would lessen the actual pain of the throbbing. Pain is pleasure resisted.

"Pain, like fear, is nature's way of saying, Pay attention."

Putting full attention on pain and noticing all the subtleties of the sensations changes it from pain to pleasure. In my seminars I ask if there is anyone who has any physical pain they would like to make vanish immediately. At a recent program a woman in her eighties named Barbie came on stage who throughout the seminar had been complaining about a chronic headache. She said, "You won't be able to help me, I've had this headache for as long as I can remember!"

Earlier in this book I talked about Non-Confronts, which is the major way that headaches are caused. I told her that I wasn't going to make it vanish, she was.

When Barbie stepped on the stage I asked her if she was ready to make her headache vanish forever.

Barbie said, "Yes."

I said, "Close your eyes and put your full attention on your headache. Tell me exactly where the pain is."

She said, "It's in my head."

"NO. Tell me *exactly* where it is. Is it at the front of your head? Is it at the base of your skull? Is it in the center of your head, is it two inches deep or is it four?"

She said, "It is at the front of my head one inch in."

"Great!" I said. "What shape is it? Is it square, is it round, is it rectangle?"

"It's round."

"What size is it? Is it the size of a baseball, a grapefruit, a golf ball? What size is it?"

"It's the size of a baseball."

"Okay. What color is it? Is it black, is it green, is it red?"

"It's black."

"What texture is it? Is it rough like sandpaper? Is it jagged like lava rock? Is it porous like a cheese grinder?"

"It's like lava rock."

"What size is it now?"

"It's smaller," she said with the slightest smile.

I asked, "What color is it now?"

"It's light brown," she said. A bigger grin was appearing on her face.

"What texture is it now?" I asked, picking up the tempo.

"It's smooth," she cooed.

"What color is it now?"

"It's white, almost clear."

"What size is it now?"

"It's the size of a pea."

"Where is it located now?"

"I can't find it." She smiled fully and had a look of complete satisfaction on her face. "You know I've had that same headache for years. Every time I started to feel it come on I would tell myself that it had to go away, that I couldn't tolerate it anymore. I realize now that the tension of trying to get rid of the headache is what made it worse."

> *"There is no object so foul that intense light will not make it beautiful"*
>
> —Ralph Waldo Emerson

Paying attention to something makes it easier to understand, and experiencing something fully will make it less powerful. It's kind of like analyzing a joke: once you do it's no longer funny. Not experiencing something fully is avoidance. Avoidance makes things worse. When you are not putting full attention on something in the present moment you are putting attention on something in some other moment. The mind cannot operate in a vacuum. It is always thinking of something. If not the present, then the past or the future.

The process of experiencing something fully works not only with things physical like headaches, it works with everything. Realize that the only reason anything exists is because of the resistance. Day exists because it resists night. Love exists because it resists hate. Light exists only when it resists darkness. Problems exist only when they are resisted. In my sales seminars I teach the salespeople that the only reason their job exists is because of the resistance of their customers. If their customers said yes to all of their requests, then there would be no reason to have a salesperson.

Have you ever been afraid to confront a challenge in your life? Have you ever put off talking to someone about an uncomfortable situation only to find that the more you put it off the worse things got? And when you finally confronted the situation and experienced it fully it was easier to deal with than you had expected or imagined? I'm sure you have. Experiencing anything fully makes it disappear. Do you have a phobia? Is there something that you are unreasonably afraid of?

> *"Fear is a little man that sits on your shoulder and says pay attention."*
>
> —Carlos Castaneda

If you want to make a phobia disappear, then experience it fully. Close your eyes and imagine the thing that you fear most is right here now. Give yourself an encounter with the thing that you used to be afraid of rather than doing your best not to think of it.

When you come and visit me at one of my live seminars you will see me do a rapid phobia removal. At a recent program I asked the group if anyone was afraid of snakes. A few people raised their hands. I told them that I have a pet python in the back of the room that I was going to bring out in a few minutes—what would they do? A woman of color stood up immediately and began walking toward the exit. I asked her what was wrong and she said she couldn't stay in the room if there was a snake there. I told her, "You're just the person I'm looking for!"

I invited her down to the stage. I asked her to close her eyes and take a deep breath. I then asked her to imagine that a very small snake with crossed eyes and no teeth was at her feet. I told her to imagine that the snake would talk to her in a cartoon voice. She giggled a little. I asked her to pick up the cross-eyed, toothless little creature and hold it in her hand. I told her that the little guy was afraid of her and that she needed to treat him gently. She began speaking to him as if he were a baby. I told her that he was very slowly getting bigger and that his teeth were coming in. I told her that he was telling her that it broke his heart to know that people didn't take the time to get to know him and just treated him like he was mean because of the color of his skin. She said that she understood and that she would protect him and that there was nothing to worry about.

I counted from one to three and told her to open her eyes. I asked her what she thought of snakes now. She told me that maybe she hadn't realized that they were just creatures too, and that they needed love and understanding just like the rest of us. I asked her what she would do if I brought a snake up to the stage now. She said she might feel uncomfortable at first and yet she was sure she would get used to it.

I said, "Great! I'd like you to meet a friend of mine." With that I had one of my staff bring out my seven-foot python, Monty. They placed the snake in her hands and she laughed. She even mentioned that his skin felt cool and smooth, kind of like her favorite pair of boots. I told her not to mention that too loudly around Monty, he's a little sensitive!

Another example of experiencing something fully is when you first meet someone who doesn't appear to be physically very attractive and as you continue to really pay attention to them it will seem as if the lines of their face and their entire persona become more pleasant. This is true for many reasons. First, as you know, we find what we are looking for, so as you look for beauty you'll find it. Also, as you put your total attention on someone and your energy is clear you will notice the things about them that make them unique. Not all works of art are appreciated by everyone and yet most do have something to appreciate. Finally, when you are putting this kind of loving, nonjudgmental attention on someone else they'll begin to respond to your expectations and start acting in more beautiful ways.

How might we as a planet be better off if we were able to experience fully what others were experiencing. Not just sympathetic—rather empathetic. Not just feeling sorry for someone, actually feeling their pain.

One day a very important businessman was preparing for a very important meeting. All of a sudden he noticed that he had not completed the report he needed for his presentation. He barked at his secretary, "Finish this up and I need it now!"

The secretary did her best to complete the unfinished project before the boss raced out the door to his appointment. A couple of hours later he came back to the office with a defeated look on his face and a worse attitude. "Can't you do anything right!" he snarled, "We didn't get the contract, so don't even think about getting a raise."

The secretary held back her anger, frustration, and disappointment and kept it bottled up until the end of the day. When she arrived home later that night she found her son had left his toy soldiers all over the kitchen. In her emotional pain that she had carried home from work she exploded without even saying hello: "Get your toys out of the kitchen. I've told you a thousand times—don't play in the kitchen. Clean up this mess and stay outside until I call you for dinner!"

The child, a little bit bewildered, scooped up his toys, tossed them in the toy box, and then shuffled sadly out the door. He sat on the back porch pouting and mumbling to himself, "Mom doesn't love me." Just as he was feeling his worst, the cat walked by. The boy, without even thinking, gave the cat a swift kick in the backside and said, "Stupid cat!" Needless to say the cat looked up with an expression on his face that said, "What the heck did I do!"

What caused the cat to get kicked? The boss being unprepared for his presentation and losing the contract of course. The moral to this story is you never know what's causing the cat to get kicked. How someone is responding to you may have nothing to do with you. When you just take the surface attitudes and energy of what someone is projecting, you will probably get yanked into their personal drama. When you observe the situation and experience it fully you begin to notice that the waiter's bad attitude, or the discourteous bank teller, or the guy who cut you off on the freeway are not reflections on you. When you refuse to give your power to people or things that you used to think were painful and just experience them as momentary occurrences, then you will become more effective. The next time someone is treating you with less respect than you think you deserve, remember to ask yourself,

"I wonder who kicked their cat?"

What if rather than responding to someone or something, you instead took the time to fully experience the circumstances and deal with them as they emerged. I mean after all, what choice do you really have? Pain is only pleasure resisted. Resist your life less, so you can create more pleasure now.

Another way to transform emotional pain into pleasure is to:

"Find your life interesting and deal with what emerges."

A few years back when I was first teaching the concept of finding your life interesting I had also just purchased my first Mercedes-Benz. I was very proud of my car and was very careful to park it away from other cars for fear of getting my first door ding. You know, the little nick that someone else's door makes when it opens up into the side of your car? Anyway, I had just finished my seminar and I was walking toward my parked car when suddenly I saw that someone had run into the back of it. As I approached I could see that they had knocked my taillight out and it was lying on the pavement behind the car. Since I had just finished teaching about finding your life interesting I knew that I was being tested to walk my talk. As I approached the car I just kind of giggled as I looked at the plastic taillight on the cement. "I've never seen a Mercedes tail light on the ground before, that's interesting!"

Just as I started thinking that I heard a very sexy female voice behind me say, "Is that your car?" Since I was a little preoccupied in checking out the damage I just muttered, "Yup, sure is."

Next I heard the same voice say, "You're not mad, are you?"

By now, because of her questions, I'm thinking, "That's interesting!"

I turned around and in front of me was an immaculately dressed, very beautiful woman in her early twenties. I thought to myself, "She's interesting." I also asked her if she had seen who had hit my car. Suddenly she broke down in tears. She told me that it was indeed she who had backed into my car. She also told me that she was afraid to leave a note or wait until the owner came back because she wasn't sure she could handle the emotional stress. She told me that she was sure the owner would get mad and yell at her. She told me that she was newly single (I thought, "That's very interesting!") and that her ex-husband would get mad at her over the smallest things and she just couldn't handle the stress right now. I told her to relax, everything would be all right. She told me she had insurance and it would cover everything and she also asked if there was anything else she could do for me. I told her as a matter of fact I hadn't eaten yet and I was starving and that she could join me for a snack if she had the time. She did and we became lifelong friends, all because I chose to find the situation interesting rather than something to get angry over.

ASSIGNMENT: When you notice something or someone today that creates an uncomfortable, unpleasant, or even painful experience for you, take the time to experience it fully. Put your full attention on them or it and become more of an observer. Be interested in what is actually going on rather than what you are feeling. Should you feel any tension in your body, then do for yourself the same process that I did with Barbie. Mentally, to yourself, define what size the negative situation is, what color, what shape. Notice that when you put attention on it and experience it fully, it vanishes.

"It's not how often you get off track that impacts your life. It's how fast you notice you are off track and what you learn that determines where you end up."

Keep in mind that you learn more when you're off track then when you're on. You're definitely going to learn more when you put your full attention on the pain at hand. I don't think that it's people who don't feel pain that have successful relationships. I know that the people who have pain are quick to notice any and put their attention on it so they can redirect the focus and deal with what emerges. I don't think it's the amount of time you spend off track that determines the success or failure of your relationship. It's how much time you spend off track before you decide it is time to get back on track that determines whether your relationship will be one of passion or one of pain.

Some people don't realize that in life everybody is off track the great majority of the time. A few months ago when I was in New York with my publisher I had the opportunity to fly back on an airline called MGM Grand Air. MGM Grand Air is an all-first-class airline. Where most planes have one hundred to two hundred seats, this plane had thirty. In addition these aren't just ordinary first-class seats, these are more like the most comfortable reclining chairs you could ever put in your living room. Not only that, there are also love seats, a full-blown stand-up bar, special private compartments, and more. They don't just serve champagne on this flight they serve Dom Perignon. They don't just serve appetizers, they serve four kinds of caviar. You get the idea. A couple hours into the flight I went up to the cockpit to say hello. The pilot and the co-pilot were talking and I noticed that the plane was on autopilot. As I was watching the plane correct itself I asked the pilot how often the plane gets off course. He told me that whether he is flying the plane or the autopilot is we were off course ninety-five percent of the time. Ninety-five percent of the time? No way! I asked him to explain that to me. He pulled out a napkin and drew a sketch similar to the one on the next page. He showed me that when we took off from New York we were on course for just a moment and that during the entire time we were on the trip we were crisscrossing the intended path. He told me it doesn't matter how often we get off path. As long as we were focused on the destination and moving closer, we would get there. He said the major adjustments are always made as we are about to land.

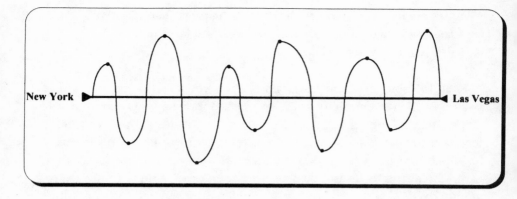

Isn't that just like your life? As long as you have a clear and specific vision of where you are going and make constant adjustments along the way you will get to your final destination. While you are on your journey it is important to select your co-pilots carefully. Since your relationships are a major portion of your life, then let them be what they are intended to be. Relationships are intended to be an oasis, a safe place you can go to when you need to regroup from all the challenges of the outside world. May all of your relating be passionate and when it's not may you learn the lessons to make them so.

> *"You learn to speak by speaking, to study by studying, to run by running, to work by working; and just so, you learn to love . . . by loving. All those who think any other way deceive themselves".*
>
> —SAINT FRANCIS OF SALES

Chapter 14

Subconscious Reprogramming for More Passion

"It's not enough to learn, one must become."

—MARSHALL SYLVER

Now that you have learned many powerful and effective strategies for relating, it's time to integrate this material for maximum impact on your life. This chapter, like the two similar ones on Profit and Power programming, is a synopsis of the material taught in this section. The material is written in a specific language syntax to have the greatest possible impact on your subconscious mind. The chapter can be used in one of two ways. One is to record it onto an audiocassette and then play it back as you relax. When you record it, make sure you allow for about two minutes at the front of the tape for you to breathe deep and relax. When you record it onto tape you will read the script in the second person instead of as it's written in the first person. "You will relax" instead of "I will relax." "You recognize that you are indeed worthy . . ." instead of "I recognize that I am indeed worthy . . ." In this way the tape you have created becomes your own personal Subconscious Reprogrammer.

Another method of reprogramming your mind with this is to use the reprogramming script as an affirmation exercise. You simply read the

reprogramming statements out loud to yourself every day exactly as they are written. This method is extremely effective because it forces you to focus your entire attention on the new programs. Often when we are listening we sometimes let our mind wander. By being an active participant in your positive reinforcement, these statements will help you stay more focused and hear what you're saying. Both methods are valuable. If you choose to use this method of reprogramming, then read the entire chapter out loud exactly as it is written.

Subconscious Reprogramming Script for PASSION:

I recognize that I am indeed worthy of passionate, healthy supportive relationships. I realize that relationships are built on agreements, and as long as the agreements are upheld, the relationship will continue. If the agreements are broken and no amendments are made, I know the relationship will suffer.

I realize that a relationship is a masterpiece, built on communication, and that relationships balance themselves out when people come together, they fulfill each other's basic needs, and are supportive. I realize that relationships are also like books in that they are for learning. Some books I read quickly, getting through the chapters only for enjoyment. Other books are novels, which I read slowly and deliberately, wanting to learn as much as I possibly can. I realize that no matter where I am in my current relationship, or in future relationships, the key is to respect the book, to put it down gently when I'm done, and that each book that I read will become easier and easier to understand and to utilize in supporting me in creating the relationship and life of my dreams.

I realize that it is much healthier to want a relationship instead of needing a relationship and I have released needing a relationship. I enjoy my own company so much that I know I can give good company to other people. I've released my demands, and I've upgraded them into desires. I've released all expectations, since I know that expectations set me up to be let down. I know how to surrender, quickly, and how to deal with whatever emerges. I experience my relationships as they are instead of how they should be.

I realize that I am totally responsible for how I feel in any given moment and that no one has the power to make me angry or frustrated or happy or impassioned, unless I give them that power over my life. I choose to give that power only to those people and circumstances that serve me and nurture me and support me.

I also know how to take charge of my own environment. If something is happening that bothers me, I think about ways of inspiring the people around me to give me what I want. I know that I always attract more with honey than with vinegar. I can charm other people easily and readily to give me what I want, and I find it easy to overlook their shortcomings, focusing only on the goodness that they bring into my life. I now take charge of my own environment, and I am totally responsible for how I feel.

I also know that it's better to be happy than to be right. I've now chosen to release the need to be right from my life, and instead on a daily basis I choose to be happy. I realize that the fastest way out of an argument is to simply say, "You're right," and then find the rightness of the person I'm talking to. I'm willing to surrender quickly and to go down a different path, realizing I can always change my mind. I know I don't have to fix anything to go for more. There's nothing about me or the person I'm relating to that's broken.

I also know that it's better to have a relationship than to spend time talking about a relationship. If I'm spending too much time talking about what's wrong, then I know I'll hardly have the time to enjoy what's right. If something happens that's outside the agreements of the relationship, I have new and wonderful ways of dealing with it. I ask my partner, "Do we have an agreement?" I ask my partner, "Would you like to change the agreement?" or I would ask myself, "Would I like to change my relationship with this person?"

I realize that anytime I fall in love with someone's potential, I'm setting myself up for disappointment, because I'm in love with someone who isn't there. It is much better to fall in love with someone as they are right now and accept the changes that come up and decide later if they're someone I still want to be with. I never fall in love with someone's potential. I see people as they are, not as I desire them to be.

I know that the truth sets me free, and I am trusting and trustworthy. I believe that people tell me the truth, until I decide that it is not worth talking to them because they lie. I also realize that being truthful with other people allows them to love me for who I really am, instead of the illusion of facade that other people might think I am. I am honest and I trust people. I am trustworthy and trusting, and I find that it expands my universe and sets me free. It allows me to feel more calm, and more comfortable. I also realize that everybody lies, and I'm quick to trust people again, or to surrender to the fact that they do lie, and move on with my life. I realize the faster I can forgive, the faster I can get back to love.

I also understand the power of listening, being genuinely interested, and without owning what the other person is saying. I realize when someone says things to me, it's their opinion, and not necessarily the facts of who I am or how the world is. I listen without interrupting, with genuine interest, and without owning what the other person is telling me.

I also operate out of a place of love instead of a place of vengeance. I recognize that punishing someone will never help me get more, and I ask myself constantly, "Is this going to make the other person feel good or bad?" I realize I can never get more by operating out of a place of vengeance, and I now operate out of a place of love.

I recognize that it only takes one person to get the relationship back on track, and if I'm the one who notices that it's gone off track, then it's my responsibility to get quickly back to love. I never assume the other person has noticed that things are off track, I surrender my ego quickly, and I say things like, "I care about you, and I want us to get closer. What do you want that can bring us back to love?" Instead of raising my voice, I maintain a position of love and focus on going for more, instead of less. I realize that I don't need to fix things to go for more.

I also know that it's easy to express what I want, and it becomes easier every day, to express it in a way that inspires my mate to give me love in the way that I want it. I am also totally willing to give my love the love that they desire in the way that they want it, or to free them up, and give them the opportunity to receive the love that they want in the way that they want it outside of the relationship. I realize that it doesn't mean that I have to transform the relationship, it simply is an enhancement that brings more goodness back to me.

I also realize that it's important to inspire my mate to give me love in a way that's meaningful to me, because I do deserve to have love exactly the way that I want it. I know that nature is give-and-take. If I keep taking, I'll run the well dry, and if I keep giving without receiving, soon enough I'll be disgruntled and frustrated. I realize that healthy relationships are both give-and-take.

I desire to have a healthy, strong, supportive relationship. I know whether or not I'm in a healthy relationship. I know that healthy relationships are designed to create more in my life, instead of less. If I find I'm devoting more time to the relationship than to the rest of my life, if I find that it's inhibiting the rest of my life, I'll now take steps to take charge, and lovingly and supportingly I'll find ways for both of us to win. I know that there are ways for my mate and me to get it all. I know that this is not an either/or world, it is an *and* world, and I know that I can simply go for more, without having to compromise the things that are important to me.

I also experience upset as an opportunity for learning. I experience challenges in my relationship as a way to bring us closer. I know that relationships are for learning, and anytime something comes up that isn't fun, I ask myself, "What is there to learn here, what goodness is here to bring me closer to the one I love?"

I know that the surest way to have my rights violated is to have rights. I recognize that I have no rights, the only way I can be wronged is to have rights, so instead I choose to have desires. I realize that what should be is what isn't, and I resolve to deal with what is. I realize that if something happens in my relationship that is less than fun, that I can create an agreement, and I can make that agreement be the basis of the relationship from that point onward, since there is no way to change the past.

All of these beneficial ideas and concepts make a deep impression upon my subconscious mind, never to be removed, to be recalled the moment I say or think the word "Passion." (*Take a long deep breath now, breathe in deeply, and speak the word "Passion" out loud.*)

I know that withholding love is always a sign of low self-esteem, and when I believe in my own never-ending abundant supply of love, I'll never hold back, and the more that I give to the world, the more I get back. I know that it's as important to know what I don't want, as what I do want. I know that my mate will communicate more with me when they know that they're communicating upon receptive ears. I also expect my mate to measure up, realizing that it's an insult not to expect them to treat me with the love and respect that I deserve. I also realize that it's impossible to have a healthy relationship unless I now respect myself and recognize my own inherent value. I am indeed worthy of a relationship that totally supports me, nurtures me, and inspires me to get more in my life.

I also realize it's important to stay together for good, and not for bad. I realize that teaching my children to love and to support each other is healthy, and teaching them to stay in relationships that are not supportive and abusive is unhealthy. I frequently find things right about the person I love, and I tell them often. In all of my relationships, I realize the more I can find right, the more people will want to give me more. I tell my mate, "Something I love about you is . . ." many times every day. I tell my mate what I love about them not because I want something in return, but because it feels good to tell them so. I understand the Taking Touch, and I give love because it feels good to give love, never expecting anything back. I realize the better I get at giving love, the more I open up my universe to receive love.

While I'm giving love, I always maintain a high level of self-respect and self-esteem. I realize that to give love in a place that's abusive is pointless, and will not support me or anyone. I also realize that giving love is a healthy way of saying that my self-esteem is high, I have plenty of love to give, a never-ending supply. I realize that self-confidence is what makes me attractive, and I stand taller, and smile broadly, and I easily and readily introduce myself to others. I recognize that self-respect is understanding my own inherent value.

I realize that sensuality is being in touch with my senses, all of them. I pay attention to how things smell and how they look, how they feel and how they sound. In my pursuit of attracting other people I present myself in ways that sound and look and smell and feel great. I realize that sex appeal is being turned on to myself, and each and every day that goes by I love myself more. I find that being alone is a wonderful place to be, and it balances itself out wonderfully with being with others.

I realize that more is always learned in pain than in pleasure, and I utilize and embrace pain for the lesson that it is, and move quickly back to pleasure, realizing that I can take those lessons with me and go for more good. I create my relationships as an oasis, as a safe place where I can go to when I need to regroup from all the challenges in the outside world. Should I have the time in my life when I am alone not by my own choice, I realize that it's all right to mourn, in fact, mourn very well, and get it done with quickly, so that I can simply say to myself the word "next," and realize that I can savor the wanting as much as the having. I realize that it's important to enjoy my singleness while I'm single, so that I can enjoy my relationship while I am in a relationship.

Each and every day that goes by I become more secure in my ability to attract other people. I become more secure in my ability to be loved, my confidence is growing daily, and I find myself looking at other people and smiling more often. I find myself now taking better care of myself, and I realize that attractiveness is an unwillingness to take no for an answer. I am constantly practicing the process of attracting other people into my life in healthy, happy, productive ways. I pay attention to how other people respond to me, and yet I realize that this is only a reflection, and that I attract what I want to attract by being what I want to attract in my life. I realize the importance of reaching out for my own personal best, to attract the best into my life. I treat all my relationships with the same respect that I would want to be treated myself.

I realize that intimacy is not the right or allowance to treat my mate as I would a stranger on the street. Intimacy requires that I treat my mate at least as good as I would treat my pets, and certainly as good as I want to be treated now. If I'm looking for a relationship, I practice treating all people with love and kindness so that when that ideal person comes along, I have the ability to treat them that way as well and attract them into my life. I am indeed a loving, compassionate, wonderful human being, indeed worthy of all the things relationships can offer me.

Today and from this day forward I find joy in the simplest of things. I realize that in relationships, the rich get richer, and any moment that I take time to appreciate the simple act of kindness someone gives to me, I realize it inspires them to want to give me more. I find myself doing small acts of random kindness, simply helping other people, realizing the more love I put into the world, the more love is there for me as well. I am indeed a happy, loving, joyful individual, becoming more inspired each and every day to touch others' lives in happy, healthy, supportive ways. I am genuinely a great listener, I trust and I am trustworthy, and I am certainly the kind of person that many people would like to know. I am a loving, wonderful, affectionate human being.

I find it easier and easier to express myself, allowing the truth to set me free. I realize that telling others how I feel and not expecting them to respond in a certain way is healthy, and it allows me to be who I am and to be recognized and loved and appreciated for the person I was created to be, a totally loving, totally self-sufficient, totally desiring human being. *(Take a long, deep breath and breathe out now and say the word "Passion" out loud. Take another long, deep breath, and as you exhale say the word "Passion" out loud again.)*

PROFIT

Chapter 15

Think and Act Like a Millionaire

I'm often asked how I went from being a poor child of ten growing up on a farm with no running water and no electricity to a multimillionaire. The story is quite simple. When I was very young I found a dime in the gutter. I took that dime and bought a single apple at the local market. I polished it and did my best sales presentation and sold the apple for twenty cents. With the twenty cents I went out and bought two more apples for ten cents each, I polished them up and sold the both of them for twenty cents each. Then my uncle died and left me $2 million and that's how I became a multimillionaire.

If you're like most people (and like it really was for me), then you had better not hold your breath waiting for your uncle to first get rich and then to die and finally to leave you all his money. Since that's about as likely to happen as you winning the lottery, then we had better get started figuring out another way to create financial abundance. That way if the uncle or the lottery comes through it will just be gravy.

In the Profit section of this book you will begin learning how to think and act like someone who has created phenomenal wealth so you can create outrageous fortune in your own life.

Did you know that 95 percent of all the money on the planet is controlled by 5 percent of the people? An even scarier statistic is that 50 percent of all the money on the planet is controlled by 1 percent of the population. It's even more scary if you're not a part of the 1 percent! It's also believed that if all of the money on the earth were equally divided among everyone, that within five years it would be back in the hands of the same 1 percent again. Why? The people that are creating wealth right now would keep doing the same things and they would keep creating the same wealth and eventually the money would go right back in their pockets.

What genetic difference is there between the people who have the money and the people that don't? You're absolutely right, none. Creating profit is not genetic. If it's not genetic then it must be mental, so if you knew what the 1 percent do, then you could do what they do, right? You are about to learn the foundational strategies of the ultrawealthy. By thinking what they think and doing what they do you'll produce similar results. Since everything is relative, even if you don't become ultrawealthy, a couple extra million would be all right, wouldn't it?

Chapter 16

Successful People Are Great Communicators

The number-one wealth habit, the greatest common denominator of the ultraprosperous, is that wealthy people are master communicators. Communication leads to wealth. Say it over in your mind and process the meaning. Since everything that you want that you don't have you will most likely get from others, your ability to effectively communicate will be your key to riches.

> **"To get what you want you must communicate with others in a way that inspires them to want to give it to you."**

The quality of your life is the quality of your communication both with yourself and with the outside world. What this means is that your ability to communicate or to persuade yourself to take specific actions, and your ability to communicate and to persuade others to take a specific action, are what give you quality of life.

Did you know that the highest paid and most powerful people on the planet are communicators and public speakers? Politicians, entertainers, superstar athletes. People who are willing to put themselves at stake in front of large groups of people and communicate in a way that inspires other people to support them. The reason that communicators are the highest paid is that the number-one fear in most of us is the fear of public speaking, of getting up in front of a group of strangers and embarrassing ourselves.

In my Total Potential Training Weekend, I motivate thousands of people to eat fire. These people, just like you, have broken through their fears and placed eighteen inches of flame into their mouth, safely and successfully. This is an extremely dangerous action and definitely should not be attempted by anyone not thoroughly trained to do so. At the beginning of the seminar, I ask everyone to tell me their greatest fears. In descending order the ones I hear most often are: number one, fear of public speaking; number two, fear of falling; and number three, fear of fire.

"What that means is most people would rather burn up than speak in front of others. Amazing!"

I don't think this is a fear of public speaking in the truest sense. I think this is the fear that the anxiety of getting up in front of a group of strangers and speaking is not commensurate with the rewards that would be gained by doing so. In fact, when I ask my seminar attendees, "How many of you would be willing to get up in front of a group of strangers and purposely make a fool of yourself every day for a year if it makes you at least one million dollars?" every single hand in the room goes up. When I point out to them that I am living proof that it could happen, then the fear of getting up in front of people starts to diminish. Do you now understand that learning the skills of communication is paramount to getting the money that you want? Your success in life will be largely determined by your ability to communicate both with yourself and with other people. Self-communication is the ability to inspire yourself to take action. Communication to others is called persuasion or influence that inspires them to want to support you on your path. In communication you will always get back what you send out. If you're having people tell you, no, too often it's because you're asking questions or making requests that are easy or fun to say no to.

"In communication you get back what you send out."

Test this out. The next time you meet someone for the first time introduce yourself by just your first name and notice what you get back. You will probably get their first name back. The next time that you first meet someone else introduce yourself by first and last name and notice what you get back. Chances are when you give your first and last name you'll get their first and last name back. If you are not getting what you want from other people it has nothing to do with them, it is what you are sending out that is ineffective. Later you will learn how to make requests that are easy and fun to say yes to. When you begin to adjust the ways that you communicate to others you will start to receive different feedback.

"Effective communicators take full responsibility for both sides of the communication."

Effective communicators never assume someone understands. They always double-check to make sure the others understood what they are saying. You're not likely to hear an effective communicator or a wealthy person say, "You just don't understand me." An excellent communicator realizes it is their responsibility to understand and to be understood. They will repeat back the other person's communication to be sure they have received it properly, and they will double-check that the person who received their communication understood what they meant.

Chapter 17

Successful People Know That Money Is Made in Their Minds First

"Empty pockets never held a man back. Only empty heads and empty hearts can do that."

—NORMAN VINCENT PEALE

Everything begins with a thought, and thoughts are turned into plans, and plans into reality. You must develop the belief that making money can only begin in your mind.

"More gold has been mined from the thoughts of men than has ever been taken from the earth."

—NAPOLEON HILL

Most great achievers in any field have turned their thoughts into profit. It's the thought that is worth millions. I have had many thoughts in my life that have netted me well over a million dollars each. I know it's easier to just surrender and believe that it's not your lot in life to have wealthy abundance and yet it doesn't have to be that way. In order for your financial situation to change you must learn to think about your current situation differently. You'll never create wealth through your labors.

"Those who think govern those who labor."

You have to learn to leverage your three key resources to create abundance. They are people, time, and the money you have presently. In the next sections you will learn how to do just that. Let's start with leveraging people . . .

Chapter 18

Successful People Create Relationships

"The riches that you want and don't have won't come from your own pocket."

—MARSHALL SYLVER

Wealth habit number three: rich people create relationships. People of wealth know the skills of bonding with others. They know how to inspire people to help them get what they want. Additionally they have a genuine love for their fellow human. They enjoy the company of others because they like themselves. Since they understand the inherent value of all people, they know that just by virtue of being human the people they meet are worthy of their attention. People who don't have the ability to bond are always judging others harshly and not accepting the other person as they are. It may seem like such a small adjustment to make to appreciate everyone you come in contact with and yet so few people actually do it. As I sit writing this I am at a resort in Hawaii. Yesterday I struck up a conversation with a man by the pool. He told me his name was Steve. He was very unassuming and seemed almost shy. Even though I was beat from a long day of writing I could tell this person wanted to talk. Since I have always had a great love for all people I was cordial and appreciative that someone wanted to talk to me. A while later he said goodbye and left. It was then that the pool attendant said, "Do you know who that was? That was the founder of Apple Computers. Steven Jobs."

"I'd rather have 1 percent of the efforts of a thousand men than 100 percent of my own."

—J. PAUL GETTY

Everything you want that you don't have you get from other people. How do you get other people to give you that 1 percent of their productivity? What do certain people do that inspires other people to want to give their hard labor up for someone else's profit? Ninety-five percent of the population is led around by the other 5 percent and they get away with it because they have a vision.

"I once met a man who knew where he was going and he invited everyone to come along."

—KENNY LOGGINS

The phenomenal success of Apple Computer had more to do with Steven Jobs's ability to get people excited than it did with technology. Many people were involved with the computer industry at the time and yet I believe that one of the major reasons that Apple did so well is that Jobs was able to make the ride so much fun that it, in the words of a famous ad campaign for the military, wasn't just a job, it was an adventure. When you're specific about where you're going, and you're so passionate that the trip looks like fun, then it's easy to invite and inspire others to want to come along.

"Either create your own journey or you'll become a part of someone else's."

By becoming so specific about where you're going it becomes extremely easy to motivate others to come on board. I'm so specific about my mission and my direction that it's not unusual for my office to receive many calls every single week from people who want to volunteer to come and work for us. I believe the reason is that by becoming specific about where I'm going, it becomes attractive to other people. Not to mention that we have a vision that allows other people to win by being a part of it. Passion is very salable. I live a passionate life by squeezing all possible pleasure from every single moment. I enjoy the journey as much as the destination. I savor the wanting as much as the having. Since human beings are motion junkies, everyone is looking for a ride that will be fun. What you need to do is create a ride that's fun and sell it with all your heart.

One of the best ways to inspire others to support you on your journey is to be excited yourself. Do you remember the story of Tom Sawyer, the one where he got the others to whitewash the fence? Instead of making the fence whitewashing a chore he made it so much fun that others begged him to let them help. One time I was returning home from Mexico and having been down celebrating a long weekend I was rather tired and I really didn't want to drive all the way back. I had just purchased my first Mercedes-Benz and I decided to inspire my date to drive. I began telling her what a fantastic car it was and I told her nothing handled like it. It's so smooth and so responsive, it's truly a joy to drive it all the way up the coast toward the States. As I began telling her about how much fun the Benz was to drive I saw her eyes begin to light up. I said, "You know that car is so special to me, I don't know what I'd do if somebody ever drove it for me now and damaged it." A few minutes later she said, "You know what, I'd really love to drive your car and I promise I'll be really careful with it. Do you think you'd let me drive it up the coast?" I said, "I don't know, the coast is windy and there's lots of rocks and I don't know if I could let you drive it. It's a ton of fun and I know you'd enjoy it, but I'm just a little concerned that you wouldn't take care of it if you drove it all the way back to the States." A moment later she was insisting that she'd take care of it and insisting that she drive it all the way back and we'd have fun. So I "surrendered" and I said, "Okay, if you have to, I guess I can let you drive back." With that, she drove, I slept, and we both won.

It is easy to get people to give you a part of their efforts when you show them how to make their efforts more profitable. If I told you that I could teach you how to make twice as much money as you are making now with the same effort and all that I want is half of the extra money, would you want me to teach you? Of course you would.

Wealthy people not only create relationships, they also genuinely want others to succeed. Since they are confident in their own talents they are not afraid of what others are doing. If someone in their field is winning they are cheering them on instead of trying to sabotage them. They let the other person's victory become their inspiration to grow. They know that when they support other people in their growth they are also setting themselves up to win. They share totally of their knowledge, time, and talents. They hold nothing back and support others as they want to be supported.

"We become like the people we surround ourselves with."

Wealthy people surround themselves with other people of wealth. They're not afraid to put themselves out there belly up to the table and be who they are. Do you do that? One reason that some people like to surround themselves with people that are not as successful as themselves is so that they can be the big shot, top dog, cat's meow. Instead they are stifling their own growth. If you really wanted to become better at chess wouldn't it better serve you to play with someone better than you that you could learn from rather than someone you knew you could always beat?

David Ogilvy, the founder of Ogilvy and Mather, placed a Russian doll in front of each of his directors. He told them, "That's you, open the doll."

When they opened the doll they found inside it a smaller doll. When they opened that a smaller one, inside that a smaller one still. Inside the smallest they found a note that said, "When you hire people that are smaller than you we become a company of dwarfs. When you hire people that are more than you we become a company of giants."

Even before you get wealthy do you have a fear of having people think they're in a higher position or a higher standard of living than you, and it's embarrassing you and intimidating you? Are you afraid to surround yourself with people of wealth? Do you think they think any differently than you do? Of course not. There's no separation between you and them. You are all they are and more. The best way to learn anything you want to learn in life is to find someone who does what you want to do well and get to know them.

Personally, I take them to lunch. I simply call them up and tell them I'm impressed with who they are and what they've done for me. I tell them I'm putting together information on highly successful people and would love to take them to lunch in a restaurant of their choice, so I can interview them. Learn to hang out where successful people hang out. Write people letters. Be where they are and you'll find a way to meet them. So right now think about someone in your area of interest that's making a lot of money and give them a call and take a millionaire to lunch or find a mutual hobby and develop a friendship.

Creating a friendship or at least a working friendship with the type of person you want to emulate is the best on-the-job training you can get. When you associate with the type of people you want to become you will discover all kinds of ways to improve your methods. People like to work with people that are fun to be with, so a pleasing personality is mandatory in order to use the association method to your advantage. I'm sure you have heard the old saying that "It's all in who you know." That statement is so true. That's why successful people make it a point to know and hang out with other successful people. In order to be successful you must start hanging out with people that can help you obtain the goals that you want. Many people might feel bad that they are hanging out with someone because of what they can get from that person. While you are feeling bad thinking about the fact that you are "using them," know that they are also "using you."

EXERCISE: Make a list of at least twenty people you could meet with who could give you information that would benefit your life. These could be people that have already accomplished what you want to accomplish. They could be people that have experience in areas that you want to grow in. They could even be people that you would consider competition. You'd be surprised at how much people like to talk about themselves. Make the list now and then call at least five of them and offer to take them to lunch. In addition make a list of at least fifty people that you want to meet just because you do. I have a list that I made years ago that has one hundred people on it from presidents to celebrities to professional athletes. I have met the great majority of those on the list and am just about to start a new one.

Now you are beginning to learn how to leverage people. In the next two chapters I will teach you the two major ways you can leverage your next two greatest assets . . .

Chapter 19

Time—
The Great Equalizer

"Wealthy people know the value of their time."
—MARSHALL SYLVER

If I gave you $86,400 and told you that you must invest it during the next twenty-four hours and whatever you didn't invest during that twenty-four hour period, you'd have to give back to me; how fast would you go to work investing that money? You know you can't make any money if you don't invest it wisely, don't you? Time is the same way. Each day you're given 86,400 seconds to do with what you will. What you don't invest wisely, you lose forever. You cannot get any extra time —you can only utilize the time you have more efficiently.

It's true that all men and women were created equal, except shortly after the birth experience things occurred that altered our equalness. Maybe we landed in the hands of a mother or father who had millions, or maybe they owed millions. The programming we hear from that birth moment on will alter our responses in our world and so too our outcomes. Even though we're only equal in that single moment there is one area that we were created equal in that will remain that way for the rest of our lives. In this one area everyone is given the same, then does with it what they will. Invested well this amenity will return huge dividends. This priceless commodity of which I speak is time.

You have the exact same number of seconds that the guy down the street has and how you use those seconds will determine what you accomplish. I quite often ask myself the question,

"What is the highest and best use of my time?"

The majority of people get so stuck on the principle of some unimportant thing that they cut off their financial nose to spite their face. Let's say that I have a personal income of $2 million per year. On a forty-hour work week, fifty weeks a year comes out to approximately $1,000 dollars an hour. Quite often I'll have something come up in the course of my business that takes me away from my ability to focus on making that $1,000 per hour. When something happens like being overcharged $20 on a printing bill or negotiating a couple of hundred dollars off on a room rental for a seminar, I always stop and consider how much time this thing is likely to take, and if it takes up to a half hour I'd better be saving myself $500. Since I earn $1,000 or more for an hour of my time, if I'm spending more than one minute worrying about losing $20 I'm already losing $20 per minute. If something comes up that makes me lose $20 per minute I need to either hand it off to someone who is paid less than $20 per minute or let it go all together.

No matter what you are earning right now I want you to imagine that you make $1,000 per hour. Is that hard to do? If it is, remember that no one with a five-dollar-an-hour belief system ever made a thousand dollars an hour. Imagine if you were the kind of a person that was making $1,000 an hour, would you handle the little things faster? Would you get less bogged down in the minor irritations and focus more on making money? If you were already making $1,000 an hour, would you be more confident in your work? Would it take all the stress away? If you really believe that you were worth that much money would you laugh more often at the people who insult you? I'm sure you've heard the expression "He laughed all the way to the bank." Wealthy people only give power to the people and the circumstances that allow them to get more. Instead of getting caught up in other people's dramas, wealthy people never waste any time being anywhere they don't want to be. In a future chapter I'll talk about making decisions quickly. Imagine you're losing $20 per minute for every minute that you don't make a decision and you'll start to make decisions a lot faster. Remember, let your yes be yes and your no be no. You can always change your mind. Also, stop jumping over dollars to save dimes.

"You can't get more by going for less. Protecting against losses is the surest way to lose."

Surrender your ego and laugh all the way to the bank. A matter of principle will never make you money. Are you the kind of person who would spend two hours of your time to get a $10 refund? Would you take a person to small claims court, and spend ten hours of your time to get $200 back? Any time you invest in going after old money stops you from going for new money.

The rich get richer. When you don't need anything people will want to give it to you. I was in a restaurant not too long ago and a well-known actor and his date walked in and were seated near my table. I couldn't help notice at the end of the meal when the celebrity tried to pay, the owner refused to take his money. The owner said he was thrilled to have a talent as big as him in his restaurant and it would be an honor to buy his dinner. I was looking at the restaurant owner thinking to myself, "Why don't you buy my dinner! This guy's worth twenty million dollars, he can afford it, why don't you give *me* a break!" People will always be more willing to give you things that they think you don't need.

When I ask in my seminars, "What do you want?" I'm really asking a two-part question. Most people will tell me things they don't have. I often think to myself if the only things people want are the things they don't have, they're bound to be unhappy. What about the things you do have? Do you want those things? Can you realize that you already have a great majority of what you want? Instead of focusing only on the things you don't have that you want, focus on the things that you do have. I think the key element in being rich would be wanting everything that you've got. All the stress would go away.

"That man is the richest whose pleasures are the cheapest."
—HENRY DAVID THOREAU

Learn to live simply and whatever you have will always make you rich. It's usually not that there isn't enough money, it's usually that there are more bills than there is money. Where can you trim the fat until you have a solid foundation? This doesn't mean that you'll have to go without to enjoy your life. It means that you have a chance to be creative and find inexpensive forms of entertainment. Quite often a museum is cheaper than a movie, and maybe a video three months after the movie came out would allow you the same satisfaction in a more intimate setting.

"What can I do right now that's positive, powerful, and productive, and moves me in the direction of getting this thing that I want?"

When your ideas are good, money will follow. A single idea, a flash of thought, can be worth millions of dollars. If in fact you knew your mind possessed the ability to produce million-dollar ideas would that create a higher level of confidence in you?

"If you knew that you were the owner of a million-dollar mind would you treat your mind with more respect and appreciation?"

Would you put less poison in a million-dollar mind? If you bought a $250,000 Lamborghini Countach you wouldn't put regular gas in it, would you? Of course not, that would destroy the engine. What about your mind? Are you poisoning it with alcohol or tobacco or drugs? This isn't a judgment because I've been there. When I used to think of myself as invincible I would do whatever I wanted. When I started realizing how much I could get by keeping my mind clear I began to become addicted to a healthier addiction. The high that I get now from doing life is greater than the high I ever got from a beer.

Think of yourself as a millionaire, right now. Since in fact you are a millionaire who simply has not had your money deposited in your bank account. Think of yourself as a person who was born a millionaire, whose destiny was to have at least a million dollars, and begin following your destiny. Start treating your Pinto as if it is a Rolls-Royce or when you get a Rolls-Royce you'll treat it like a Pinto. Act as if you are a millionaire now and start to do the things that millionaires do. If you already were a millionaire, what would you do differently? What differences would other people who knew you when you had no money point out to you now that you do have money? What advice would you give to someone else to help them make more money? Imagine youself giving advice to your friends and they listen to what you say. How would your friends change? Do you have friends that want you to be a millionaire? Would they be happy for you or would they be jealous of your success? If you really want to be a millionaire you must keep friends that will inspire you and not sabotage you. Remember, money starts with a thought. Use your imagination to explore what you would do if you were a millionaire. Some people are afraid to dream big because they don't want to be disappointed. Imagine you have a million dollars in the bank with more coming in. Where will you spend your weekends? Who would you now help out by giving them money? How will this money affect your life? What will you do for the rest of your life? If it's hard to do that, remember that a lack of money could be an incredible inspiration.

Have you ever had to come up with your rent or risk being kicked out of your home and then somehow you found the money? Have you ever had to make a car payment by a certain date or they'd take your car away and somehow, some way you came up with the cash? Have you ever noticed that your income usually expands to meet your bills? Have you ever purchased something and were afraid you couldn't afford it only to find out later that somehow, some way you found the money to take care of it? If you are this kind of person who always seems to just barely get by and barely pay your bills each month, then you're probably the kind of person who waited till the last minute to finish your assignments in school too. You like to come in under the wire. In fact, it's a thrill for you.

I used to be the same way in school. It wasn't until I realized that the whole time I was waiting to do my assignment I was getting less enjoyment from my moments. In other words every single day that went by that I wasn't doing the thing that had a deadline to it I was worrying about the impending deadline. So instead of truly enjoying my free time I would spend that time worrying about the assignment. Then when the time came that the assignment was due I would scramble to finish my project and turn in substandard work.

While writing this book certain circumstances arose that made it take much longer than anticipated. Due to this fact a long-awaited holiday in Hawaii became the place where the book was finished. I was supposed to spend eight days relaxing and instead I was under the time crunch of a book deadline. Rather than doing a little here and a little there I did the entire task the moment I got off the plane until I was finished. This allowed me the rest of my vacation guilt-free and satisfied. In the next chapter I am going to talk about **Worst Things First**, which is the practice of doing the things that you are worrying about now so you can focus your attention on the tasks at hand.

Know the value of your time and decide it's worth the same as that of any other millionaire. Know that in any given moment you are either getting more of what you want or less. Constantly ask yourself, "What is the highest and best use of my time?" Maybe you are the kind of person who is always busy and yet never seems to be getting anything done. If you are always putting out fires, then you need to learn the simple skill of . . .

Chapter 20

Priority Management

To master time is to master your universe. Since it's impossible to manage time you must manage your priorities. When Charles M. Schwab was president of Bethlehem Steel he confronted a management consultant named Ivy Lee with an unusual challenge. He said, "Show me a way to get more things done. If it works I'll pay you anything within reason." Lee handed Schwab a piece of paper. He said, "Write down the things that you have to do tomorrow." Schwab did it. "Now number these things in the order of their real importance." Schwab did that as well. Lee said, "The first thing tomorrow morning start working on number 1, and stay with it until it's completed. Next take number 2, and don't go any further until that one's completed, then proceed through number 3, and so on and so forth.

"Now, if you can't complete everything on schedule in the same day don't worry about it. At least you'll have taken care of the most important things before getting distracted by items of lesser importance."

The key to priority management is realizing it's not time management. You cannot manage time, you can only manage the order in which you get things done. To begin your priority management habit what you want to do is every single night list the things you need to get done. Evaluate their relative importance in the order you need to do them. Give them a specific number. After establishing your priorities stick to your plan of action. Begin item 1, and do it until it's done, then move to number 2, and so on. In this way you'll be assured of accomplishing the things that are the most important to you on a day-by-day basis instead of getting caught up in the fires that need to be put out.

Sometimes people will shift their priorities because the things that they need to accomplish are challenging. It may be that you put off certain tasks that you know need to get done. I have a philosophy that I use called:

"Worst Things First."

What that means is you take care of the toughest things first because usually it's the toughest things that create the greatest rewards for you. After Ivy Lee taught Charles Schwab this process, he did this every working day. Lee told Schwab, "After you have convinced yourself of the value of this system, have your men try it. Trust it as long as you like and then send me a check for whatever you think the idea is worth." In a few weeks Schwab sent Lee a check for $25,000. Schwab later said this lesson was the most profitable one that he'd ever learned in his business career. If life were a chess game, then time is your opponent. Make sure that every single move and moment matters.

Priority management is the ability to do the most important things first, then move on to the things that are less important. You've now learned about priority management. Ask yourself this moment: "Is the thing that I'm doing right now the thing that absolutely must get done?" If not, shift your focus and concentrate on the things that matter, even if you'd rather not have to deal with it. Also ask yourself, "Am I spending time in the present worrying about something in the future?" If you are, either surrender it to the future or do it now because . . .

Chapter 21

He Who Hesitates Is Poor

"Let your yes be yes and your no be no—you can always change your mind."

—MARSHALL SYLVER

Successful people make decisions quickly. They are fast to make up their minds and slow to change them. There's an expression that says, "If you want something done, give it to a busy person to do." I've noticed that ineffective people never seem to have enough time to get anything done. Where the movers and shakers seem to not only have time to do their own jobs, they're also the ones who volunteer for boards or philanthropic programs. How do they have so much more time than the underachievers? The reason is they waste very little time in the decision-making process. Wealthy people make decisions quickly.

Most people spend months deciding whether or not to get into a business, later finding out their hunch was right and now it's too late to capitalize on the idea because so many others are doing it. You must remember, unless you are a true visionary, when you get an idea it's already been put into the universe and that means lots of others are sharing the same idea. It's the person who capitalizes on the idea first who wins. That's why in the entertainment industry you will suddenly read about five different projects in development and all five are slightly different variations of the same idea. The idea was put out into the universe and writers began picking up on the vibrations of the ideas.

The first question to ask in the decision-making process is: "Will this decision move me closer to or further from what I want?" If the thing that you are making a decision on has no downside (potential for loss of time, money, or resources), then the decision is always yes.

"Maximize the potential while minimizing the risk. You can never get more by saying no. You can hold a current position by saying no, but you can only move forward by saying yes."

I had an experience recently with a couple of company managers. These were subcontractors who wanted to provide management for one of my companies. I'm one who spends very little time hashing out the details of an agreement, because I know invariably that the details will change as time passes by. This management team on the other hand wanted to create a twenty-year contract and dragged out our negotiations over four months. There were many reasons that the both of us could have said no and not reached an agreement for another four months. Since they couldn't make decisions on the littlest of things, just to get moving I ended up saying yes to things that in the short run really didn't matter. What ended up happening is that after they finally came up with decisions and we began working together, after only two months we decided to end the contract and our working agreement. It took us longer to decide on the details of the agreement than it took for the agreement to become invalid.

The reason ineffective people take so long to make decisions is that they're afraid they'll make the wrong decision. The problem is since they're so afraid they'll make the wrong decision any decision they make they think is wrong. Since they are looking for the wrongness of the decision, eventually they find it. If the ineffective person waits too long the world will eventually make a decision for them. Not making a decision is making a decision. The money-making opportunity will go away or expire and then the non-decision-maker will say something like, "See, it wasn't meant to happen. Good things never happen for me."

Effective people who produce lots of money make decisions quickly. They don't worry about making a mistake after they have made the decision. If things don't work out the way they planned they will make another decision to get them out of their present challenge and take with them the knowledge that they learned from the previous decision.

The key is to: "Fail Forward Fast"

You can never be sure the decision you're going to make is going to be the right one. It takes making the decision and moving along the path to find out whether your judgment was effective or not. Since you won't know whether the decision was a good one or an ineffective one, you may have to change course no matter which decision you make. So, wouldn't it be better to make the wrong decision now so you would realize that it's inappropriate sooner and make a different decision that will help you to fail forward fast?

Here is a graph that shows how making decisions quickly will always put you in a place to win better than making no decision at all.

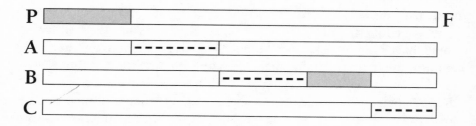

Let's imagine you have a life (just kidding) and let's imagine you have a decision to make. The top line represents your life from present to future. The next three lines (A, B, C) represent possible choices. Let's pretend that the old you didn't make decisions very quickly so you simply made no decision (gray area). Finally you chose decision A. After a period of time you realize that decision A (dashed portion) isn't work-ing for you so you choose decision B. You realize that B isn't the effective decision for you either (dashed portion), but because you are afraid to make another wrong decision you don't make a shift to C until a little more time has passed (gray area). Finally you choose C (dashed portion) and enjoy the decision for the rest of your life. In the above example there are only two times when you are really losing; in the beginning when you don't make any decision and during the time when you know that decision B is ineffective (both gray areas) and you don't make another decision. By looking at the above example it's easy to see that you could have enjoyed more than twice as much of the effective choice if you had made your decisions more quickly. Decide to decide.

"Even if you're on the right track you'll get run over if you just sit there!"

—WILL ROGERS

EXERCISE: For the next few days when faced with decisions make them quickly. Especially simple ones like what to have for dinner and what video to rent. When you start to make your decisions more quickly you will have much more time on your hands. In addition, start paying attention to the people around you who seem to get a lot done. Notice how much time they take to make decisions.

When you are quicker to make decisions then you will have more time to prepare yourself to . . .

Chapter 22

Seize Opportunity!

"Doing downtime work insures uptime victory."
—MARSHALL SYLVER

Sometimes it seems as if you are unprepared, when in actuality you are. Does it seem like opportunities are few and far between? Does it also seem like when they come up they do so at the worst possible time, like those times when you aren't quite ready for them? Some people appear to be lucky because they are in the right place at the right time. In reality we all have moments of opportunity that come up and whether or not we are prepared to take advantage of the circumstances is the difference between good luck and bad luck. One of the reasons that successful people have the ability to seize opportunity in advance is that they expect to win in advance. They believe that the preparations that they are making today will definitely be utilized tomorrow. The unsuccessful person has the mind-set of "Why bother trying, it's not going to make a difference anyway?"

Throughout this book I have constantly told you that the mind will move in the direction of its dominant thought. When you are expecting opportunity to occur and you are preparing for it, not only will you be ready when it does pop up, you will also find it in more places since that is what you are looking for. The reverse is also true. When you are unprepared for opportunity you will look the other way when positive circumstances arrive because you don't want to have to face the truth that through your own inaction you are missing out on what you want.

For years I tried to get my own television show for my motivational products. I went to all of the big producers of these shows and each time in some way I was turned down. Instead of cursing my bad luck I kept using the time between my meetings to get myself better prepared. In show business this is the same as the act who can't get an agent until they don't need an agent. Every time I would get turned down by a producer I would go and refine my product and my show until I knew that I was irresistible. It made me realize the power of uptime/downtime.

Uptime is when you have to be at one hundred and ten percent of your capacity. It's when you're making that presentation, or when the person of your dreams comes through the door, or when the chance encounter with the individual that could put all of your plans in motion occurs. Unless you are ready for those times it will seem like they are bad luck when the only thing necessary to turn them into good luck is preparation. **Downtime is the time spent preparing for uptime**. Downtime is the time you spent making the slides or handouts for your presentation. It's the time you spent working out at the gym to be more appealing for the person of your dreams. It's finishing the project that has not yet been sold so when you have that chance encounter you are ready. For me, uptime is when I'm on stage and right now as I work on this book. The book will live for many decades after its completion. Downtime for me is the time I spend preparing for seminars, rehearsing for my entertainment production show, or researching new information. Uptime is the moment of truth where I give birth to the thing I have labored over. It is the uptime that matters.

Wealthy people take care of the details before they need them. When you prepare for your victories as if they were certain, they become so. When Steve Wynn builds a new casino property in Las Vegas he is putting hundreds of millions of dollars on the line. Do you think he would do that if he was afraid he was going to lose? Have faith that your downtime efforts will be rewarded in your uptime pursuits. Know that what you are doing today will determine how tomorrow goes. If you're going to be rich, realize that 95 percent of your time is going to be spent preparing for the other 5 percent. Opportunity is when preparation and circumstance meet. Spend your downtime getting ready for your opportune moments. Most people have many opportunities for a better life, yet they just don't realize or see the opportunity when it comes knocking. When you have done your downtime work, then when opportunity knocks you'll throw open the door.

If you're a salesperson it's too late to learn sales skills when the customer is in the showroom. If you're a writer it's too late to finish the book when you run into that publisher at a party. If you want to sell your idea for a product, spend your time between meetings enhancing your product. If you want a promotion in your company, and none are open right now, then spend the current time learning the skills that you'll need for the promotion so that when it does open up you'll be ready. The Boy Scout motto is "Be prepared." It means going the extra mile in work to be the best that you can be. By going the extra mile you're not only setting a good example for the company, you are also setting yourself up to win. This is a good way to build self-confidence. It will also be an important factor in enhancing your life.

> *"When the student is ready the teacher appears."*
> —ANCIENT BUDDHIST EXPRESSION

The above saying could just as well mean that when you are ready for success, then success will appear. During my career I have had many letdowns and heartaches. Many times I thought that I was ready for my big break and it just didn't happen. Rather than get frustrated (okay, I got a little frustrated!), I would tell myself, "Marshall, you must not be ready yet. What can you do to make yourself more attractive when the opportunity comes up again?" Earlier in this book you created your ideal day. What can you do right now that is a step in the direction of that ideal day? I know that some of you are thinking what if I put all this time and energy into preparing for opportunity and it never comes. My question to you is: "What if opportunity comes and you aren't prepared?" If you don't prepare yourself for opportunity, one thing is certain, you won't win even when you get the chance. Downtime is for training, development, and preparation. Go to a communication seminar, read a book on persuasion, get your body and mind healthy right now so you can seize opportunity. Make your Subconscious Reprogramming tape from the script at the end of this section. The law of nature is that if you don't embrace opportunity it will be embraced by an opportunist.

ASSIGNMENT: Take the time right now to specifically define at least five downtime actions that you can take in the next twenty-four hours that will move you toward what you want in the big picture. If you want to be an author, maybe it's writing one chapter. If you want to get healthy, maybe it's a one-mile (or ten-mile) walk or run. If you are working on creating a new relationship, maybe it's creating that Subconscious Reprogramming cassette or going out and meeting at least one new person or even just getting a haircut. Five downtime actions per day for one week will create a massive shift in your preparedness for opportunity. *Doesn't doing something for yourself feel great!*

Talk about seizing opportunity! There once was a crime boss who for security reasons hired a deaf-mute accountant in the belief that if the accountant were arrested he wouldn't be able to testify against him or tell people where his money was coming from. After five years of service, it became obvious to the crime boss the accountant was embezzling money, in fact almost $10 million. One day the crime boss went to the accountant and said, "I want my money." The accountant sat there looking at him as if he didn't know what he was talking about. The crime boss pulled out a gun and screamed at the top of his lungs, "I want my money." Realizing that he wasn't getting anywhere because the accountant sat there looking at him blankly he called for an interpreter, to sign to the accountant what the request was. The interpreter came and the crime boss said, "Tell him I want my money." The interpreter signed to the accountant and sure enough the accountant signed back, "I don't know what he's talking about." The interpreter told the crime boss, "He says he doesn't know what you're talking about." The crime boss got more angry and he said, "TELL HIM I WANT TO KNOW WHERE MY TEN MILLION BUCKS IS." The interpreter signed, the accountant signed back, "I don't know what he's talking about." The interpreter said "He says he doesn't know what you're talking about" again. By now the crime boss was furious, he cocked back the hammer on the gun, put it in the accountant's mouth, and said, "You tell him I want to know where my money is, or I'm going to blow his head off. This is the last time I'm asking." The interpreter signed to the accountant. The accountant signed back frantically, "The ten million dollars is under the floorboards, under the bed in my house." The interpreter turned to the crime boss and said, "The accountant says, he doesn't think you have the guts to pull the trigger!"

Chapter 23

Wealthy People Do What They Love

"Do what you love and the money will follow."
—Marshall Sylver

Ask yourself this question: "If I had a magic box and every time I opened it, it would give me a never-ending supply of money to do whatever I wanted to, what would I do with my life?" If people tell me they love to travel, then I say the key to their riches is to focus on something to do with travel. Or they say, gee I like to surf all the time, then I direct them to look at something to do with surfing, maybe opening a surf shop, or becoming a professional surfer. Look to what you love and the money will follow. Many people hold the mistaken belief that it's not possible to do what they love every moment of the day. I agree, and yet it is possible for every person on the planet to do what they love most of the time since people find personal satisfaction in so many ways. Quite often I'll see people having fun doing a job I could never see myself doing, let alone enjoying.

"The best way out of a job you don't like is to do a great job."

I remember one time watching the trash men pick up the trash in front of my home. The two guys that did it made it look like art the way they had carefully choreographed the passing of the trash cans and the pulling of the truck switches. It was a thing of beauty to watch them working and you could tell that they were having fun. One trash day I made it a point to come out and wait until the trash truck came up the street. I wanted to find out what these guys were thinking that made them look like they were having so much fun working in the grime of their job when friends of mine that worked in sparkling office buildings were whining about slaving away. When they got to my house I asked them why they put so much production into it, and they told me that it was more fun that way. They told me their day went faster. They also told me that they decided one day that if they were going to be what they called "sanitation engineers," then they would be the best on the planet. The last thing they told me is that even though this was their day job and it paid them twenty bucks an hour it also helped them get ready for their career in show business as a singing and dancing duet. They were practicing their dance moves so that when the opportunity arose they would be ready. Wow! These two men looked to me to be two of the happiest people I had ever encountered. They were able to take the time that they were doing something they had to do and make it be and support what they loved to do, which was perform.

When I was seventeen and working as an announcer at a beautiful-music station in San Diego I was offered a job at the local rock-and-roll station. At the time I knew the rock-and-roll station would be more fun and yet something told me that having the opportunity to talk more on the air rather than play more music would be better for me in the long run. I am sure glad that I did because the training that I received at "Beautiful and Relaxing KJOY" set up the foundation for all of my work as a public speaker.

Life and Life Maintenence

I want you to now ponder a concept called **life and life maintenance**. The majority of people spend the majority of their life working so they can enjoy the few hours that are left. If you spend sixteen hours a day on your job so you can go home and spend ten minutes with your kids, then it seems to me the life maintenance of your job and the life that you are maintaining are out of balance. The best way to maintain life and life maintenance balance is to make sure that life maintenance is life. In other words, love what you do. Make your vocation your vacation. I know that there is no way I could possibly work seventy-hour weeks if I didn't love what I was doing.

Given the opportunity to do anything for a living I would do what I do. I absolutely love doing my show on casino stages and colleges throughout the country and the world. Given the choice I would happily spend at least one weekend per month on stage inspiring people to go for more. As a hobby I write and create my books, tapes, and television shows. Even though I have long passed the point where I would ever have to work again, I choose to do what I do because I love it.

Can a person really do what they love and earn a living? Mike Whitaker loved fishing for bass. Purely on faith he took his life savings of $5,000 and founded Operation Bass. In less then ten years he had an organization that had over $3.5 million in revenues and became the country's largest organizer of fishing tournaments. *Yes you can.*

ASSIGNMENT: PART ONE: Write a paragraph about all the ways your current work supports your lifelong dreams. Leave out anything to do with money and focus on what you can do at your present job to support what it is you have a real passion for. If you want to be a writer and you are currently working as a secretary, then recognize the chance to practice your typing skills as one way your job supports your passion. If you are a supervisor in a machine shop who longs to play in a rock band, then pay attention to the ways that you can inspire the best possible "performance" from your subordinates. You'll find what you are looking for, so keep looking for the ways your current job supports your dream, listing at least five ways.

PART TWO: Make a list of at least ten things that you could do to make money that have to do with what you love. As an example, if you love to travel you might list travel agent, tour guide, travel editor for magazine, import-export buyer, speaker, flight attendant, pilot. It's your life, so the more options you can come up with the more possibilities you'll have.

You never get more time. The only thing you can do is become more valuable. Master your time in a way that will be beneficial to you and your growth. Could you do twice as much work in one hour and get paid twice as much? Wealthy people get paid for what they produce, not for how long they work at producing it. If Stephen King got paid by the hour, don't you think it would take him a year to write a book? He gets paid by the book, he gets paid for what he produces.

You don't get rich by how much time you use, you get paid for what you produce. While you are leveraging your time and the resources that other people can offer you'll get more done faster. When you start producing more in a shorter amount of time you will have more money. Now that you have some strategies to leverage those two resources, (people and time), let's move on to how we can leverage the third, money . . .

Chapter 24

Wealthy People Leverage Money

"Either make your money work for you or you will always have to work for your money."

—MARSHALL SYLVER

I've already told you how hard it was growing up in my house. Even though it was tough my mother did her best to give us special treats whenever possible. Whenever she would get any extra money she would do something special for the kids. Maybe buy us a new game or take us to the drive-in. Since we usually only had enough to survive I'm sure it was also her way of giving herself some of the pleasures needed to make life more than just bearable. Because the extra money was always spent whenever it would come up there was never anything left to be saved.

When I first started making a decent amount of money I noticed something strange. Even though I had more than enough to pay my bills it seemed that at the end of the month there would still be nothing extra left. I realized that I had fallen into my mother's habits. Every time I would get some extra cash I would spend it on pleasure. A weekend trip here, a new camcorder there, an expensive night on the town. Since unexpected bills do come up from time to time (car accidents, things stolen) I found out more than once I was again short of cash. Earlier I told you that your income will expand to fill the bills you have coming in. If you have a fair amount of experience in just getting by, you understand that the phenomenon works both ways and that:

"Bills expand to equal the amount of cash you have coming in."

You get a raise and think that you'll start having extra money and at the end of the month you find out that you don't. You are left being short the same as you were before. If this sounds like you, then this process will benefit you.

Years ago I wanted to buy my first home. I knew that I would need at least a $30,000 down payment. I had never saved $30,000 in my life. So I set down a schedule to save the money over six months. Since your arithmetic is quick, I'm sure you have already computed that's $5,000 per month. This number seemed out of reach and yet on faith I proceeded. Do you have a bill basket or a bill file or a bill drawer at your house? A place that you go to maybe once or twice a month to pay the ones that are in the file? I do too, and what I did was added my new bill called "Down Payment" to the file. This $5,000 per month bill seemed out of reach and in fact in the first couple of months I was tempted to just ignore it. I stayed with it, though, and started looking for additional ways to make sure this particular bill got paid with the rest. A funny thing started to happen. Since my mind was focused on the need to generate and hold on to an additional $5,000 per month I started paying more attention to the frivolous things that I was spending my money on. I also started noticing opportunities that I hadn't noticed before. I think too, that whereas before I would put only as much energy into my work to produce at a specific level, since I had to come up with the additional money, I put a little more energy and a lot more creativity into what I was doing. I started risking more. I asked my clients for more money for my services, I developed new markets for my products, I found ways to leverage my resources of time, money, and people to get more done in less time. By giving myself the bill called "Down Payment" I strengthened and enlarged the abilities I had all along.

If you have ever worked out you know that muscles have memory. What this means is that once you build up a muscle it is easier to build it up again. The same is true with making money. When you start to flex your prosperity muscles you will start to experience yourself at a different level. Since I now knew it was possible to make the extra money, each month it got easier. In fact, now I didn't let up my focus until I met that new amount every month even after the initial six-month period had passed.

Another practice that has greatly enhanced my ability to keep the money I have earned fell right in line with creating future bills. For the first years of running my own business I would pay the bills out of the monthly income and then I would use what was left as my income. What happened is the same thing. At the end of each month there would be nothing left to grow the company with and or to get ahead myself. A process I had heard about for years was to:

"Pay Yourself First."

What paying yourself first does is let you know that you are as important as the other bills you pay on a regular basis. When you own your own business it is a regular paycheck that the company pays you like any of the other employees. This lets you always live within your means and see your company grow. I never paid much attention to how much I was spending on a monthly basis when I was just "taking from the till." When I started paying myself first I again noticed that the income expanded to pay the bills that were there. Even if you work for someone else you can pay yourself first.

Paying yourself first is just the first step in leveraging your present money. When you work for someone else you must also pay yourself first. You must also have a specific plan to make your money work for you. No matter what your current financial situation you must live within your means while going for more.

This means that to get ahead you must put:

    10 percent into savings,
    10 percent into reducing debt (extra payments on big items), and
    10 percent into something that has risk and the potential for
        greater future payoff.
    You then use the 70 percent left for your living expenses.

I know what you're thinking, "Marshall, I barely get by now. Where's all this extra money going to come from?" The secret is it's not extra.

Right now your mentality is to just get by. Since you are just getting by you cannot ever get a firm foundational foothold. On your current path you will always be on a treadmill going nowhere. Unless you shift your lifestyle now it will get worse. Since you are living at the peak of your current means, when you have any extra money you feel guilty about spending it and you don't get the enjoyment out of it that you want and deserve. What this process will do is make a minor adjustment in how you are living now so you will be able to make a major adjustment later. It does mean you will probably start paying attention to where money is going and be more on the lookout for greater opportunities for savings and income. A penny saved is a penny earned. (Just be sure you are saving more than you could earn using the same amount of time and energy.) It does mean that you will most likely start doing better work so as to become more valuable. It does mean that you will be living a lifestyle that is different from the one you are now, and yet isn't that what you are looking for? Here's the reason the above formula will get you ahead faster than you realize. First, saved money is both a comfort zone that allows you to think clearer (you'll always know that you aren't totally broke); it also compounds the money by gaining interest. Your money becomes a source of income. Money used to reduce debt will pay off hugely in the long run by saving you tremendous money in the interest paid out to others on borrowed money. A few years back when I used this method to pay off my car early, the savings were in the thousands. Lastly, the risk money is money that could pay off in huge ways and would probably be spent on frivolous items for instantaneous gratification. I promise you that nothing is more gratifying than making tons of cash. The risk could be in any number of forms. It could be buying stocks (there are places you can start a portfolio for as little as $50), it could be on materials you need to start a side business that you enjoy, it could be investing in some private venture or person that you believe in. Just make sure it has the potential for a payoff greater than what you would get in savings.

You must give the "savings," "debt reduction," and "risk" bills priority over other bills in order to ever get ahead. You must adjust your expenses down and your income up to be able to do this. It may be a challenge at first and yet in the long run you will thank me and yourself for the discipline.

ASSIGNMENT: I have two assignments for you. The first is to make your current financial foundation more solid. If you are in the habit of being just able to pay your bills, rejoice! You already have half the skills neccesary to utilize this process. The next step is to just pay the bills in the best possible order. Start today by creating a bill called "savings," one called "debt reduction," and one called "risk capital." Although 10 percent is what's recommended it doesn't matter what amount you start with as long as you remember some is better than none. Simultaneously with this at least write out a simple budget. If you have never done this, then the process of writing it out alone will increase your awareness of where your money goes and how to most effectively channel it. A little later in this book I will elaborate on the skill of keeping score.

The second assignment is even more fun. This is where you will start making even more money. Make a list of at least *ten* ways you could increase your income just 10 percent. If you work at an hourly wage make sure none of the ten is working overtime. It's time to start shifting from one who labors to one who thinks. I know you've worked hard; now it's time to work smart. Asking for a raise could be one of them. Should you ask for a raise, remember you won't be paid more money unless you provide greater value even if you are underpaid now. Instead of getting angry get creative. When you ask for the raise specifically state (without beating around the bush) how much you want to make and that you are willing to do what it takes to get it. Ask what you need to do to get that amount. If the answer is there is no way, you have something to ponder.

Also think about what side venture you could become involved with that is fun and has the potential for income. Start by looking at your hobbies. How can these create an income? If you work for someone else how could you give them more value? If you work for yourself, how could you better serve your customers? Whether you are selling a service or a product you are selling a service. You are selling what that thing does for your customers.

How might you leverage your three resources—time, money, or people—for greater production? What ways could you get more from any of the three so that you could make more? What is the highest, best use of your time? Years ago I had to stop doing one-on-one sessions because they weren't as profitable as the other things I was doing. Even though I was making the huge sum of $1,000 per hour, it still wasn't what I could make doing seminars or television shows.

What's the best use of your money? Is it working for you or are you working for it? When you make the giant leap to compounded interest you will have an additional employee making you money with no extra effort on your part. How about other people? How can you best use their resource to leverage your time? Be the thinker that governs those that labor. You cannot get rich until you do.

I've given you lots of possibilities, now come up with ten ways you could expand your income if you really had to. Do it now or all your reading is in vain.

Chapter 25

Wealthy People Know the Score

"It's hard to know if you're winning if you don't keep the score."

—Marshall Sylver

Wealthy people know the score. They do their homework, they know what the competition is doing, and they know how to get the advantage. They know who is winning and what they are doing to win. They gather all the information possible. They know what they owe and just what they have coming in. They operate on a budget. Just how successful do you think a corporation would be if money were spent haphazardly on whatever came up? How do your family books hold up under this kind of scrutiny? How many friends do you know who buy into the theory that they are not good with money? In seminars this is a frequent topic. When one doesn't claim responsibility for the money he has now, why would the universe waste more time with such a foolish person? If this sounds familiar, you must have heard it early on in life, and when you practice Subconscious Reprogramming you will be able to release that belief and establish the strength of a more profitable philosophy. If someone said to you, you can really learn how to save on what you're making now, wouldn't you want to learn?

No matter what your current financial situation is, set down a budget right now and practice staying within it. In addition, for just one week keep a complete record of everything you spend. How much you spent on food this past week, on gas, on entertainment. You'll begin to relax about where your money is going and in the process you will learn that . . .

Chapter 26

Wealthy People Handle Stress Differently

"The man in the penthouse and the man in the gutter have the same amount of stress. It's just a matter of what you choose to stress over."

—MARSHALL SYLVER

When I taught the above to a recent seminar group a woman stood up and asked, "Do you mean to tell me that when I own a penthouse apartment and a ski condo in Aspen and a limousine and driver I am going to stress out as much as I do now trying to pay the rent on my apartment?" I told her yes. If what she feels now as she is trying to pay her rent is something that she calls stress, then later she'll feel the same thing when she's trying to pay for the penthouse.

"Let what used to be your stress be the excitement that inspires you now."

Quick, if your heart is racing, your breath is short and fast, and your face is scrunched in an unusual fashion, are you in stress or ecstasy? I guess it depends on what you're thinking, doesn't it? Having to get up in front of a thousand people and teach them for five straight days, would that be pleasure or pain? I guess it depends what you're thinking. You've just been paid a huge advance to complete a book and the book is due in days, stressed or jubilant? I guess it depends on how much money and how many days or maybe just on how you think. Everyone feels stress. I have as much stress in my life now as I did when I was searching for macaroni and cheese money in the couch. The only difference is that now when I stress it has the potential for much bigger gain. Instead of wondering where my next meal is coming from now I wonder are we going to do $20 million or $30 million in gross income. I stress just as much, it's just a whole lot more fun to be stressing these days.

"Our success in life is determined not by how much stress we can tolerate, but rather by how much stress we welcome into our life and enjoy."

When you realize that deadlines and obligations are not things that have to create a tightness in your stomach or a tension in your muscles, then you will begin to take on more of the things that have the potential to give you great rewards.

Wealth is a state of mind. When you think you're rich you stop stressing about things that are unimportant. If you knew that you were going to make tons of money do you think you would spend so much time fretting over little details? Wealthy people keep things in perspective and recognize that everything is relative.

Two expectant fathers were nervously pacing the floor of the delivery ward waiting room. One said, "This is tough luck, we were on vacation."

"The other one said, "What are you complaining about? We were on our honeymoon!"

When you are building wealth it is important to know that it's not money that makes you rich. Rich is a state of mind. When I was growing up a hundred dollars seemed like a lot of money. When I got older ten thousand dollars seemed like a lot. When I became a millionaire, a billion seemed like a lot and a million didn't. Unless you start living rich right now you will put yourself on a never-ending treadmill. Like a hamster in a cage you will work day in and day out and feel like you are not getting anywhere. Take a look around you and notice how rich you really are right now. If you are able to look around you, then that would mean that your eyes are working. You're very rich. Do you have a roof over your head? You are abundant. Did you take a vacation this year more than five hundred miles from your home? Then you are doing something that less than five percent of the population can ever afford to do—you are wealthy.

Another way that I remind myself that everything *is* relative is to put it into the grand perspective. The expression "Don't sweat the little stuff and it's all little stuff" is very true. I mean how much is any one moment going to matter in the long run? When I find myself getting stressed over something in any area of my life I close my eyes and take a trip. I imagine that I am floating up over my body. I can see it beneath me and as I continue to float up I can see my house around me. As I continue on my upward journey I then start to see my city and I can just barely pick out which one is my house. I continue further and soon I am looking at a top view of what my state looks like, then my country. As I continue my ascent I can now see the entire planet as I'm traveling rapidly through space. Soon the earth too becomes small and suddenly my whole solar system becomes just another single star. Somewhere around this time I begin to realize that the thing that I thought was so important in my life is not even a speck of what really is and doesn't deserve the energy that I was putting on it. Then slowly as I come back to full awareness and open my eyes I giggle and just deal with what's immediately in front of me.

Chapter 27

Wealthy People Persist and Take Immediate Action

"Just keep swinging the bat. The odds are that sooner or later you'll connect with the ball."

—Marshall's oldest brother after Marshall's
three years of Little League and not one hit

After Fred Astaire's first screen test in 1933, the memo from the MGM testing director said, "Can't act, slightly bald, and can dance a little!" Astaire kept that memo over the fireplace of his Beverly Hills mansion.

A football expert said that Vince Lombardi "Possesses minimal football knowledge and lacks motivation."

It was once said of Albert Einstein, "He doesn't wear socks and forgets to cut his hair. Could be retarded."

Socrates was called "an immoral corrupter of youth."

Failure makes excuses. Success just keeps swinging the bat. I finally did get a hit. Not because I was a great baseball player. I got a hit because I kept stepping up to the plate. No, I will never be a professional ballplayer, and yet I got a hit. Against everything I believed in I got a hit. During all those years of reinforcement of not getting a hit I thought I would never get one and then I did. The odds are if you keep taking action, sooner or later something is going to work.

Wealthy people are persistent and take immediate action. When a successful person decides on an idea and a plan, he will do whatever it takes to accomplish his objective. He sets down a plan of action and takes advantage of every opportunity that will get him to his plan.

Have you ever thought about how persistent a postage stamp is? When you lick the stamp to the envelope it sticks to it until the letter arrives at its destination. Wealthy people are as persistent in their actions. When they decide something is right for them they will stick to their actions like the stamp sticks to a letter.

Aristotle Onassis was one of the world's richest men. He reportedly had a plaque on his desk for employees to read that said, "Find a way or make one." Wealthy people swing the bat. They jump into the ballgame and put their plan at risk. By swinging the bat they just might get a hit that will take them around the bases and home for the score. Even swinging and missing will give you feedback that will be valuable. Life is about experiences and the more experiences you have reaching your plans the more you'll understand what you want and don't want in life.

I once hired the services of a man named Don Wayne. He is a consultant to entertainers such as myself and to one of my favorites, David Copperfield. I am sure you know that David is one of the greatest magicians of all time. While Don and I were having discussions, I asked him who would be the best person to talk to to get a network special produced. He gave me the name of a producer. The next day I went and called the producer, then I called Don and told him the outcome of my conversation with this television producer. Don laughed and said, "I can't believe you called him so fast." I said, "Why not, Don, you gave me his name." He said "Marshall, you and David Copperfield are exactly alike. Both you and David will take twelve projects in a year and bulldoze your way through all twelve and maybe four will turn out successful." Don said that he himself always focused on one project and worked out all the details to insure its success. I said, "Gee Don, I'm not sure if my arithmetic is right, except it seems like David and I are four to your one. I think we're winning."

The reason that some people aren't persistent is that the scariest moment is usually right as you are about to get what you want. I was recently down in Playa Blanca, Mexico. I took myself and my younger brothers down there to celebrate their birthdays. While we were in Playa Blanca, we practiced trapeze and tightrope and other circus acts as a part of the activities they had at this resort. There is a moment when you're flying on the trapeze when you must let go of the one you're coming from or there is no way to connect with where you're going to. Like a trapeze artist, sometimes you must let go of what is known to get that which is new.

Chapter 28

The Power of Being Unique and Doing More Than You're Paid For

"If they can't get it anywhere else you determine the price."

—MARSHALL SYLVER

Wealthy people understand the power of being unique and being the very best. Their uniqueness comes from their own minds. Instead of copying the work of others they focus on what is unique about themselves. They make no apologies for who they are and they focus on being their own personal best. They also always give more than they are paid for. They go that extra mile and do more than their competition.

> *"When you build the very best property on the very best location, using the very best materials, there is no money people will not pay for the very best."*
>
> —DONALD TRUMP

What can you do right now that will increase the quality of what you do and give more than you are paid for? Whether you work for yourself or for someone else, there is always a market for someone who is the very best at what they do. Go for excellence and the money will follow.

Chase money at the cost of excellence and the money will go to the person who is refining their craft. What can you do right now to increase your excellence or talent? Take a seminar? Read a book related to your work? Increase your health? Someone has to be the very best in your field, it may as well be you.

> *"Personally I have never received a promotion in my life that I could not trace directly to recognition that I had gained by rendering more and better service than that for which I was paid."*
>
> —RALPH WALDO EMERSON

Wealthy people do more than they're being paid for, always. They always underpromise and overdeliver. The best way out of a job that you don't like is to do a great job. This will help build your self-confidence about your abilities and give you the chance to improve your skills in the process.

You learned earlier in this book that the best way out of a job you don't like is to do a great job. If you want out of that job and you're doing a great job, chances are you'll be promoted to the next level. Even if you don't get promoted in that company to another place, what will happen is that somebody else from another company will notice you're doing a great job and they'll hire you away. They'll give you a job you do want.

When I was a teenager I swore that I would never, ever pump gas. Well, shortly after I made that vow, I was cleaning somebody's windshield in a gas station, and I was doing a great job with it. In fact, I had determined to myself that if I had to be there I'd be the very best gas station attendant I could be. One day a regular customer came in who I had been giving great service to and this day it paid off. He leaned his head out of the window and he said, "You know what? You always give such great service, I was wondering if you had ever considered a job in radio." I said, "Not until now, sir. Yet maybe if you've got something for me, we can talk." He said, "Maybe I do. I'd like you to come down to my office and talk to me about working on my radio station." I did and the rest is history. I went down and I spoke to Mike Burnett, and he gave me the job at KJOY.

I was seventeen years old and I've never looked back. Always do more than you're being paid for and you'll get what you deserve.

Chapter 29

Wealthy People Have Plans Instead of Goals— Seven Steps to Powerful Plan Setting

"A dream becomes a goal the moment you write it down. A goal becomes a plan the moment you break it down into doable steps. A plan becomes reality only when you take action."

—MARSHALL SYLVER

Wealthy people have plans instead of goals. Instead of aiming for a goal they have plans specific to the accomplishment of their desired outcome. Right now you're going to learn a process called **plan setting**. The reason I call it plan setting instead of goal setting is that I believe a goal is something you aim for and a plan is something you do.

Since your subconscious mind is just a computer, it is not able to determine what you "really" mean. Do you think it is more likely for your subconscious mind to think you would follow through more effectively to complete goals or plans? Which contractor would you hire to build your new home? One that showed you his goals or one that showed you his plans? If the contractor said, "I have a goal of building you a three-bedroom house. My goal is to have it done by the end of the year and the goal is to have it close to your budget." You'd think the guy was crazy. Since the mind accepts the program as it is presented to it, you must make sure that you're focusing on the right concepts. When a football team wants to score a touchdown they develop plays that will take them down the field and across the goal line. That's their objective. How they get it across that goal line is their plan of action.

> *"If you don't know where you're going you might wind up somewhere else."*
>
> —YOGI BERRA

Your mind always moves in the direction of its dominant thought. Without a plan of your own, you'll become a part of someone else's plan. No matter what it is that you want in your life right now, you must begin to create a specific plan to accomplish it. We're going to learn how a creative plan-setting process can pay off in dividends.

To start making your plans a reality get out your ideal workday and your ideal day of play. You are going to select five different items and select them with this criterion. I want you to select one big thing that you want now and that you believe you will have and can accomplish within five years. You're also going to select three things that will be a major challenge for you to accomplish within one year. Finally, select one thing that you can, when you put your mind to it, complete within one month.

List the five items in the space below:

Five-year plan: _____

Three-year plan: _____

Three-year plan: _____

Three-year plan: _____

One-month plan: _____

The first element of plan setting is:

**The closer the plan, the more precise you
need to be; the further it is, the more general.**

Here's why. Since it's not an immediate plan, all you are doing is putting out into the universe what you want. Your subconscious mind will go to work creating a plan for you to accomplish it. Furthermore, during the next few years you will gather more information about this thing that you want to accomplish, and even though you may not feel like you are doing anything to accomplish it, your mind is in the information-gathering stage.

On the other hand, if you are plan setting for something you want in a month, you need to have all the details immediately. When I was putting together a tape series, I wanted to challenge myself and made a plan to have the complete series from inception to completion within six weeks. This meant I had to design all of the artwork for the cover and the cassettes and I had to write all the copy as well. I had to list all of the steps and time-activate them so I could keep track of whether I was ahead of or behind schedule. I also had to plan time for recording and outside production. The music had to be created and all the manufacturing had to be done. All of these things certainly would have gotten done eventually. To get them done faster and with less possibility for mistakes, the precise plan that I wrote out let me know when I was winning the game and when I needed to focus a little more. The series ended up being completely produced in just five weeks, due in large part to my focusing step by step.

At the beginning of each month I set down a specific plan of what I am going to get done that month. I find that a one-month planning schedule is effective because it trains you to complete what you have set out to do. When you get in the new habit of finishing something just because you wrote it out in your plan, then you will start getting more and more done. One-month plans are also very powerful because if you don't finish your plan you are able to start anew next month. Also, you really can get a tremendous amount done in thirty days of focused work. In my own life, some of my thirty-day plans have been: write and produce a new tape series, write and produce a new script, lose five pounds, rewrite this entire book, create a new seminar.

I suggest you start by only setting one major project per month until you can accomplish this easily and readily. Then move up to two or three. If you have more than three projects per month, they're not really projects, they're more of a daily to do list—things that can be accomplished in a day. Make that one special plan as vivid as possible. Make your descriptions and your plans as full of detail as you can. Use descriptive words in your plan that will excite your imagination.

When I was creating a tape series, I described the packaging with me pictured in a dramatic pose. I described the silver letters and purple highlights and that the project would be done by September 25. I described the hard-driving, motivating music that would be artistically created to make people want to take positive, powerful action, and that music would be completed by September 29. The more you can use dramatic statements covering every detail of what you're accomplishing, the more powerful will be the effects on your subconscious mind in directing you to your desires.

The second element of plan setting is:

List action quotas instead of production quotas.

List what you'll do instead of what you'll accomplish. The distinction between an action quota and a production quota is that an action quota is something you can be guaranteed of and a production quota is something that the outside world determines. For example, if you are creating a plan to lose weight, working out for thirty minutes three times per week is an action quota, whereas losing ten pounds is a production quota. Working three hours per day on a script is an action quota, selling a screenplay would be a production quota. Calling ten new potential customers in one hour is an action quota, closing three new sales is a production quota.

In the beginning of any game it is important to set yourself up to win. As you start to give yourself action quotas that support your production desires what will happen is that suddenly you will start producing the results you are looking for. Remember that anything you do often enough you will get good at. Also remember the Training Cycle for yourself and make sure that you are also working on improving performance each time you perform the action.

"Practice doesn't make perfect, perfect practice makes perfect."

If your plan is to make $5,000 this month, and you're in sales, the first thing you must do is determine how many calls it takes on average to close the amount of sales that will earn $5,000. Then break it down by week and then by day and then all you must do is make the calls and the money will happen. At first you may not be as effective as you want to be. You may not make your $5,000. The thing about setting action quotas instead of production quotas is that at the end of each day you will know if you personally did what it takes. For example, if you make $500 commission per sale and it takes you on the average ten presentations to make one sale, then you will have to make at least one hundred presentations to make your $5,000. Remember that you do not control the world. You only control yourself. So remember to set action instead of production quotas.

The third element of plan setting is:

Plan high.

The thing that you are planning must be inspiring. Instead of making a plan to "get out of debt," make a plan to "have $10,000 in the bank." In his wonderful book *The Greatest Salesman in the World,* Og Mandino said, "It is better to aim for the moon and strike only an eagle than to aim for an eagle and strike only a rock." (Og must not have been a friend of the ASPCA!) What he meant was that as you set your plans, set them high so that they are exciting to you. Let them be something that you will feel fantastic about when you are done.

Plan high and at the same time keep it reachable so that your subconscious mind can go to work. It won't do you any good to plan for a million dollars right now if you're only making $25,000. It would be more effective to plan for $75,000 or $100,000 so that you can work out a step-by-step plan that leads you to the next step.

The fourth element of plan setting is:

Chunk it down.

"Nothing is particularly hard if you divide it into small jobs."
—RAY KROC, founder, McDonald's

When you chunk a plan down into doable steps you set yourself up to win. What happens is that you will have many minor victories that will begin to add up.

"When you take care of the little things the big things will take care of themselves."

When you want to earn $50,000 per year, for example, then you must figure out that you must earn at least $1,000 per week. A thousand dollars per week means that in an average week you must generate an average of $200 per day. Two hundred dollars per day means that in an eight-hour day you need to earn $25 per hour. The first thing I would do to begin earning $1,000 per week is find a way to earn the $25 per hour. When I got confident in my ability to earn $25 per hour, then I would group eight of those hours together and earn $200 for the day. When I was able consistently to earn $200 per day I would group five days together so I could have the experience of earning $1,000 per week. It is said that your first million is the most difficult to make. Once you know that you can, it gets easier. (I suggest you just skip the first one then and go to the second!)

Now that you know how much money you need to make per hour, per day, per week, the next thing you need to do is determine what action quota it takes to generate that amount. Stick to your action quota and the money will come in. As an example, should it take you ten calls on an average to make that $200 a day, then make sure your action quota is at least ten calls per day. In the beginning you might not produce as much money, but it will catch up to you because you'll become more effective. When you have accomplished your action quotas you will always finish your day feeling secure in the knowledge that you did all that you could do.

How do you chunk down something else besides money? I'm sure that you might have written down in your Expansion Thinking exercise a place that you'd like to go. If I wanted to go on a trip, I would chunk it down in the same way. I would set down a step-by-step action plan. Step one might be, "Go to the travel agent to find out cost." Step two, "Determine what the investment would be for where I want to go." Step three, "Determine how long it will take me to save that investment." Step four, "Create a monthly bill for my bill file called, 'Trip.' "

After I've made my plan, I start working out the other details to keep the plan exciting. Every plan you can come up with can be chunked down step by step. No matter what you want, you can write out an action plan into digestible portions that will be workable and keep you motivated in moving toward its triumphant completion.

The fifth element of plan setting is:

List personal alterations.

Whatever it is that you want that you don't have, there's probably a reason. Since you cannot change the world the only place to go for change is inside of you. In order for things to change, you must change. A personal alteration is the shift you must make to align yourself to live congruently as if the plan were already a given. I know the only people who like change are babies with wet diapers. Sometimes the toughest thing to do is to admit that one of your habits is stopping you from getting what you want. When I decided that I had a mission to teach people to live their lives with passion and excitement, I knew that I would have to be the epitome of what I was teaching. I would have to walk my talk. At the time, I was a smoker who was fifteen pounds overweight. On my own list of personal alterations I wrote the things I knew were slowing me down. I knew for certain that I would have to become a nonsmoker and that it would serve me to make my habits more consistent with who I knew I was created to be. Something else I did was to cancel my cable TV subscription so that I wouldn't waste any time watching shows that wouldn't support my vision. To this day I rarely watch TV.

By taking a hard look at myself and making the personal alterations I knew were helpful, I have made my journey much smoother in the long run. If your desire is to make more money, your personal alteration might be to prioritize your day or it might be to be at your office consistently on time or to learn better networking skills. Whatever it is that you want, I guarantee you that you can come up with at least three personal alterations that will make you more effective. Most of us can come up with many more. As I'm sure you've already figured out, these personal alterations are actually new habits, habits of success.

Take the time right now to write down three personal alterations, maybe losing weight, maybe becoming a nonsmoker, maybe being on time and making more calls that will help you move toward your plan setting. Write down your alterations and take at least one step toward being who you need to be to reach your plan.

The sixth element of plan setting is:

Repetition.

You need to program what you want on a subconscious level and the best way to do this is to read the core element of your plan every day. Most of the books you'll ever read on success will tell you to affirm that which you want every day. The reason the books tell you this is that it works. You know that you will always move in the direction of your dominant thoughts. By placing your plan in the front of you, in the front of your thought process, you will find ways to help it to its successful completion. As you're thinking on a subconscious level, you'll be solving the challenges related to what you're doing. You will see a newspaper article, meet someone, or simply create in your own mind the elements you're looking for. Read your plan every single day. It will create a sense of urgency on your part, a constant reminder that you have a project to complete and you will do at least something every day to move you in that direction.

Post signs of encouragement all around your home and place of work. Bill Gates, the founder of Microsoft, calls this random discipline. He practices changing his habits quickly just so his mind accepts the fact that it's easy to change. One way of doing this is to write out the core element of your plan in twenty-five words or less and put it around your home, your work, and anywhere else you spend time. The point in reading plans daily is that they become an obsession and your subconscious mind begins to accept it on every level that you can both accomplish your plan, and that you deserve to.

The seventh element in plan setting is:

Put yourself at stake.

Commit to others what you're going to do. The more people you can tell, the greater your commitment and the more likely you are to accomplish your plan or acquire their help. It's a strange thing that human beings who would never let someone else down will let themselves down. Are you the kind of a person that if you tell someone else that you'll do something, then it's as good as done, and yet if you tell yourself that you'll do something, then only maybe you will? You are not alone and that's all right, you just need to start telling other people what you are going to do for yourself. Years ago I saw a billboard in Las Vegas put up by one of the casino owners who wanted to become a nonsmoker. He put on the billboard, IF YOU SEE ME SMOKING IN THE NEXT 90 DAYS, I'LL PAY YOU $100,000. How's that for putting yourself at stake? You can bet he accomplished what he set out to do and he never paid the money. Since most people have a huge fear of being embarrassed in front of other people, the more people you can commit to, the more likely you'll be to finish what you've set out to do. Of all the elements of plan setting I have found this to be the most effective.

Chapter 30

The Power of Persuasion and Influence

"Elegant persuasion is when the other person thought it was their idea."

—MARSHALL SYLVER

Would you like to be more persuasive? Who wouldn't. Would you like to have the skills and abilities to get other people to both buy in to your concepts and ideas and to motivate them to want to give you what you want? I bet you do. Part of leveraging the resource of people is being able to persuade them to support you and your vision. Being persuasive is not a quality that some people are born with and others aren't. You don't have to be an outgoing, gregarious person to be influential. In fact, some of the most powerfully persuasive people are soft-spoken and appear delicate. It's the person that doesn't appear to be persuasive that usually gets what they want. Gandhi persuaded an entire nation to put down their arms and be peaceful. History is full of teachers who have persuaded troubled kids to stay off drugs and realize the value of an education. On a daily basis you are going to use the power of persuasion and influence to: get your kids to clean their room and be more responsible, get your employer to give you a raise, inspire your lover to respect you more, get the car dealer to give you a better price, and even get the best table in that popular restaurant.

In a moment I am going to give you the basic strategies for persuading others. Before I do, though, it is essential to understand what you need to know and do to effectively influence others.

1. **Know your desired outcome.** Unless you have a specific idea of what you want the end result to be, you will risk being influenced by the other party if they have a clearer idea of what they want.

2. **Keep emotions out.** This is difficult for most people. We humans are jerked around by our unconscious response to the actions around us. It is essential to understand that getting angry (I have the right to this, dammit!), or even overly excited (Geez, I really want this car no matter what the price) in any situation only diminishes your power. Think of being influential and persuasive as a game. The more you practice the game the better you get. Becoming angry during any game, whether it's golf, chess, making money, or creating love, separates you from your primary resource of effective thinking.

3. **Persuasion is inspiration, not manipulation.** The best kind of persuasion is when the other party thinks it was their idea. Influence is an elegant process. When you think of yourself as an artist you will get more. A salesman could get a great white shark to experiment with being a vegetarian. A master of influence would get the shark to believe that being a vegetarian was their idea and get them to convince all of their great white shark buddies to be vegetarians too.

4. **There is no failure, only feedback.** The most persuasive people on the planet still don't get what they want sometimes. Since they view the process as a game they experience every encounter as a learning experience. "What can I do next time that will get me what I want?" They pay attention to what results they are producing and adjust accordingly.

5. **Be responsible for your results.** Hand in hand with keeping emotions out and experiencing failure as feedback, you must have a belief that if you aren't getting what you want it is your duty to make a shift. Years ago I was wanting an appointment with a very famous producer. I placed repeated phone calls and none of them got returned. I shifted my approach and faxed him a letter. When that didn't work I overnighted him a letter. When still I got no response I went to his office and waited all day in his lobby. Maybe because he knew that I wasn't giving up I finally got the five minutes with him that I had been asking for. Which leads us to . . .

6. **Change strategies until you get what you want.** Take control of

your destiny so that you can create what you want. There is a way for you to get what you want—it's just different from how you have been doing it. Make a shift, it works. Ask in a different way, ask a different person, ask many different people for parts of what you want until you get the whole.

7. **Know what you are willing to give up to get what you want.** You won't necessarily have to give up anything to get what you want, but it is important, however, to know what you are willing to give if you have to. You must also recognize that by dovetailing what you want and what the other person wants you are more likely to be persuasive. Knowing what you are willing to give up in advance will also be a stopgap to insure that you don't give up more than you want to.

8. **Desire to be more persuasive and enjoy the process.** The distinction between manipulation and influence is your intention. When your intention is good, then you are doing the other person a favor by persuading them. To know whether your intention is good ask yourself this question, "Would I want to be persuaded to take the action or hold the belief that I'm asking others to hold?" If the answer is yes, then you are morally and ethically obligated to be as persuasive and influential as possible.

"Put your request out loudly and frequently into the universe."

Wealthy people are always promoting themselves and what they are doing. Since they are proud of what they do, they let other people know what they're going for. By putting it out you open the doors of opportunity for others to share your passion and give support to your plan. Tell other people the things you want to accomplish and enlist them in your process. Excite them like Tom Sawyer did whitewashing the fence. Make your ride the most fun one of all.

9. **Know what the other person wants and align your desires with theirs.** When you can give other people what they want they will be eager to give you what you want. What you want and what they want may not be the same thing. The only way you can be sure is to ask. In the next section I will give you strategies for finding out exactly what the other guy wants.

"In no deal did I ever figure our own profit first. I always mapped out a proposition where the dealer or the jobber would make out better

than we did. . . . We must give them the thick end of the stick. No matter how thin our end is, remember we have thin ends coming in from everywhere and many littles make a lot."

—WILLIAM WRIGLEY, JR. OF WRIGLEY'S GUM

I've said throughout this system that everything you want that you don't have you get from other people. I call the process of getting what you want from other people the **Persuasion Equation.**

The steps of the Persuasion Equation are:

1. Gain rapport with the other person.
2. Elicit the other person's outcome.
3. Give the other person a specific directive.
4. Give the other person more information.
5. Give the other person the directive in another way.

On number 1, gaining rapport: People tend to like people that they are like, and people tend to not like people that they are not like. You are more apt to agree with someone you trust and have affection for. You are more likely to resist someone you have nothing in common with or someone you don't like. We tend to be attracted to people that we have similarities to. There is also a certain amount of human resistance to people who are different from us. Obviously, this is seen all over the planet in the wars between countries, racial challenges, and gender conflicts. I have a belief that if Martians were to land on this planet today and threaten the people of earth, all war on this planet would cease immediately. I believe that all of the people of planet earth would bond together to protect ourselves from the greater difference. The key in gaining rapport and persuading another person is to become like them, so much so that they want to agree with you because you are so much like them. The first element in persuading another person is gaining rapport.

The second element in persuading another person is finding out what they want. Obviously you know what you want. You decided what you wanted before you started the process. It is essential to find out what the other person wants so you can align your desires with theirs or at least make your request look like what they want. We call finding out what they want "eliciting their outcome."

Step 3 in the Persuasion Equation is getting agreement, or getting them to commit. In most instances if you have done a great job with the first two steps, then this step will be more of a directive telling them to take a specific action. If you do not get agreement in step 3, then you would move on to step 4. Step 4 in the Persuasion Equation is giving them more information if you didn't get them to commit in step 3. After you have given them more information, then step 5 is giving them a directive in another way to commit. Since reality is created through validation you must give them greater validation that this is the right thing for them to do, and then give them a directive (close them or get them to commit) so they know what they need to do to win.

The reason there is a need for rapport is that it creates a higher level of trust. When a person has a high level of trust in you, they will have less resistance to new ideas, concepts, products, services, or whatever it is you are wanting to persuade the other person to believe, support, or invest in.

The basic premise for gaining rapport is the ability to find commonality with another person. Commonality could come in many different ways, like discovering that both of you went to the same high school or that you both favor the same team in the Super Bowl. It could be that you share common spiritual beliefs or that you both have the same hobbies. Any similarities that you can bring to the other person's attention, whether they were obvious or needed some digging to get to, are possibilities for rapport. When there are no apparent similarities it is still possible to create a degree of commonality that will create a greater connection between you and the person you desire to influence.

One of the fastest ways to gain rapport is a process called mirroring and matching. Mirroring and matching was developed by two men named John Grinder and Richard Bandler based on the work of a hypnotist named Milton Eriikson. In mirroring and matching, we keep in mind that we communicate primarily on three different levels: the words we select, the tone we use in delivering those words, and the way we use our body. Roughly 40 percent of your communication with another person is comprised of the words and tonality that you use, 60 percent the way you use your body. There are a number of things you can either mirror or match or duplicate from another person to inspire a closeness or a rapport with that person. In your verbal communication the three primary things you want to mirror and match or duplicate are, first, the words that the other person uses. For example, if someone comes up to you and says,"Wow, that's a totally rad idea, man," you'd be silly to say to them, "Yes, it is an extremely exquisite concept, wouldn't you agree?" What you're going to do is alienate them and make them think you're different from them or maybe even that you are making fun of them.

Secondly, you need to mirror and match their volume. How loudly, how softly do they speak? If they're loud, then chances are they may be hard of hearing or it may be that they believe someone speaks loud because they're being honest. So if you spoke softly, you'd alienate them or make them think you were being dishonest. The third element of their verbal communication you want to mirror and match is the speed of their delivery or their pacing. Some people speak very quickly, and if you spoke very slowly to them, you'd make them feel uneasy. To gain rapport, therefore, you want to speak at the same rate that they speak and the same volume using the same words.

Since this is a crash course in mirroring and matching I'm also going to give you the three primary things you want to mirror and match about someone's physiology, or the way they're using their body. The first thing you want to mirror and match is their body position. As you're speaking to them, are their legs crossed, are their hands crossed, are they leaning against a rail, are they standing up with their hands behind them? Whatever it is, mirror and match exactly what they do as you are speaking to them. The second thing you want to mirror and match are their gestures. Do their hands move about a lot, do they reach out and pat you on the shoulder? If they're gesturing a lot, and they're patting you on the shoulder, be sure you gesture a lot and pat them on the shoulder to let them know you're the exact same kind of person they are with the same desires and concerns that they would have. The third element you want to mirror and match is eye contact. How often do they look you directly in your eyes? Do they maintain lengthy contact with you or do they look away? Some people think that the longer you have eye contact with someone the more honest you are. This may or may not be true. Some cultures find it absolutely rude to stare into another person's eyes; in fact it's a sign of respect to look down. The important thing is, whatever the other person is doing is what you want to mirror and match, thereby gaining greater rapport.

"A tactic known, is a tactic blown."

—General Douglas MacArthur

Mirroring and matching is not mimicking. Mimicking means they know what you're doing. If they know what you're doing, cease and desist immediately. If they know you're trying to mirror and match them, you've got to stop because you won't gain any rapport; in fact they will even resist you more.

Another effective way to gain rapport with somebody is to get them talking about themselves and what's important to them. Ask them questions about themselves and be a good listener. As mentioned above, it's also important to find things you have in common. Do you both have large families? Did you both grow up in a specific place or do you both have similar interests outside of your work in the thing that you're persuading them with? Rapport is about finding commonality and finding ways to let them know that you're just like them.

After you've gotten rapport, the next thing you want to do is to find out what is important to them. Let's imagine you're wanting to persuade someone to lend you money, and you're willing to pay them back with interest. Yet you've still got to make it attractive to them to lend you the money. The second thing you'd want to do after you had gained rapport and trust is find out what it is that they look for in an investment. When you're listening to someone's outcome keep in mind:

**"People will always give their
needs in descending order."**

The reason people give their values in descending order is they want to be sure they get the most important thing out first, and that way if you interrupt them or they trail off, the least important will be last. For example, if you've asked them what they'd look for in an investment and they said, "I look for security, I look for a 10 percent to 20 percent annual return on my dollars, and I look for something that's fun for me, that I can have a personal stake in," since people give their greatest needs in descending order, the most important thing to that person in investing in something is security. The second most important thing is the amount of return (in this example it's 10 percent to 20 percent), and the third most important thing is something they can have fun with or have an ownership stake in.

People always give their needs in descending order unless they specifically tell you they have a certain number of needs or values. In other words, if someone were to say to you, "I have three things that are important to me about an investment," what they are doing is telling you they want you to listen until they've told you all three things.

Quite often, however, people will tell you they don't know what they want. What do you do when that happens? Glad you asked! I'm about to give you a very powerful and effective strategy for getting information from other people and for getting information from yourself. This process is so powerful I considered devoting an entire chapter to it. That would have made the book much longer and increased the price, so what I decided to do is condense the strategy and throw it in at no extra charge. What a guy! All seriousness aside, you must experiment with this process to understand its power. It's called the:

"I don't know" strategy

Have you ever asked someone else what they wanted and gotten the reply, "Oh, I don't know"? Of course you have. Have you ever had the experience yourself of wondering what to do in a given situation and said to yourself, "I just don't know what to do"? Again, of course.

Can you imagine asking a person that you wanted to persuade to lend you money, "What is it you look for in an investment," and they said, "I don't know." The reason the "I don't know" response comes up is twofold, and they are both defense mechanisms. Number one. They may not know what is available to them. If they told you they were looking for a 10 percent to 20 percent return on their investment and you were willing to offer a 50 percent to 100 percent return on their investment, they would have sold themselves short. So one reason a person will tell you they don't know what they want is they're not sure what is available to them. The other reason a person that you are about to persuade will tell you they don't know what they want is they are afraid you just might go out and get it for them. So if you fulfill all their conditions they might not have any way to resist your request.

So here's the way I deal with people who aren't willing to give me information when I'm requesting it from them and they say to me they don't know. Let's imagine I've asked this person from whom I want to borrow $50,000, "What is it you look for in an investment?" and they say, "I don't know." I'd say to them,

"I know you don't know. If you did know what you look for in an investment, what would it be?"

And they'll tell me! The reason this works is I'm giving them permission not to know and also making it okay for them to tell me whatever it is they want to tell me.

With others
They say: **"I don't know."**
You say: **"I know you don't know.**
If you did know, what would you want?"

or for yourself
You think: **"I just don't know what to do!"**
You'd think to yourself: **"I know I don't know. If I did know what to do
I would . . ."** Then do it.

Next time you're out with a friend and the friend says, "Let's grab a bite," and you say, "That sounds fine to me, where do you want to go?" and they say, "Oh, I don't know," you repeat back to them, "I know you don't know. If you did know, where would you want to eat?" and they'll tell you. It's that simple. It's going to be a lot of fun and I know it's something you will use in the future. Keep in mind again that a "tactic known, is a tactic blown." You'll probably only be able to use this once or twice with an individual before they catch on to what you're doing. But then again even when they know what you are doing they just might appreciate your ability to help them choose and to get what they want.

Should someone notice what you are doing explain to them that you are practicing a method that you just learned for helping minds get unstuck. Tell them that you use it on yourself and it works really well. Tell them that sometimes when you are sitting at your desk or you're out taking care of things you have a hard time motivating yourself to do the things that you know you should do. Tell them you ask yourself this question: "What should I be doing right now?" Should your mind answer back, "I don't know," then you simply ask yourself the question, "I know I don't know. If I did know, though, what would I do?" The moment your mind gives you the answer, go forward and do that thing.

Eliciting the other person's outcome means finding out what the other person wants. Once you know what they want and they trust you, the last element of the Persuasion Equation is giving them a directive, getting agreement, or getting them to commit. Getting them to commit means that we want them to experience the thing that we're offering as the thing they want. We need them to envision this thing that we have available to them as the item, the concept, the service that they've been looking for. Again, let's imagine I wanted to persuade a person to lend me $50,000 and I wanted to make what I had available to them attractive to them and what they were looking for. The first thing I'd want to do is feed back to them their elicited values. I'd want to talk to them about the security of the investment and how they would be paid back before anybody else, out of the first funds that came in. Secondly, I would want to point out to them that this would be accepted as a personal loan and guaranteed with a return of the investment between 10 percent and 20 percent and maybe even greater. Lastly, I would find a way to involve them in the process, maybe even get them to come to meetings where decisions were made on how the money in the project was going to be invested.

No persuasive process is complete without getting a person to take a specific action. You must tell them what you want them to do and give them the chance to do it. In the example of the loan, you would want to have an agreement or letter of intention drawn up with blank spaces to fill in percentages and any other variables such as payback period or terms. When you are persuading someone you must know what you want and give them explicit directions as to how to give that to you.

"An ambiguous request will get an ambiguous response. A specific request will get a specific response."

Small commitments lead to large commitments both with yourself and other people. This is especially true with the Persuasion Equation. When you can get someone to agree or say yes to part of your presentation, then it will be easier to get them to say yes later. One powerful way to get minor agreements from another person is a process called

A.R.C.ing Statements

A.R.C. stands for Affirmative Response Conditioning. What this means is I get them to give a positive affirmation to something I want them to commit to—so much so, it becomes a natural response for them to say yes to the final request. An A.R.C.ing statement is a statement *and not a question* used to affirm a positive response.

Four types of A.R.C.ing statements:
1. Standard: You say, "It's a great day isn't it."
2. Inverted: You say, "Isn't it a great day."
3. External: They say, "Isn't it a great day?" You say, "Isn't it."
4. Silent: You ask a question while you nod your head yes.

The distinction between a statement and a question is the tonality at the end of the sentence. A question turns up and a statement turns down. Let's take a closer look at the four different A.R.C.ing statements:

The first is called a standard A.R.C.ing statement. It goes like this: "It's a great day isn't it." Notice that wasn't a question. A question would have been, "It's a great day, isn't it?" The only distinction between the two is the tonality or the way that I delivered the information. When I say that in a statement there is a natural tendency for the listener to say yes. Now in the instance of wanting to borrow the $50,000, I might say, "This is a really exciting proposal isn't it," getting them to affirm, "Yes it's exciting." "I know you can really see the security of the way I've structured this can't you." That's a different A.R.C.ing statement. "I'm certain you realize that a 25 percent to 30 percent investment is well beyond what you're looking for isn't it." If you kept using all these A.R.C.ing statements again and again people would notice what you were doing sooner or later wouldn't they." "And I bet it would drive them crazy wouldn't it." "And more often than not they'd strangle you and say 'Knock it off' wouldn't they." So the key here is to use a little bit of variety.

The second type of A.R.C.ing statement is inverted. It's just the opposite of a standard A.R.C.ing statement. Instead of saying, "It's a great day isn't it," you'd say, "Isn't it a great day." So you can sprinkle throughout your presentation inverted A.R.C.ing statements such as, "Don't you love the ability that you'll have to keep your hands on your investment and be at stake in this process." Or, "Isn't it clear to you now how powerful this investment is going to be and how secure you can feel by making it right now."

The third kind of A.R.C.ing statement, the external A.R.C.ing statement, means that when they say it, it's true. It might be that after making your presentation they lean back in their chair and say, "Wow, you've really done a great job with this." Instead of just smiling at them, you look them square in the eye and say, "Haven't I." Or they say, "This seems pretty secure to me," and you look them square in the eye and say, "When you're right, you're right."

The fourth kind is the silent A.R.C.ing statement. Since you communicate 60 percent of your communication solely through your physiology, this type is by far the most powerful. A silent A.R.C.ing statement would consist of looking at a person, smiling at them, getting complete eye contact, and simply nodding your head up and down. You may have looked at them and said, "You like the investment?" You look them in the eyes, you smile and nod your head up and down. People have a natural tendency to be led by the other person's actions. In other words, they'll follow your action because they trust you.

Check this out the next time you get on an elevator and someone else gets on with you. The moment they get on stand the way they're standing. If their hands are in their pockets and their feet are spread, put your hands in your pockets and spread your feet the same way. The moment they look over at you, glance over at them, look them square in the eye, smile and nod. At minimum you'll see their head begin nodding up and down. The funny thing about nodding your head up and down is our body says as much to our brain as our brain says to our body. Nod your head up and down right now. What's the single word that pops into your mind? It's the word "yes," isn't it? Yes is imposed on the subconscious mind by a simple nod of the head.

You can combine the silent A.R.C.ing statement with any of the other A.R.C.ing statements to make it more effective, whether it's standard, inverted, or external, by smiling and nodding your head up and down while you make the statement.

ALTERNATE ASSUMPTIONS: AN EITHER/OR QUESTION THAT ASSUMES AGREEMENT.

If people are saying no to you it's because you're asking questions that are fun or easy to say no to. Part of being persuasive is the ability to avoid asking questions that can be said no to. Instead of saying "Do you want to invest $50,000," you might say, "Do you want to invest $50,000 or would you feel more comfortable with $25,000?" Or you might ask, "Would you want to invest the $50,000 all at once or would you rather split it between two weeks?" The moment they answered either one they are committed to you. Then you say, "Great, let's just sit down and take care of the details." Instead of asking the person, "Do you want to go to lunch with me," you ask them instead, "Would you like to go to a Chinese restaurant or the deli today?" Ask either/or questions that assume a positive response and the positive mental expectancy will cause the other person to be more inspired to say yes to you. When you want something from somebody, no matter who they are, there's only one way you're going to get it and that's to learn to ask in a way that is going to inspire them to say yes. Be specific about what you're asking for, be persistent in the ways that you ask. Make sure you're asking the right person, and learn to work with the resistance.

All resistance is, is someone testing the validity of your request, so their resistance doesn't mean no. It's simply a request for more information. In the process of persuasion, accept whatever happens, stay charming, and keep asking. If after all that you still aren't getting what you want, then change your strategy or your approach or at least change who you're asking.

Now that you are aware of the tools and strategies for increasing profit in your life, it is important to reinforce these procedures through Subconscious Reprogramming. When the mind accepts these strategies as true you will, on a daily basis, bring more profit into your life.

Chapter 31

Subconscious Reprogramming for More Profit

"It's not enough to learn, one must become."
—MARSHALL SYLVER

Now that you have learned many powerful and effective strategies for increasing your wealth, it's time to integrate this material for maximum impact on your life. This chapter, like the two similar ones on Passion and Power programming, is a synopsis of the material taught in this section. The material is written in a specific language syntax to have the greatest possible impact on your subconscious mind. The chapter can be used in one of two ways. One is to record it onto an audiocassette and then play it back as you relax. When you record it, make sure you allow for about two minutes at the front of the tape for you to breathe deep and relax. When you record it onto tape you will read the script in the second person instead of as it's written in the first person. "You will relax" instead of "I will relax." "You recognize that you are indeed worthy . . ." instead of "I recognize that I am indeed worthy . . ." In this way the tape you have created becomes your own personal Subconscious Reprogrammer.

Another method of reprogramming your mind with this is to use the reprogramming script as an affirmation exercise. You simply read the

reprogramming statements out loud to yourself every day exactly as they are written. This method is extremely effective because it forces you to focus your entire attention on the new programs. Often when we are just listening we sometimes let our mind wander. By being an active participant in your positive reinforcement, these statements will help you stay more focused and hear what you're saying. Both methods are valuable. If you choose to use this method of reprogramming, then read the entire chapter out loud exactly as it is written.

Subconscious Reprogramming Script for PROFIT:

I know that 1 percent of the population does indeed control 50 percent of the money, and yet that 1 percent has nothing on me. I am all that they are and more. I realize that the number-one skill in making more money is the ability to communicate and that communication equals wealth. I realize that the highest paid people on the planet are those who can communicate easily and readily. I've released all of my fear of public speaking and I am now secure in my ability to communicate with others. I realize that in communication what I get back is what I send out. I choose to send out to the world the communication that I deserve and desire phenomenal wealth.

Each and every day that goes by I become more effective at communicating, paying close attention to how others respond to me. I realize that dynamic communicators are responsible for both the sending and the receiving of communication and I'm willing to take that responsibility, realizing that I'll be rewarded accordingly. I know that the quality of my life is the quality of my communication, both internally and to the outside world, and I find myself thinking many times throughout the day, "I deserve money. I'm worthy of more."

When other people pay me compliments or give me gifts, I simply say the words "Thank you," fully secure in the knowledge that I deserve them. I realize my self-communication is of the utmost importance in the creation of money and I desire to make more money so that I can support myself and those that I love in ways that are positive, productive, and powerful. I realize that whatever I send out will come back to me manyfold and so I send out into the world the communication that I desire to support others in their pursuit of abundance as well.

I realize that money is made first in the mind, that everything begins in thought, and that thoughts are things. I have learned to think about awesome wealth and all of my situations differently. I realize that I will never create incredible abundance through my labors alone. I know that I am now learning to leverage my key resources, people, time, and money to get more of what I want.

I also realize that in order to be wealthy, I must create more relationships. Each and every day that goes by I find it easier to relate to other people. By listening to what they say and supporting them in what they're going for, I inspire them to help me in what I'm going for.

I realize that it's easier to begin with the end in mind, and so because my vision is strong, my purpose definitive, and my desire great, I inspire other people to support me. Because I know where I'm going, I invite others to come along.

I realize that it is better to surround myself with people that I want to be instead of surrounding myself with people I am better than to feed my ego. I desire to surround myself with people of wealth. I desire to be near people that are doing things right to learn what they're doing and do them in my own life.

I realize that in order to create phenomenal wealth, I now make decisions quickly. I let my yes be yes; I let my no be no. I know that I can always change my mind. I know the sooner I make a decision, the sooner I'll find out the effectiveness or ineffectiveness of that decision; so I now make decisions quickly. I also understand the value of my time.

I choose to focus my time on going for more instead of protecting myself from loss. I realize the only way to lose is to protect myself from loss and I choose to go for more. I realize that to spend twenty minutes on saving a dollar is ridiculous. My time is more valuable than that. I also realize that no one with a five-dollar mentality ever put a thousand dollars in their pocket. I realize at this moment that I am indeed a millionaire whose money has simply not been deposited in my bank account. I make decisions quickly and I create relationships easily. I know the value of my time, and because of that, I refuse to jump over dollars to pick up dimes.

I choose to let go of those people and occurrences that have cost me money and I choose now to focus on going for more. I know that the rich get richer, and the more I can appreciate the dime in my pocket, the more I'll appreciate the dollar. I also realize the enjoyment of accepting abundance from others and I eagerly accept their gifts and their praise. I realize that it is better to have desires than demands and I desire things in my life and yet enjoy what I have now. I know it's not necessarily that something costs too much, it's in that moment I might not be able to afford it, and yet I desire to create plans and strategies that allow me, step by step, to create the things that I want.

I am totally responsible for what something costs and I know that in any moment I can do something powerful and productive that moves me in the right direction of getting what I want. I know that being a workaholic will not produce money; it will produce lots of work. I know that those who think govern those who labor.

I also know that when my ideas are good, money will flow to me. So I enjoy thinking and creating, brainstorming with myself and other people, realizing that a single idea, a flash of thought could be worth millions of dollars. And because I treat my Pinto as if it were a Rolls-Royce, I will not treat my Rolls-Royce as if it were a Pinto.

Right now I choose to live impeccably. I choose to live the life of a millionaire in abundant wealth, to walk and talk and think as if I were already the wealthiest person on the planet. All of these beneficial ideas make a deep and lasting impression upon my subconscious mind, never to be removed, to be recalled the moment I say the word "Profit." (*Take a long, deep breath right now. Breathe in deeply, and as you exhale, say the word "Profit" out loud.*)

I realize that lack of money can be an incredible inspiration and so I never let the lack of money slow me down. In fact, by putting myself at stake, I realize it inspires me to go for more and I do go for more. I realize that in each and every moment I must be ready to seize opportunity so in any moment that I'm not making money, I'm becoming better. I'm teaching myself. I'm learning new skills.

I'm meeting new people that will impact me and help me on my journey.

I realize that to seize opportunity I must be prepared and I spend my time preparing to make money as well as making money in the moment. I realize that I must do what I love and the money will follow. No risk, no goodies. And in any moment I am either making money or losing money.

I realize that money is a product of doing a great job and there's nothing wrong with making money. I am in the habit of doing more than I'm paid for. I'm in the habit of giving a little more, helping a little more, providing more than I promised.

I know that wealthy people keep score and I choose from this moment forward to keep track of my finances. I choose to pay attention to where my money goes and know how to use it wisely. I realize that in order to create phenomenal wealth I am now more persistent. I realize that to create great wealth, I must risk and step up to the plate. As I swing the bat, I realize each and every time brings me one step closer to getting what I want.

I never ask myself the question "Can I?" I now ask myself the question "How can I?" I realize the power of being unique and I choose to be the very best at what I do. I know that there is always a market for someone who is willing to be the very best, and since someone is going to be the best, I now know it can be me.

I know I get paid for what I produce and not how long I work and I'm constantly looking at my life and finding ways to do things better and more quickly so that I can enjoy more of my life. I realize that it's easy to change habits and I can change my habits easily and readily.

Instead of goals, I have plans that are broken down step by step. I'm always promoting what I'm doing. Since I'm proud of what I do, I tell others often and I eagerly persuade them to become involved in my product, service, inspiration, or mission.

I know that I'll always get more by doing more, and when I do more, I have more fun, because I love what I do. I choose to do things that are inspirational to me and, in turn, they inspire others.

I know that some is better than none and better late than never. I'm willing to surrender quickly when I know I'm off track to put myself back on track again. I know that an object in motion tends to stay in motion and I now avoid negative input. I avoid the television and the radio and the newspaper. I'm secure in the fact that if anything is important, I'll find out about it soon enough.

I always focus on going for more instead of going for less. I constantly ask myself the question: "Do my current actions move me closer to the things I want or further away?" I know what I need to do now and I know that money will not buy me happiness. I must appreciate where I am now because (where I'm at later will be where I'm at then.)

I know that I am indeed a wonderful, deserving, incredible human being. I am certainly worthy of an abundant, wealth-filled life. I already possess the tools necessary to create an awesome amount of money.

I enjoy going for more. I savor the wanting as much as the having and I let them think I'm weak when I'm strong and strong when I'm weak. I realize the journey of a thousand leagues begins with a step and everything begins in thought.

I chunk down all of my plans into step-by-step, doable portions. I realize that each and every moment I spend going toward what I want indeed brings me closer to that attainment. I post the things that I want around me on notes and papers so that I can read them every day. I commit to myself and to others with a deadline the things I want to accomplish.

I know the more I commit to other people, the more likely I am to accomplish what I want, and I eagerly commit those plans to others in a way that inspires them to support me. I realize that unless I give service or knowledge or support to my people, they cannot assist me in my challenges and in my plans.

The only reason someone says no to me is a fear of loss. I realize that all decisions are made first on an emotional level and then backed up logically. I realize the art of inspiring other people is to first gain their trust and rapport. I do this by being empathetic, by understanding their needs and desires. I accept whatever happens in my request and I keep asking. If I'm not getting what I want, I simply change my strategy or the person that I'm asking. I am indeed worthy of abundance and wealth beyond my wildest expectations.

I stay focused and on track because I'm inspired and I enjoy my life. I realize that wealthy people inspire cooperation through genuinely enjoying other people. It's easy for me to create relationships because I have a genuine interest in what other people are doing. I recognize the more interested I am in other people, the more interested they will be in me, and they desire to support me because of my vision and because of my focus. Each and every day that goes by, these beneficial ideas and concepts make a deep and lasting impression upon my subconscious mind, always to remain to be recalled the moment I think the word "Profit." *(Take a long deep breath and breathe out now and say the word "Profit" out loud. Take another long deep breath and as you exhale say the word "Profit" out loud again.)*

POWER

Chapter 32

What Power Is

"Power is for use."
—MARSHALL SYLVER

Robert Schuller asked, "What would you do if you knew you couldn't fail?" Another great thinker, in fact, a man destined to be the greatest thinker of all time, took it one step further when I asked, "What would you do if you knew your results?" Power is the ability to take action now. You have many useful tools for the creation of passion and wealth in your life, whether you create the kind of relationships and financial abundance will no longer have to do with what you know; since you now have the knowledge, it will be based on what you do.

This entire book is only a catalyst, a beginning, in creating the life that you want. Without consistent action it is useless. This section of the book is dedicated to focusing on the elements of power. Power is for use, and you would never have been given the abilities and intelligence and hunger for achievement that you have if you weren't expected to use them. If I asked you to get out of bed every morning and put your feet flat on the floor and say, "What a glorious day filled with love, opportunity, and potential!" would you do that every day for a year? Due to the fact that you probably just gave me an underwhelming response, let me ask it in a different way. If you knew that getting out of bed, putting your feet flat on the floor, and saying, "What a glorious day filled with love, opportunity, and potential!" every single day for one year would make you an extra million dollars and create the relationship of your dreams, would you do it? Of course you would! The question you have is you don't know for certain that it would make you a million dollars and create that relationship, do you? You also don't know that it won't.

What if it did, and you never did it. What if that was the one thing missing and because it was so simple, you never did it on a daily basis. It's obvious that something is missing from your life's equation or you'd have what you want right now. It's obvious that something isn't there in your relationships, your wealth, or your well-being or you would have success on your terms in these areas. You've learned all through this book that everything begins with thought and one key ingredient of thought is faith.

Faith is not believing in something without evidence. Faith is proceeding in the face of adversity with merely the slightest amount of validation.

"The stress of an action diminishes rapidly after that action is performed."

Your greatest rewards are always preceded by your greatest stresses. After you have done that thing that caused you to feel stress and probably a certain amount of fear, how did you feel? What did you think to yourself? You probably thought, "What was I so stressed about?" In one of my seminars we do a walk across twenty feet of broken glass. Most people get extremely anxious about the walk beforehand but afterward will always tell me it was much easier than they imagined. Of course it is! Hell isn't outside of you—what you are thinking and what you are imagining is almost always worse than what is.

When I was about to change careers from being a professional magician to serving my fellow human beings I took a leap of faith. I was extremely well paid for my magic talents and didn't have any idea how much I could make in the service of others. When I was creating my nationwide television show there was no guarantee of its success. What if after the years of working on it the message had gone unnoticed? Obviously it didn't, so my faith paid off. When I created my huge hypnosis production show it took many months and many hundreds of thousands of dollars to create. Many times during the process I had the passing thought, "What if no one is interested?" Since no one had ever created a show with lasers, pyrotechnics, dancers, magic illusions, and hypnotizing large groups from the audience, maybe the truth was it couldn't be done or that no one was interested. The proof was in the pudding and again my faith paid off. As I am writing this book I have had the fleeting wonder of "What if nobody reads this? What if the message isn't carried through the printed word the same way as through my spoken word?" I know that hundreds of thousands of you will get the message that I am just like you. You have as much intelligence, opportunity, and wherewithal as I have; and if I can do it so can you.

"Faith = Follow-through"

The thing that kept me going through each of those long projects was knowing that I really didn't have a choice. Unless I was willing to admit I didn't want what I was going for I had to finish each one of those projects. If you knew that going without cigarettes for twenty-one days would make you a nonsmoker would you do it? If you knew for certain that ten days after letting go of that totally unhealthy relationship that the person of your dreams would knock on your door, would you let go of the unhealthy relationship now? If you knew that one year after writing out your ideal day of work and play you would see them unfolding in your life, would you take the thirty minutes to complete it? Faith is follow-through. Circumstances in my life created my undying belief that you must finish what you start or all of the previous energy was wasted. This doesn't mean if what you have been doing on faith isn't getting you what you want you should continue. You must have the acuity to know whether you are getting what you want. When you know beyond a shadow of a doubt that you are going to get what you want, then you will enjoy the journey as much as the destination. Savor the wanting as much as the having, just insist on the having too.

"Faith must be reinforced by reason."
—GANDHI

The power of faith is suspending judgment long enough to gain the rewards available. Even though we can't see the wind we know it exists when we see the movement of the trees. You know it's possible to have passion in your relationships, and tremendous wealth in your pocket, because other people just like you have it in their lives. You're all that they are and more, the only difference is they aren't making excuses, they're making progress. The next time you have a brilliant idea or an exciting impulse follow through. Don't let your fearful voices within talk you out of your potential gains.

"Live a life of adventure rather than a life of maintenance."

I want you to think about the first time you really felt powerful in your life. For me it is when I was about seven years old. I had the need to be different. It comes naturally in a family of ten if you ever want to get recognized at all. I borrowed a magician's book from the library and learned a few magic tricks. When I started displaying my new skill everyone wanted to know how I created the magic. I suddenly knew something they didn't know. I felt powerful. What do you remember about the first time you held power in the palms of your hands? For me that feeling of power has been the driving force in my life. It's still my first love. I love to perform on stage. The thrill of bringing enjoyment to people is an empowering feeling. That feeling is what gives performers the desire to keep going on.

Not appreciating what we have now robs us of our abundance even when it exists. If we don't appreciate it, do we really have it? It also stops us from getting more. Who would you rather give to—the person who doesn't even notice your gift or the person who has a never-ending amount of gratitude? If I were doing a show and someone threw a quarter on stage and I got all excited, jumped up and down, and said, "Thank you, thank you, thank you!," I guarantee you someone else in the audience who saw me get all excited would say, "Did you see what he did for a quarter? Quick, throw him a five spot and see what he does!"

"You must appreciate where you are now because where you're at later will be where you're at now, then."

Chapter 33

Self-Mastery, Tools, Action: The Three Steps to Creating Everything You Want

"To yourself you are what you think. To the outside world you are what you do."

—MARSHALL SYLVER

When you can control what you think, when you have the proper tools for the task at hand, and have the ability to take immediate action, then you can create absolutely anything. Having one or two of the elements isn't enough; you must possess all of them.

SELF-MASTERY

Self-mastery is the ability to control your thoughts, habits, and disciplines, physically, emotionally, and mentally in order to create a successful and satisfying life. It's the ability to take full responsibility, to know that no matter where you are or what your circumstances are, *you* did it. It's the ownership of your actions. When we take the responsibility of our actions, we empower ourselves to live up to our own standards and values. My entire Subconscious Reprogramming system has been designed to continually program you to take complete responsibility for all areas of your life.

The biggest element of self-mastery is controlling the brain boogie or psychobabble that goes on in your subconscious mind at the rate of fifteen hundred words per minute.

"Every thought creates a physical response in the body."

It's impossible to think a thought and not have it affect your body in some way. This is the reason this book has continually focused on getting you to think in different ways. Since every thought has a physical response and every physical response impacts your world, the first step to total power is to **have complete control over every single one of your thoughts**. Even minor physical reactions and responses will make major distinctions in the long run.

In a moment I am going to tell you a story that will cause your body to physically respond. As I tell you this story visualize it in your mind. Recently, I was driving through a citrus orchard near my home. As I looked around me, I saw thousands and thousands of ripe, juicy, plump lemons. When driving through a citrus orchard one of the first things you'll notice is the wonderful scent. As I made my way, I kept staring at those juicy, plump, ripe lemons. It was a hot day and I was thirsty. I couldn't resist. I pulled my car off to the side of the road, got out, and I hopped over the fence. I walked up to the nearest tree full of lemons.

I reached up to the tree and I plucked the biggest, juiciest lemon I could find. The scent was luscious as the stem burst away from the fruit. The sour, tangy, juicy citrus scent filled the air. I sliced the lemon in half with my pocketknife. The sticky, tangy, tart juices squirted all over my hands. I tipped my head straight back and I began squeezing the lemon into my mouth. My mouth exploded as the tarty taste hit my palate. I swallowed hard as my mouth tightened. The tartness was over-whelming. My mouth puckered up and my body reacted. As I bit into the lemon, my whole face puckered up.

As I was telling you this story I bet that you too could feel your mouth getting moist and puckering up, couldn't you? If you didn't feel the physical response of your mouth salivating it was because you sped through the story without taking the time to form the mental pictures.

Do you now understand that if a simple story like this one about the lemon that has no emotional impact in your life can affect you to that degree, then other "stories" that the world tells you can affect you physically as well? It is up to you to determine which stories you will and will not give emotional strength to. The more you internalize and identify with the stories or data input you receive the more impact they will have on your life. Conversely, the less you internalize and identify with them, the less impact they have. Have you ever noticed that if someone is saying something negative about you that you know is absolutely untrue it doesn't have as much impact on you as something that has only a touch of truth? The mind cannot decipher between what is real or what is imagined.

Every thought has a psychosomatic response in the body. What you think in the mind will be telegraphed to your body, and it will respond to that as if it were true.

If I were to convince you that the sky was purple, then that color you'd see would be purple to you. Anytime you saw it in the future you would believe that the sky was purple.

"Men are not prisoners of fate, they're prisoners of their own minds."
—Franklin Delano Roosevelt

The reason I wrote this book and designed my Subconscious Reprogramming system was to help you break free from these destructive voices that hold you prisoner. My purpose is to instruct you in reprogramming yourself to have voices within that will inspire you in a supportive and reinforcing manner. That way you will develop the habit of moving forward. You will actually become aware of feeling uneasy when you are sabotaging your own success.

The first element of self-mastery is **undying belief**. What you focus on expands. When you focus on health and believe your body is functioning perfectly, you begin to do things that create greater health. When you believe that you're healthy you'll be more apt to move and to exercise. The more you move the healthier you get. You must affirm that you are getting healthier all the time.

When you believe you are powerful you will create a commanding presence. This type of power comes from within. It is the foundation for building one's self-confidence. It's typified by the person who walks into a room and immediately lights it up in some kind of unique way. With this heightened awareness, you will have a command of your own well-being, and what other people say and do won't affect you. When you are at a gathering you won't worry about how you are coming across, you'll assume people are thinking pleasant thoughts about you and most people will repond to your kindness with kindness. If they don't, then you'll have the awareness not to buy in to their drama.

The second element of self-mastery is **personal programming**. Personal programming is any "I" or "I am" statements that you think or say and believe to be true. When you affirm statements like, "I have a bad memory," you actually inhibit your ability to remember. Since your subconscious mind is just a computer you will be programming it to forget. Your subconscious mind does not have the ability to make judgments, so if you gave your computer a program to have a bad memory, it would simply let go of any data that it received. If you say to yourself, it's really hard to make money in this day and age, you'll actually impede the flow of money into your life and you'll look for evidence of the difficulty in getting it. You will not be able to see the natural opportunities when they present themselves to you.

People have a natural tendency to want to be right. When you think something to yourself on a subconscious level your mind will support you in being right and begin looking for the evidence to make it true. Since we always find evidence to support whatever we choose to believe, we find the validation to support our reality and proceed accordingly. From this moment on pay close attention to everything you say to yourself or to the outside world that has the words "I" or "I am" attached, and realize that in that moment you're molding your future.

Other people will either intentionally or inadvertently program you as well. If someone says to you, "Do you ever notice how people on the freeway make you so mad when they cut you off?" The moment you agree you're actually allowing their programming to interfere with yours and your mind will react according to their programming the next time you are cut off while you're driving. Now, you might not have really cared whether anyone ever cut you off, yet, in that single moment when you agreed with the other person, you received the effects of that agreement or program. It's up to you to decide which programs you will and will not accept.

When you buy in to a friend's fears and failures you're also subconsciously reinforcing your own fears and failures in life. That's why it is important to be aware of the programs of your friends. You need to associate with people who are going to help you obtain your desires, not confirm to you that your desires are hopeless. If you buy in to that philosophy you choose to be programmed without even realizing it. In every moment we choose what programs we will let in or what programs we will never let into our subconscious thinking.

Personal programming is knowing that you and you alone are in charge of your thoughts. It's directing your thoughts to the ends of your own choice. When you think you can do it, your mind will open up to the possibilities of what can be. The mind is eternally at work. It builds us up and tears us down. It makes us feel like a million bucks or a complete failure. It brings us joy or sadness, prosperity or demise. Heaven and hell lie between our ears, and how you experience your life will be based not on what is, but rather on what you believe to be.

Self-mastery is not simply having a positive mental attitude. While having a positive mental attitude is one of the elements of self-mastery, it's not enough. I know many people with a positive mental attitude who keep doing the same things in the same way and getting the same less than desirable results. They have such a positive mental attitude that they just keep hoping things will turn out and smiling dumbly as their life passes them by. Personal programming is the ability to observe or be aware of what you're getting by what you're doing. Through making adjustments based on what you observe, you will then start creating outcomes in the way that you want them.

The final element of self-mastery is **passion**. People who are masters of themselves are passionate. They possess an emotional intensity that's magnetic. They move with a definition of purpose. They're so excited about what's happening in their life that they desire to share it with others. I believe that we teach what we most need to learn. Teaching something holds you accountable to know it better than your students.

I hold a personal development course called "Certification" at which the attendees get certified in hypnotherapy and can immediately go out and earn a tremendous income with the skills they've learned. Even though this is true, most people who take the course don't do it for a new job, they do it for their own personal development. If you wanted to become a nonsmoker and I taught you how to teach others, it would inspire you to remain a nonsmoker so you'd be congruent in your teaching. We teach what we most need to learn.

"Reality is created through validation."

The more evidence we have to support a belief, the more impact the belief has on our lives. Children who grow up in the ghetto and who see no signs of wealth other than that of the drug dealer or the pimp begin to believe that the only way to create money is through dealing or pimping. That belief becomes reality and a whole life gets formed around the lie.

Some five hundred years ago there was a man named Chris who was trying to get a deal funded, and everyone said, "No way, we're not giving you the money. You're nuts, the world's flat. Haven't you seen the maps? There's a dragon on the edge, you'll be eaten alive." Christopher Columbus set out to find a faster way to India, since he believed the world was round. As he set out for India he got side-tracked, landing in the Americas, which goes to prove you must deal with what emerges and take the benefits of what you get. In that moment when Columbus found the Americas he proved that the world was round, not only for Christopher Columbus but for the entire world. Now was the world always flat and it became round or was it always round and became true for them in that moment? Obviously it was always round. Even after Columbus proved the world was round some people didn't believe it. Was the world flat just because they didn't believe it was round? It was flat to them. They plotted their trips on a flat map that represented a flat world. They stayed clear of the dragons and existed as if the world were flat. Even though it truly was round they existed as if it were flat.

"Not believing in something doesn't make it not exist."

No matter what your current situation is there is a way for you to get what you want, yet it requires that you take a new and sometimes scary action. If you've ever lost something at your home and you can't find it anywhere, the key to finding something is to look in a place you haven't looked.

"To find what we can't find we must look in a place we haven't looked."

I've noticed when some people can't find things they continuously look in the same places and aren't able to figure out why they're not finding it. The next time you can't find something, instead of looking in the places you thought you'd left it, list the places you haven't looked yet, and look there. Truth is you'll have discipline or regrets. Either you will now do what it takes or ten years from now you'll wish that you had. I'm certain you know when you're helping yourself to get the things you want or when you're throwing a wrench in your own gears.

TOOLS

The next element for creating what you want in your life is having the proper tools. While self-mastery is the mental aspect of creating anything, the tools that you use are the physical aspect. It's very difficult to stay in a masterful state of mind when you aren't getting what you want. How much fun do you suppose building a house would be if you had no hammer and had to use your hand to pound the nails into the wood. Even though you may have lots of passion and mental self-mastery you would soon be so bloodied and bruised you most likely would get discouraged. Tools aren't always physical, sometimes the most powerful tool is knowledge.

Throughout this book I have given you many mental tools for the creation of passion and wealth. Like a hammer that is left on the workbench, the power of the tool lies not in the tool itself, rather in its use. Certainly your life can never be the same after reading this book. There are too many new ways of thinking and being presented here for them not to have at least some powerful, positive impact on your life. Generally the tools for a task will be both physical and intellectual. When persuading others, the tools might be the A.R.C.ing statements or alternate assumptions that you use to gently inspire a person to agree with you and fulfill your requests. If you wanted to write a book the tools might be a computer to help to speed up the creative process and the knowledge of how that computer operates. If you are writing music your tools might be the instrument on which you compose and the audio recorder that gives you the necessary feedback to let you know if you are on track.

What are the tools for the outcome that you want to accomplish? You don't have to wait until all of the tools are at hand to begin the process of creation, and yet it is powerful to know what tools would make your task easier and more enjoyable. At a recent seminar I came across a man who wrote screenplays who had no clue as to how to use a computer. In this day and age it astonished me. He told me that it takes him three months to write a sixty-page script. Three months? That's twenty pages per month, that's five pages per week, that's one page per day! Since a large part of what I do has to do with the creation of the written word it flabbergasted me to believe anyone would still do their word processing on a typewriter. I praise the day that I picked up an Apple computer and kiss the ground that Steven Jobs and Steve Wozniak walk on. I was initially afraid of computers and at the same time could never imagine how long my current projects would take if I were still writing on a typewriter. This book alone would have taken twelve months instead of eight weeks if I had to use Wite-Out every time I made a mistake. (Just the thought makes me go AAARRRGGG!)

What tools could make your task easier? If you are wanting to create a new relationship and you are not sure what the current fashion and clothing trends are, then a consultant in that area becomes a tool. If you are an aspiring stand-up comic, then a local comedy club's amateur night becomes a tool. If you are working on creating a specific outcome right now take a few moments to list what tools might make that thing you want to create easier to attain.

ACTION

"Do it like there's no one watching, do it like you don't need the money, do it like you just can't lose, just do it."

—Nike ad

The last element in getting everything you want is the most important and yet it is the only one that cannot be taught in this book. When you have become a master of your own mind and have assimilated the proper tools you will still not have what you want until you take action. For all the successful people on the planet, it is this one element alone, the ability to take consistent action toward what they wanted, that made a distinction.

The Ultimate Scorecard

I have a philosophy that keeps me on track. I call it the ultimate scorecard. It goes like this: you're always either winning or losing. You're always getting more healthy or less healthy. You're always using your time wisely or you're wasting your time. You either did it or you didn't. You're either getting closer in your relationships or you are pushing them away. You're always getting richer or poorer. When you're using this strategy you become highly effective and there's no gray area. In other words if you told someone you'd meet them at 5:00 o'clock and you show up at 5:01 you're late. You must be willing to do whatever it takes. This means no alibis or excuses.

When the Mongols would go to war they'd sail to their enemy's shore with their wives and children. Once there they'd burn their ships, thus forcing their fate. They'd either win the battle or go out fighting. They set themselves up to win or to lose. How's that for motivation? How's that for putting yourself at stake? Using the ultimate scorecard is a very effective means in helping you be totally honest with yourself. It will also increase your credibility with others. When you say something is done it's as good as done. When you begin to live in this way you will astonish yourself at the increase in your productivity and happiness.

Ask yourself this question: "What can I do right now that is positive, powerful, and productive and moves me in the direction of what I want most?" Effective people recognize that in any moment they're faced with decisions that either assist or hinder them in their successes. The only way you can truly do something totally ineffective is to do nothing.

By taking some immediate action you'll either succeed at what you set out to do or you'll learn a way that doesn't work. Either way, what you are doing is beneficial to your plan. You are taking action. If you succeed, all the better, and if you feel that you've failed, then look at your mistakes and grow. Successful people stumble all the time. The more they stumble the more chance of success.

"Anything you don't do right now isn't going to get done."

Learn to fail forward fast. Any action focused on your desired outcome is more effective than no action. Power people know that they must take action on their thoughts. People of power know that in order to win you must be willing to lose. You can't win a game if you don't play. Do something now, for tomorrow never comes, and you alone are responsible for your success. There's no time like the present, take action now.

Chapter 34

The Elements of a Habit

"Success is a habit."

—MARSHALL SYLVER

"A habit is something done often, hence easily."

—DICTIONARY DEFINITION

Do you like to play games you're not good at? Me neither. What's the best way to get good at something? Right again, do it often. Sometimes we get really good at doing things we'd rather not do; we call those things bad habits. Sometimes we find ourselves consistently doing things that support us; we call those good habits. What is it about habits that seem so magical? Like looking behind the curtain and finding out the wizard is only a man, let's take a look at what habits are in order to take away their power.

Element one: Habits are chosen. Even though it may not seem so, you have chosen every single habit you have. A habit is a choice not a chance. Every time you respond in a given way it gets easier to respond in that way again. Most people think of the ineffective actions that they take consistently as habits and the effective actions they take consistently as disciplines. However, they're both the same and formed the same way. The gift of knowing that you've chosen all of your habits—good and bad—is that you can now decide to choose habits that serve you.

The second element of a habit is that it's usually programmed through emotion. The reason that habits are usually programmed through emotion is that all persuasion occurs first on an emotional basis and is then backed up with logic. This is how people start smoking. They have the emotion of wanting to be accepted and then back it up with the logic that smoking is one way to fit in. It's obvious that if we considered smoking from a logical point of view it makes no sense. To become a habit the action must either be repeated by discipline or emotionally triggered. Let me give you an example of each.

A habit takes roughly twenty-one days to form. When you want to begin responding in a given fashion, what you must do is consistently perform that action for at least twenty-one days. Somewhere around the nineteenth, twentieth, or twenty-first day you will suddenly realize you have been doing it naturally. Someone who wishes to become a non-smoker that can maintain their smoke-free lifestyle for twenty-one days is well on their way to success. The first few days might have been easy and then once the initial motivation of becoming a nonsmoker is worn off, the next few days get increasingly more difficult. Around the four-teenth day, the person usually goes absolutely bonkers and probably has a cigarette. Now if they're smart, they'll get past those first fourteen days and let each day go by day by day. Because somewhere around the nineteenth, twentieth, or twenty-first day the individual begins to forget what it was like to be a smoker and a new habit is formed. They forget what it's like to smoke cigarettes and suddenly they become a habitual nonsmoker.

Phobias are a different kind of habit. A phobia is an unsubstantiated fear that was programmed through emotion. No one takes consistent conscious action to form a phobia. The only way you can form that unsubstantiated fear is to begin responding to it and reinforcing it. That first time someone reacts in fear to a given stimuli is called the "initial sensitizing event." Seeing a snake for the first time is not enough to form a phobic response to them. There needs to be a heightened emotional state tied to the initial exposure to form the phobic response. Then what happens is that it is reinforced by another similar event and similar emotional response until the thing that caused the initial reaction is long forgotten and a phobia is formed.

RAPID PHOBIA CURE: Close your eyes and let your body relax. While you are in that relaxed state, let your mind drift back to the earliest moment you can remember having that particular fear. When you go back in time and begin to remember that fear, chances are you will be reexperiencing it. Instead of actually being in the action, imagine you are watching the situation on a movie screen. Imagine you see the you on the screen becoming frightened and responding the way you usually do. Just as when you are watching a scary movie and you feel scared, notice that you feel the same emotions watching yourself in the movie. Now imagine that you are the producer of this movie. Imagine you are sitting up in the balcony and you can see yourself on the screen and you can also see yourself in the audience responding to the movie on the screen. Just as a director is never frightened by his own movie, you watch the person in the audience respond to the movie knowing that you wrote the script to make them respond this way. Next, in your imagination have you as the director yell, "Cut!" Rewind the film and run it backward. Notice how strange it looks and how funny it sounds. Look down at yourself in the audience and see that the you in the audience is laughing too. Now make the movie go forward in slow motion and in black and white. Notice that the you in the audience gets bored and is unaffected. Start the movie once again and this time let the you on the screen switch from the victim to the hero. See yourself doing or facing that thing that you used to fear. While you do, listen to the music playing to a joyous crescendo. Look down at yourself in the audience and say the word "Power" out loud. As you see yourself and the screen as the triumphant victor and you see yourself in the audience as the happy spectator, say out loud again, "Power!" Every time you say the word "Power" you reenforce the new program you've just created.

Now go out and reinforce the new habit. When you are about to come in contact with the old thing that used to cause you to respond phobically, simply fire off your mind trigger and say the word "POWER!"

The third element of a habit is that it must be rationalized as being appropriate to the conscious mind. The conscious mind must accept the fact that it is appropriate to have that habit. *It's appropriate to smoke. You see, all my friends smoke and it's cool and I want to be cool too.* Or, *it's appropriate to be afraid of snakes. Snakes can bite me and hurt me and they've scared me so many times I just don't want to be around snakes.* Or, *it's okay for me to eat this third bowl of ice cream and this second piece of pecan pie because, you see, I really want them and I'm bored and nobody talks to me anymore because—well, because I'm fat.* It's got to be rational-ized as appropriate by the conscious mind or it can never become a program of the subconscious mind. This is not to say that later on the conscious mind won't say this is a sickening habit, I'm tired of overeat-ing, I'm tired of smoking, I'm tired of being afraid of snakes to the point where I don't even want to see them in a zoo. Once the subconscious mind has accepted this program, it's become a habit now and the alter-nate habit must be disciplined as a habit for change to take place.

The fourth ingredient of a habit is that it must be repeated to the point of ease. You form a habit either by responding in a similar fashion many times over or you discipline it. Each and every time you respond in a given fashion, it gets easier to respond in that fashion again regard-less of whether you responded initially by accident and then reinforce-ment or whether you responded initially by hardened discipline to achieve the habit that you wanted.

The fifth element of a habit is that it is something done seemingly without thinking. This is because the grooves in your subconscious mind get so deep that the thought or the habit simply follows the path of least resistance.

All of these are elements of a habit. When a habit truly becomes a habit is when you've reached what is called unconscious competency. The scientist Abraham Maslow came up with four levels of competency, and they go as follows:

Unconscious Incompetency
Conscious Incompetency
Conscious Competency
Unconscious Competency

The first level of competency is unconscious incompetency. That's when you don't know that you don't know. This is when you are a child and you don't know that you're supposed to know how to tie your shoe. You simply don't know that there's any reason to tie your shoe.

What happens is that one day you're walking along at around three or four years old, and as little kids often do, you've got your tongue hanging out of your mouth, you're bopping along, you're happy as a lark, you're smiling about the birds, laughing at the way things look to you, and all of a sudden you step on your shoelace, you fall on your face, you bite your tongue, you cry, and you say to yourself, "There's something here I don't know." At that moment you've reached what's called conscious incompetency.

Conscious incompetency. You know consciously that you're incompetent. Then your parents or one of your siblings teaches you how to tie your shoes. Soon you can tie your shoes except your face kind of gets scrunched up into a funny shape and your tongue usually sticks out of your mouth as you focus all of your attention on what you're doing. When you can tie your shoe and it takes all your concentration you've reached the next level called conscious competency. You know that you know. You consciously focus your attention on the task at hand and you perform it competently.

A few years go by and you put your shoes on every single day and by doing this every single day you start doing other things while you're tying your shoes. Maybe you read a book or maybe you talk on the phone while you are tying your shoe. When you can tie your shoe without much effort you've reached unconscious competency. You no longer need to think on a conscious level how to perform a specific action. At the point of unconscious competency a habit is formed. We can get good at things that serve us or at things that don't. Whatever we do becomes our habit.

A man came to one of my seminars because he was completely terrified of asking a woman out on a date. He couldn't even talk to a woman that he was interested in without shaking and stuttering. Needless to say he hadn't had many dates. I asked him to teach me to be him. I said, "What would I have to say to myself and how would I hold my body and what would I have to do to produce the same results that you're producing?" He said the first thing I'd have to do is when I look at someone I'm interested in I'd have to immediately say to myself, "She probably doesn't go for guys like me. The next thing I'd have to do is imagine everyone is looking at me and then imagine when I strike out they all laugh. And the next thing I have to do is look down, when she looks over, so that she won't try to talk to me and embarrass me when I ask her for a date and she says no." After he'd rambled on for a few minutes, I got the picture.

"An object in motion tends to stay in motion, whether it's a baseball or a thought or a lifetime."

The power comes when you decide to change the results of your mind and redirect them in a way that will be positive to your mental health. This man's mental image of himself was ineffective. He was so caught up in his fears that he was going to make sure they happened, and they did until he was able to reprogram his thinking. I decided to challenge him on his belief system of himself.

I asked him if there was anyone in the audience that he might like to have lunch with at the break. He said yes. I asked which person it was. He said he couldn't point her out because he'd be too embarrassed. I thought to myself, "This is going to be a fun one!" Finally after much coaxing he pointed to a very beautiful woman in the group. I asked her to come forward and sit in a chair on stage. After she was seated, I asked him to ask her for a lunch date. He stood kind of frozen in place.

Since he couldn't move, I told him that I would ask her out the same way he told me he would. In other words I would become him. I looked at her and said out loud, "She probably doesn't go for guys like me. Jeez, why is everybody looking at me. I just know everybody is going to laugh at me when I strike out. Oh heck she's looking at me! I'd better look away so she doesn't think I'm staring." Then when I finally walked up to her I said, "You probably don't want to go out with me do you?" She said "No!" and everybody laughed.

Next I asked him if there was anybody in the room that he thought would have no problem asking this girl for a date and getting it. He smiled and said, "You, Marshall." I smiled back and modestly agreed. I also asked him how he thought I would go about asking her for a date. What would I be thinking to myself and what would I do? He said, "Well, the first thing you'd be thinking is that girl would be lucky to be on a date with me!" I laughed as did the rest of the audience.

He said, "The next thing I'd do if I were you is smile and wink at her

PASSION, PROFIT, & POWER 249

confidently and raise my eyebrow like you do." I told him to go ahead and see what response he got. When he did she outwardly blushed.

He said, "It looks like it's working!"

I said, "It's got to work better than the plan you gave me!" I told him to go ahead and ask her for a lunch date in the way he thought I would.

He walked over to her and said, "Hello you beautiful example of female perfection. I was just standing over there and thinking to myself that my entire life would be complete if I could share twenty minutes with you over a cup of coffee. Would you like to go now or would you rather wait until the lunch break?"

Needless to say the entire group was floored, especially me. This guy did me even better than me. Everyone applauded him and the woman agreed to have lunch. Later on during the weekend every time I saw him he was talking to another woman. I guess he could never go back to his old self since the new self was so much fun.

ASSIGNMENT: Select a mentor for the thing that you want to be better at, whether it's asking someone for a date or getting youself to go to the gym more often. Make a list on paper of the things that they do that you don't. Even if those things seem difficult, are they possible? If you had to do them could you? Make the determination to start pretending you are the mentor that you want to be in that chosen area. If you were that person would you walk, talk, think, or act any differently? I've already shared with you how I one day decided that I was the greatest hypnotist of all time. When I made that decision I knew that I could no longer smoke since a great hypnotist wouldn't. I wrote down a long list of the things that the greatest hypnotist of all times would and wouldn't do. As I started living my life as if I were already that person, other people and the world started treating me as if I were that person. *Ponder this: if I already was the person I wanted to be, what would I do differently?*

How do we change habits? How do we become more effective? Since you now understand where habits come from, I'm going to give you a formula for forming new and powerful habits that will serve you and nurture you and add to your effectiveness as a human being. Needless to say, changing a habit can certainly be more of a challenge than forming it in the first place. On the other hand, the rewards are so great that I highly recommend that you accept the challenge.

The first thing you must do is to decide on exactly what area you're going to focus your attention on first. Maybe you are overweight and you smoke and you sit around watching television all the time putting off what you want to do and you really would like to improve your golf game and also possibly be a better lover.

In order to get a win under your belt I recommend that you start with one habit at a time and then move on to the next. Working on too many things at once can be frustrating and takes all the fun out of transformation. Once you've decided which habit to start with focus on exactly what it is that you want. Focus on how life will be after you've acquired that new habit. To do that, the easiest thing to do is list the benefits you will receive from your new habit. What I recommend you do is take out a sheet of paper right now and begin listing at least ten things that you will have when you have formed your new habit. Remember: anytime you get rid of one habit you're forming a new habit.

As an example, say you want to stop overeating and you want to form the habits of a slender person. Those ten benefits might be, "I'll be more attractive, I'll have more fun when I go out, I'll be more confident, my clothes will fit me nicer, I'll be able to dance more, I'll have more energy," and so forth. Whatever your personal benefits are, list at least ten. The more you can list, the easier the process of transformation will be.

"You can accomplish just about anything if you have enough reasons."

—JIM ROHN

List the things that you want in the positive tense. Always list what you will have instead of what you won't. As an example, "I will be slender and attractive," as opposed to, "I won't be fat."

I want you to list all the things that are barriers for obtaining new habits. These would be things that might be triggers for the old habit. List next to them how you can remove those barriers. For example, if you're someone who wants to stop smoking, a barrier might be when you go out at night with friends and everybody lights up. The thing that would break through that barrier might be a written agreement that you carry that you have all your friends sign saying they promise not to give you a cigarette. You must confront these barriers and find a way around them. For me, when I smoked, every time I got on the phone, it was a natural habit to pick up a cigarette and begin smoking. Every time I drank coffee, I'd smoke. So I had to plan in advance a way to overcome my desire for a cigarette at those critical moments.

Once you have listed the reasons you want your new habits as well as the strategies for overcoming the potential challenges, you are ready to move on. Isn't creating our life on purpose fun? The next area has to do with programming that subconscious mind. You must program your subconscious mind to start changing those elements of your mind that cause you to respond in that specific negative fashion.

Chapter 35

Create a Habit Buster

"Turn your habit into a conscious decision."

—MARSHALL SYLVER

The next thing you need to do to change a habit is to form what I call a **habit buster**, something that allows you the opportunity to make a conscious decision about your actions. Habit busters are things that you invent to help you decide to decide.

My favorite habit buster is utilizing something called a wrist or a pack band. In cigarette smoking they're called pack bands because they go around a pack of cigarettes. In weight loss and nail biting we call them wristbands because they go around your wrist. (The creative staff was up all night coming up with those names.) If you were wanting to change the habit of gambling it might be something that you put in your wallet that made you stop and make a conscious decision every time you were about to pull out cash to gamble with. If you wanted to break the habit of calling the person that you had an unhealthy romance with, it might be a card over the telephone that says, "Make the choice that's best for you."

What a habit buster does is it sends up a signal. It's like a red flag going up every time the person moves back to their old habit. The wrist or pack band is about an inch and a half wide and has a number of lines on it. In my nonsmoking program and in my weight-loss program not only does this band have a bunch of lines on it, it also has a little space that says "plan date."

The plan date is the date you'll give up your habit and form a new constructive habit to replace the one you are giving up. In weight loss it has a "plan weight" on it so that you know what you're aiming for. Let me explain how the band works.

With the smokes in your pocket and a pack band on your cigarettes, you reach for your cancer sticks. The first thing you do every time you smoke is look at the pack and make a note of what time it is. You write down the time on the band. What this does is it causes you to stop and think. It breaks down the habit. That's why we call it a habit buster. It breaks the habit down into a conscious decision.

Once you're making a rational, intelligent, conscious decision for those things that are better for you, you begin forming new habits. When you look at your pack band, it sends the signal up that says, "Hey, wait." You write down the time. When you write down the time it gives you the opportunity to decide whether you want that cigarette or whether you can wait three or four minutes, half an hour or a day or forever. It gives you the chance to think about what's more important to you: becoming a nonsmoker as you planned, or having that cigarette.

In the case of smoking, should you decide that you want to wait, beside that time you wrote down, you'd place a little star and put your pack away. The next time you'd reach for a pack, you'd pull it out, you'd look at the pack band, you'd look at the time, you'd write down the time, and you'd make your decision. Do I want the cigarette or not? If you want the cigarette, you put a little black dot beside the time on the pack band, and then enjoy your cigarette. I mean if you are going to do something you don't want to do you might as well enjoy it. You've said, "I'm making an intelligent decision to have this cigarette." When you start keeping track of what you're doing, that moves you in the direction of who you want to be, and you will be less likely to beat yourself up over what you're not doing.

Have you ever had a tough time getting up in the morning? I used to have a tough time getting out of bed because I really enjoyed sleeping in and dreaming. I used a mental habit buster that got me out of bed in the morning. Mental habit busters are a process of self-hypnosis that are extremely effective. How I used it to get myself out of bed is I would think to myself, while my eyes were still closed, "In a moment I am going to count from 1 to 5. The moment I say the number 5 I am going to jump out of bed filled with energy ready to face the challenges of my day. I will put my feet on the floor, clap my hands together and say, "What a glorious day filled with love, opportunity, and potential!"

Then I begin counting in my mind from 1 to 5. Number 1, all right, you're getting ready. All right, number 2, you're going to get out of bed in a moment. Number 3, your body's coming back to life. Number 4, you're almost up. And when the next number comes, number 5, I say, "number 5," I jump out of bed, my body automatically responds, and I get out.

By triggering my mind and forcing myself to respond in the beginning to getting out of bed when I say the number 5, it makes getting out of bed that much easier. Now, of course while I'm lying in bed my mind is fighting with me saying, "You don't have to get up when you hear the number 5." Then I'd start counting and by number 3 I'm saying, "This is ridiculous. You know you're going to lie there." The key is, though, that when I reach number 5, my body responds because I insist on that response and in doing what it takes. When I say "number 5," my feet hit the floor, my hands go into the air, I smile at the heavens, and I say, "What a glorious day filled with love, opportunity, and potential!"

The key to using a mental habit buster is to be consistent. Insist to yourself that you will respond whenever you use it. Soon it will be so ingrained in your subconscious that it will be difficult to resist.

Chapter 36

The Six Steps
to Forming
Diamond-Hard Habits

Step No. 1: Commit. Affirm your new habits to the world. The greater your commitment to the world, the greater the success in your new habit. By confessing your new habit you set yourself up to have to succeed because you now know that if you don't you'll look foolish among your friends. This is effective because many of us have no difficulty whatsoever in letting ourselves down, yet something funny occurs when we commit to other people. We get the job done. Commit to as many people as you can. Just commit.

One of the reasons the pack bands and wrist bands are so effective as a habit buster is that every time you think about the band you consciously reevaluate what you are doing and what you want to accomplish. Another reason they work is that other people will ask you what the bands are for. When you explain them you are confirming your new habit to someone.

Step No. 2: Take action now. Decide when you are going to have implemented your new habit. If it is something that has a definitive stop date (such as becoming a nonsmoker) or start date (such as working out) determine when that will be. If it is a habit that is ongoing, then the start date is now. Post your affirmations and read them out loud daily. Your affirmations are the subconscious programs that you wrote.

When you are really committed you will also create a Subconscious Reprogramming cassette.

Step No. 3: Know your outcome and focus on it. Even before you've actually changed your habit tell yourself it's happening now. Just like the ultimate scorecard says, you're always either winning or losing. You're either going toward or away from the thing you want. In this very moment you're either losing weight or gaining weight. If you don't believe that ask yourself this question: are you putting something in your mouth right now? When you want to change a habit there is a moment that you must affirm to yourself it's already done. I want you to say to yourself the words "I am _____" and fill in the blank with whatever it is you want to become. It might be "I am a nonsmoker" It might be "I am confident in my dealings with other people." It might be "I am a money magnet." Where the blank space is, insert what you want to change and say the words "I am _____."

Affirm that the change is occurring in the present. You can never change something in the future. It is ineffective to program your subconscious mind to say, "I'm going to become a nonsmoker," "I'm going to be confident," "I'm going to make money." You're either doing it in the present or it's not happening at all.

Step No. 4: Use repetitive action. Sometimes you don't think you're getting somewhere, when actually you are. When you've been doing something wrong for a long time, doing it right is going to feel wrong to you. Be persistent. Focus on your change even if it feels awkward at first. Stay with it; soon enough it will become natural.

Two frogs fell into a bucket of cream. One of them, realizing it was hopeless to get out because he couldn't reach the top by jumping, gave up and drowned in the cream. The other frog, even though it felt uncomfortable and he felt like he wasn't getting anywhere initially, kept jumping up and down in the cream. Very soon the cream turned to butter, which gave him the foundation from which to launch his body out of the bucket and save his life. Keep repeating that new action even if it feels awkward.

Step No. 5: The moment you get off track get back on. If you're wanting to lose weight and you noticed you just put that third piece of banana cream pie in your mouth, then the time to change your habit isn't after you've finished that one piece, or tomorrow or the next day, it's right now—don't even finish that bite. If you notice that the bite is in your mouth and you realize it doesn't help support you and your desire to lose weight, spit that bite out into a napkin. If you're not going to spit that bite out, then enjoy every bit of flavor that bite has to offer, without guilt, realizing it was your choice. If you're wanting to become a nonsmoker, and after you've made the decision, a few days later you notice you have a cigarette in your hand, the moment you realize the cigarette is there is the moment to make the decision to either stop or, guilt-free, to enjoy the cigarette. Either way you are making the choice, and if you truly want to change your habit, the moment you realize you're off track get back on. Changing habits isn't a matter of not getting off track, it's how long it takes you to notice you're off track and how quickly you get back on.

Step No. 6: Forgive yourself with the proper self-talk. In other words, if you do get off track, say to yourself, "That's not like me, I'm taking charge of this area of my life. I'm strong, I'm powerful, I am a nonsmoker." Don't say, "Oh, you're such a loser, you can't ever stop, I can't believe you're still smoking, what a jerk." That's only going to depress you and make you want to have cigarettes more.

Right now I'm going to share with you the fastest way to change any habit and to create confidence beyond your wildest dreams. The next few words can change the way you do things forever. To totally take charge of your life and to command complete control over your destiny, you must learn to:

ACT AS IF.

From reading my book or from seeing me on my many television appearances, do you think I'm a confident individual? Do you? I'll bet you do. What if I'm not? What if I'm scared to death in my television presentations? What if I'm terrified and I am just acting as if I were confident? If I act as if I'm confident enough and enough other people tell me I'm confident, because I'm not confident I'll believe them, and I'll become confident. If you want to change a habit, learn to act as if the habit has already changed. If you want to be nonsmoker act as if you are already. Think what a nonsmoker thinks, do what they do with their hands, buy what they buy when they go to a convenience store and act as if you're a nonsmoker right now. If you want to be more confident in your dealings and your relationships with others, learn to act as if you are already confident. If you're having a tough time with this concept and you're not quite sure how to act as if you are already the thing you want to become, look around at someone who is already what you want to become. Look at someone who is already slender, already a nonsmoker, already confident, already wealthy and do what they do, act as if you're that person already.

Chapter 37

How to Structure Mega-Powerful Subconscious Programs

By now you know that the things you think determine what you do on a daily basis. Since the mind operates in a very specific fashion, the way you structure your new subconscious programs will greatly determine your level of success. What follows are the rules for structuring Mega-Powerful Subconscious Programs.

Rule No. 1: Use positive, not negative, words and images. In other words, eliminate all negative words. Use the positive present tense to move in a positive direction. In your affirmation, instead of saying, "You do not toss and turn for hours before you sleep at night," which would be creating a mental image of a restless night, you'd be much better off making an affirmation that says something like this: "I sleep as if I were floating on a soft, beautiful cloud and I sleep easily and readily." What it does is create in your subconscious mind the proper picture of your desired result.

To give you a couple more examples, an effective program would be "My breath smells as fresh as that of a nonsmoker." The ineffective program would be "My breath doesn't stink." An effective program would be "I am slender and attractive." An ineffective program would be "I'm not fat."

By saying "I'm not fat" your mind moves in the direction of your dominant thought and your whole focus will be on that statement or the affirmation of the single word "fat." When you say, "I don't stay awake at night," the whole focus is on the affirmation of staying awake at night.

If I were to tell you what not to do it wouldn't tell you what to do. If a parent tells a child, "Don't talk back to me!" the child still won't know what the desired behavior is. In fact, programming yourself or others to "don't" do something will actually make the undesired behavior more pronounced since it creates a vacuum in the mind. By telling the mind not to do something it creates a space that when unfilled will suck the only program lingering right back in and reinforce it to a greater degree. Always use the positive versus the negative.

Rule No. 2: Use the present tense. When you're structuring an affirmation, structure it as if it's already been accomplished. "I am calm and relaxed." "Someday" or "soon" or "will be" or "when I'm ready" are not active suggestions for your subconscious mind to act upon. They're indeterminant and ambiguous. In other words, it doesn't say when it's going to happen.

Use the present tense similar to these examples: "I sleep easily at night" as opposed to "I will soon find myself sleeping easily at night." A program in the present tense is "I am now becoming a nonsmoker." Or after you've made the commitment; "I am now a nonsmoker." An ineffective program would be "I am going to become a nonsmoker." Or after you've become a nonsmoker, "I am going to stay a nonsmoker" because that gives you an out because you're saying you're going to do it, not that it's already done.

Rule No. 3: Affirm an action instead of an aptitude. As an example, an effective program for becoming a more powerful public speaker would be "I speak more clearly and with purpose" versus "I'm able to get my point across and people understand me." Getting your point across is an aptitude, something you have no control of. The only thing you have any control of is your actions. So affirm an action instead of an aptitude.

Rule No. 4: Focus your attention on one area at a time. You'll make it harder on yourself than neccesary by working on too many habits at once and you can speed along your great change into the powerful person that you truly are by accomplishing one goal at a time. Focus your program on one thing at a time. By choosing one specific area of programming you have a much better opportunity to be successful.

Once you've reached your goal and have a new habit, it will have a dramatic impact on your acceptance of the next program you create.

Rule No. 5: Use all available details. Example: If you want to form the powerful habit of enjoying public speaking, which indeed is a very strong habit to possess in the business world, you might program yourself in this way: "I love to entertain," "I love to be the center of attention with all eyes focused intently upon me," "I enjoy knowing that each and every ear in the room is hanging on my every word," "I enjoy the lights when they're turned on me and I enjoy being in front of a large group of people," "When I hear applause, the creative resources of my mind float easily and readily creating new and wonderful impactive statements to deliver to my obviously excited audience," "My voice is clear and resonant, ringing through to the final row, and my presentation is concluded with gracious applause."

By using programs that describe the full circumstances, they become more exciting to your subconscious mind.

Rule No. 6: Use obtainable goals. It's always best to aim high in anything you do. In other words, make sure that you're not underselling yourself. But at the same time, when you put your goals or programs for your new habits and plans too far out of reach, they become frustrating to the subconscious mind and frustrating to the individual as a whole. Sometimes it's not appropriate to suggest perfection.

Example: "You always plan your time exactly" is an impossible goal for the mother of ten children who all have individual activities. Trying to program that in that circumstance would only lead to frustration to that person wanting to get more done with their family. When you use words in your affirmations like "always" and "every time," make sure that it is something that you're capable of doing. "I always sit down when I eat." "I always set my utensils down between bites." "Every time I chew, I get every bit of flavor that particular bite has to offer." You see, these are obtainable goals. An unobtainable goal will lead to frustration and rejection of a new habit.

Rule No. 7: Be exact. If the result you want to produce is measurable, such as a body weight, a golf score, or an income, suggest the exact weight, score, or amount. It's not effective to tell your subconscious mind to lose some weight or to better your golf game by a few strokes. Your mind will believe that only partial success will be acceptable and you've accomplished a new habit. When you tell your subconscious mind exactly what you want, you're programming a target, a plan, a goal in your mind to accomplish that.

Rule No. 8: Use the first person. When you say your program out loud, always speak in the first person. Instead of "You are confident," make sure your program says, "I am confident." The only time you would speak in the second person is if you were recording your programs onto cassette in the second person saying, "You are more confident" so that you could hear that program back and respond accordingly.

These are the rules for Mega-Powerful Subconscious Programs. Now that you've decided on what habit you want to change, you focus on an outcome. You list your benefits, you've found out what you'll have once you've changed that habit. You list the barriers that you've had in the past. All the things that you know cause you to respond in less than a way than you would like. You list how to get rid of those barriers.

Now, I want you to take the time out right now to write. Write out at least ten programs using rules I've just given you. Remember to be simple, use positive, exciting, descriptive words, affirm action instead of aptitude, and use all available details. Make sure that they're obtainable goals. Be precise on your change instead of the change of others. Make sure that when you're programming something, you use the first person unless you're using a cassette, in which case you would use the second person.

Chapter 38

Words to Remove From Your Vocabulary

There are certain minor shifts you can make immediately that will produce instantaneous results. What follows are some words that you must now remove from your vocabulary forever to make your self-communication (programming) and your communication with others more effective.

TRY

The first is the word "try." Try implies failure. If you try to do something it's not the same as determining you are going to do it. In my seminars I will ask one of the participants to try to pick up the slide projector controller from my hand. When they reach forward and pick it up, I say, "No, I said try to pick it up, you picked it up." As they reach for it again they usually don't pick it up. They quickly come to the conclusion that there is no state of trying, they either did it or they didn't. Try is a word that everybody uses to get themselves off of the hook. It's the fail-safe that says, "If I don't do what I said I was going to do at least I tried." How often have you set out to do something and because you didn't finish what you started you used the excuse "I tried"? When you send a message of try to your subconscious it believes that something isn't really important: that disempowering word "try" will set you up for failure.

An excellent example of this is in *The Empire Strikes Back.* In the movie there was this little green guy named Yoda who was teaching Luke Skywalker how to use the Force. In one of the scenes he and Luke were practicing in the swamp and Yoda said to Luke, "Levitate the spacecraft." Luke said, "Master, I'll try." Yoda said, "Try you mustn't . . . do you must." Do you must.

Pay attention to people who say the word "try" to you. If someone tells you they'll try to get back to you tomorrow you can pretty much count on the fact that they won't. When they say, "I'm going to try to get back to you," get them to commit. Tell them, "I know that you're busy and does that mean I'll hear from you tomorrow, or won't I?" Once you get their commitment they'll be ten times more likely to follow through. Power people take responsibility for their actions. How many times have you invited a person to a party and they said they'd try to make it. Usually these are the people who don't make the party, isn't it? Try is a word that people use when they want an excuse for not completing what they started or for not doing what they didn't want to do in the first place.

CAN'T

Can't is another word that needs to be eliminated from your vocabulary. Can't means: don't know how to or don't want to. Whenever I say the word "can't" to myself, I immediately ask myself a question: "Does it mean I don't know how to accomplish this, or does it mean I don't want to put forth the effort needed to accomplish it?" If I really don't want to put forth the effort to accomplish the task, I'll release it and with it the stress of not doing what I decided not to do. Remove the word "can't" and decide whether you don't know how to and will learn, or that you don't want to and release it.

BUT

But should also be removed from your vocabulary. But negates everything that goes before it. "Gee, I want to earn a lot of money but it's a lot of work." "Gee, I want a better relationship but sometimes they're unreasonable." " I want to go but I don't know anyone."

Anywhere you use the word "but" replace it with the word "and." "I really want to earn a lot of money and it takes a lot of work." "I really want to make my relationships more fun and sometimes it seems they're unreasonable." Remove the word "but" and replace it with the word "and"—and notice how your communication will improve.

Pay attention to what other people say. If they say, "You know what, I'd really like to get together with you, but I have other things going on." Realize that what they're really saying is at that moment they don't want to get together with you.

Wimp Words
(As in Wimpy Wimpy not Hefty Hefty)

The following two words are words that present you in a less than confident light. What they do is take away your power so you seem unsure of yourself and your outcomes. Whom would you rather be in a relationship with or do business with, people who are confident and know where they are going or people who are uncertain and unsure. We all feel more confident when the other person feels confident. Removing these wimp words from your vocabulary forever will enhance the way people perceive you and give you the power that you deserve. The first word is:

HOPE

"I hope things work out for me." "I hope I make the team." "I hope I get a bonus." Hope is a wimp word because it betrays a lack of security and confidence. Can you imagine going to a doctor who said, "Take off your clothes, lie down on the table, we're going to cut you open, and I sure *hope* we find out what's wrong with you." EEEKKK! You'd be terrified of that doctor. You'd think to yourself, "He'd better *know* he's going to find out what's wrong with me before he starts cutting into me."

"According to Dante, on the gates of hell are the words, 'Abandon hope all ye that enter here!' I wonder if the gates of heaven say the same thing."

People who hope their lives will change are people who do nothing for themselves. These are the same people who believe God will take care of them without realizing that God already did by giving them the ability to take care of themselves. Not only is hope a wimp word, it is just one step short of wishing on a magic lamp. It may give you a pleasant feeling but it lacks all the definition of purpose that knowing provides. Replace the word "hope" with the word "know." "I know I am going to get what I want because I'll just keep moving until I do!" "I know that man will agree with me because he will sense my conviction." Be a person of power and action; release hoping and start knowing. Next wimp word:

IF

If I get what I want, if I win the lottery, if they like me, if the new raisin and grapefruit diet works, EEEKKK again! Since your subconscious mind believes to be true whatever you tell it to be true, then "If I ever create a relationship," "If I ever get rich," "If I'm able to figure out what to do with my life," "If I wasn't so stressed out" tells your subconscious you are not going to get, be, do, or figure those things out.

If, like should, is what isn't and you must deal with what is. If is a word that people use to rationalize their regrets. "If only I had done this or that. If only you hadn't done that, then everything would've worked."

If is a word that puts conditions on what you want to accomplish. It makes you wait until circumstances are perfect. It makes you hesitate in going for what you want. Replace the word "if" with the word "when." "When I create a relationship," "When I find the wealth that's rightfully mine," and "When I know consistently how to deal with the stresses in my life, then I'm moving forth on a positive path" sets your mind up for positive mental programming. Focus on what's working and go for more. When infers the confidence that something is going to occur. When sends a signal to the subconscious that you are in the process of doing what you are affirming.

Chapter 39

Being the Best
That You Can Be

"There is always a market for the very best of something."
—MARSHALL SYLVER

Success is not something you're born into. I personally know many people who were born into riches but never learned how to take care of themselves or their inheritance. The ability to have a healthy, well-balanced life, physically, mentally, and emotionally, provides for passionate, profitable, and powerful relationships.

Success strategies aren't genetic qualities that some people have and others don't. Michael Jackson wasn't born with the ability to dance. Robin Williams wasn't born a creative genius. Ray Kroc, the brains behind the McDonald's Corporation, wasn't born into riches. It takes drive, desire, discipline, and dedication. Say these words: "I commit to being the very best at what I do." Let go of excuses and put yourself at stake.

A friend of mine owns a seafood restaurant in Southern California. And even though the fish is kept in tanks, right up to the point where it's prepared, quite often he complains the fish taste flat. One day while in his restaurant I observed the fish and realized why they were tasting flat. Even though they were kept alive, they looked like they realized they were on death row. They were listless. When he put a predator into the tank with the fish, they suddenly lost their listless look and started moving to save their own lives. It's the same for us. We can go through life listless and not do much with our abilities or we can put our lives at stake and go for more. When we put our life at risk we will be forced to live out of our comfort zone, which will create a need for us to accomplish more in life.

When you put your desires and dreams at risk and you prepare for the when in your life, you will be ready to capture opportunity when it comes knocking at your door. Have something at stake. Tell others what you are committed to. Let them know exactly what you're going to accomplish and when you're going to do it. The more people you tell the better. Remember it's the people who make excuses about the economy in their area or the weather that become poor salespeople. Other people complain about their health without paying attention to the fact that they did it, not you. You're responsible for your own life and it's up to you to choose to go for more no matter what happens.

Han Solo, in the movie *Star Wars,* said, "I don't want to know the odds." Take the responsibility for your own success. Can you imagine what kind of a player Michael Jordan would have been if he had sat around drinking coffee and smoking cigarettes between games because the odds were in his favor? Refuse to let the odds demotivate you. Ask yourself "Can I?" and ask yourself "How can I?" Instead of asking if it's possible to get more, ask yourself how it's possible to get more. What you can conceive, you can achieve. It all begins with what you think and what you choose in any given moment.

I challenge you right now to decide to never settle for what you think you can get. I challenge you to go for what you want. When others ask how things are doing you always answer "fantastic," "perfect," or "awesome." This does many things. First your mind is instantly programmed to find what's fantastic, perfect, or awesome in the moment. Secondly, it lets people know what kind of person you are. That you're the kind of a person that's in charge of your life. When you use these words you decide how you're going to respond in any given moment and that you are not going to buy into another's pain. These words also indicate that your life is going right on schedule. It arouses curiosity in the other person's mind when someone tells them they are fantastic. The other person is going to wonder what has happened to you to make your life so perfect. How many times have you said to someone that you are fantastic and they respond with a question? Why are you perfect? What has happened that has made life so enjoyable?

Thirdly it attracts people to you. When people feel that you are confident and sure about how you feel they will want to be around you because it is uplifting to them. People will always want to be around a person that is fun and positive rather than a person that is always complaining about their situation. When you are at a party don't you congregate around the people who are exciting and fun? When you develop these types of words you will stand out and you will make an impression that will be remembered for a long time after the encounter.

Small commitments lead to large commitments. When you're having a challenging day and you're not able to get out these words, at least program your mind to move in the right direction. If you are having a very challenging day, when someone asks you how you're doing simply say, "Getting better all the time." Since your mind will always move in the direction of its dominant thought, this will force your subconscious mind to start looking for what's getting better and soon you'll feel awesome.

I was recently on a one-week cruise in the Caribbean. While I was working out in the ship's gym, I saw a sign on the wall that said, "Working out is as easy as right foot, left foot." What it meant was you put your right foot through your shorts, then your left foot. If you're having a tough time getting to the gym, don't beat yourself up. Instead take it one step at a time. Go to the gym and put your shorts on. The first step is getting to the gym. If this seems like an impossible task, then instead of working out just go to the gym and watch other people work out. Eventually while you're there instead of doing a full workout just pick up a couple of weights or ride the bike for a little while. By taking a single step in the right direction you'll set yourself up to take action.

Let your credo be, work hard and play hard.

You get much more pleasure from all of your life. Focus your entire attention on where you are now. If your mind is going to be somewhere else, you might as well go there, since no one is winning.

To win at the game of life you must find whatever happens in your life as interesting and deal with what emerges. You really don't have any choice. Deal with it joyfully. Send a message to the world that no matter what happens, you can handle it.

Your success in life will be in direct proportion to your ability to embrace stress. The more stress you can joyfully endure, the more rewards will flow into your life. Like a cornucopia of riches. See your problems as challenges, puzzles that have a solution. That once found, deliver to you the jackpot that you deserve.

Have you ever been doing a jigsaw puzzle and as you were doing the puzzle, thought, there's no way to solve this. You got stuck a certain way through the puzzle and said, "Forget it. They didn't put all the pieces in here. They left a couple out." And you were convinced that a 500 piece jigsaw puzzle only had 475 pieces. Then as you were looking at it someone else came along, saw the puzzle and said, "This piece here looks like it might fit" because they looked at it differently. Because they saw something maybe you didn't notice or looked at it in a way it didn't appear to you, they found a piece that fit and with that piece fitting, more pieces fit until suddenly the puzzle was completed. All the pieces are there, you can win. No matter what happens accept your life as the game that it is and realize you must not only play to win—the key is to have fun playing.

Chapter 40

What You Focus On Expands

"Your mind moves in the direction of its dominant thought."

—Marshall Sylver

Truly all you have to do is have fun and be happy. Since what you focus on expands, focus on what's right. Let go of what's not fun. Focus on the good of others and you'll find more good. Focus on their shortcomings and you'll find plenty. Be kind to yourself, and appreciate what you do that works, and take steps to teach yourself better ways to deal with what doesn't. Surrender to the fact that things are the way they are and use your energy to go for more instead of focusing on what isn't. Realize that everything happens for a purpose and it serves you. Victory goes to the person who plays the game the best and not to the person who gets into the right game. Champions can win at whatever they do. Excellence is an attitude and a way of life. Play as if there's no time out in this game. Use all your available resources. Everything counts. There's no rehearsal. Learn to play when the game gets tough and you'll be able to play the game when it's easy.

I have a personal trainer named Lee Goldsmith who helps me stay on track physically. Lee is probably one of the greatest physical trainers in the country. One day I was complaining that I wasn't feeling well and wanted to cut the workout short. He said, "Marshall, anybody can work out when they feel good. The difference is when you aren't motivated and you still work out. That's when you'll see some gains." Default good and bad and realize it is always you that decided what is good and what is bad. Let go of good luck or bad luck and realize it is you who chooses what it is.

There is an old story about a farmer living in the hills of Kentucky with his son. Their sole source of income was plowing the fields with a plow horse they'd had for many years. One day as the son was plowing the field, the horse reared up, broke away from the plow, and ran off into the foothills. The neighbors said, "Wow, that's bad luck. Now you're not able to plow your fields and harvest your crops and feed yourselves." The old farmer said, "Good luck, bad luck, who knows." Five days later, the plow horse, being strong and study from plowing the fields for so long, returned with five wild mares. The farmer and his son captured all the horses and hooked them up to the plow. Now they were able to plow the fields in a fourth the time and harvest that many more crops. The neighbors all said, "Wow, that's good luck. You've got all those horses." The old farmer said, "Good luck, bad luck, who knows." One day as the son was strapped into the plow, all six horses pulling him through the field, the wild mares got spooked, reared up, and dragged him through the field, breaking both his arms and both his legs and putting him in the hospital. The neighbors said to the farmer, "Oh, that's bad luck." The old farmer said, "Good luck, bad luck, who knows." While in the hospital the son was attended to by a beautiful, sweet, young nurse. They fell in love, they got married, and if you've ever been married, Good luck, bad luck, who knows. The moral to the story is, things are as we see them and we decide what is good or bad for us.

Learn to pit your greatest values against your unwanted habits. Ask yourself, do you want to eat that second piece of pie or would you rather have more dates? Do you want to smoke or do you want to be a superstar vocalist? Do you want to gamble or do you want to have financial independence? You don't have to fix anything to go for more. You can begin going for more right now. Go for more, embrace change, step out of your comfort zones. Do something different today and put yourself at stake.

Say these words out loud: "No risk, no goodies." Smile, and say it often: "No risk, no goodies." Risk today, risk and call someone who you've been putting off making amends with. Risk today and ask for what you want from other people. Risk today and take a chance on yourself. Risk today and use what you've learned. Risk today and ask for the support you want from others. Remember that tomorrow never comes—if you don't do it now you aren't going to do it. It only gets done in the moment that you do it—now. There is a power to commitment. There is a power in telling the world I'm going to do this in this moment. The moment that you make a decision to proceed forward, providence has a funny way of taking over. The universe has a way of aligning and allowing you to accomplish what you set out to do. Commit today and commit often, commit to as many people as possible to get what you want.

Chapter 41

Satori:
Life Is a Series of Nows

"There is nothing better than the here and now."
—MARSHALL SYLVER

Total power is the ability to live the majority of your time in the present. Another word for this is "satori." Satori is a Zen Buddhist term that means to be here, now. An excellent example of satori is skydiving. The moment you step out of the plane while you're skydiving, I guarantee you, you won't think of anything else. Your rent could be due, your mate could have left you, you could have been angry about something that happened to you in your childhood, it doesn't matter. The moment you step out of that plane over a mile in the air and begin falling over a hundred miles per hour, you're not going to think of anything else.

The Buddhists tell a story about a man who was running from a ferocious tiger. While he was fleeing the tiger he fell off a very high cliff. Just beyond the edge of the cliff the man reached out and grabbed hold of a single vine growing out of the side of the ravine. While dangling dangerously moments from his death, he looked up and saw the tiger above him, he looked down and saw the jagged rocks hundreds of feet beneath him. At that moment he also noticed a big juicy ripe strawberry growing from the vine he was holding. Knowing he was just moments from his death, he reached out, grabbed the strawberry, and ate it as he fell.

Another state of satori is when you're in total physical pleasure; in the climax of physical ecstasy, you'll think of nothing else. Ineffective people spend the majority of their time in time other than the present. They think about the past. What they should have or could have done. (They forget what might have been isn't necessarily what would have been.) They live in an imagined future worrying about what might happen and work hard to control that future. The past and the future are what isn't and you have to deal with what is. Constant living in the past is what creates depression, constant living in the future is what creates anxiety. The act of living in the past or future is a Non-Confront of living in the present. You remember Non-Confronts don't you? That's when you don't want to deal with something and the only time you can deal with something is in the present. How much more enjoyable would your life be if you let every moment be a celebration and no matter what the circumstances focused your attention on the present?

"Living in the present is the best use of the past and gives us more in the future."

I have a minister friend who while writing his sermons always thinks about how much he's missing making love to his wife and wishes he had more time to do it. Whenever he's making love with his wife he thinks about the sermon he should be writing. He misses both experiences totally. If you're going to think about playing while you're working, the quality of your work is going to suffer. If you feel guilty about playing when there's work to be done you can't possibly enjoy the sweetness of unbridled pleasure.

Any second spent dwelling on a less than enjoyable moment from the past robs you of the potential to enjoy the present. The present moment will never be available to you again. You cannot get it back. If your parents, your ex-lover, or your children did something to you in the past that caused you pain, and you spend time dwelling on it in the present moment, you're robbing from yourself. Live in the moment. Experience the moment for what it is.

The past does not equal the present or even the future. When you find your life less than perfect it is because you are not living in the moment. To me this is a living hell. How do we get out of this hell? You must find something perfect in your life right now.

When I'm having a hard day and it seems impossible to be in the moment, I stop and look at my hand. When I look at my hand, what happens to me is that I realize that my hand is an incredible mechanism. This creation, which can pick up objects or manipulate a keyboard or paint a portrait, is such a piece of perfection that it's hard for me to think that I don't have anything in my life. As I look at my hands I realize that I'm using my eyes and the miracle of the two makes it a perfect day for me. I'm lucky to be living this very moment.

It's the same in relationships. If you're in a bad relationship, and you're looking for something perfect, I guarantee you, there is something perfect about the relationship. Sometimes it's not easy to find it. Sometimes the perfection is pain. Suppose you are in an abusive relationship. Maybe perfection is finally learning to stand up for yourself and saying, "No more. I will not tolerate this for another moment of my life." It is painful but maybe had you not learned your lesson now you might have gotten into a worse relationship that might have ended in death or permanent injury. It always seems that our own pain is worse than the other guy's, and if we can focus on the things that are perfect, all of a sudden we can find our way out.

Another way I get back to the present is I get in touch with my senses in that moment. I'll reach my hand out and touch the surface of my desk. I'll focus my vision on something near me and really notice the details. I'll really listen to all the sounds around me and discern what they are. The only sense I don't come in touch with when I want satori is the one most people use without realizing it, that is the sense of taste. Many people will eat something when they're feeling lonely or bored or frustrated because the act of eating stimulates your senses at least momentarily to come back to the here and now. The moment you put a piece of food in your mouth you taste the food and you're in instant satori. Obviously if you're an overweight person and you want to lose weight this is a counterproductive way to get back to the present.

By being here, now, means you will put your full attention on the present moment. If you're at work you work hard so when you play you can play hard. The added bonus of living in the moment is that you begin to notice things that other people don't. It'll seem like you get more time, because you'll enjoy your moments more. You'll begin to notice details of how things really are, and you'll gain a greater insight into what you should or can be doing. There's no way to change the past and no one can possibly deal with the future until it becomes the present. So your first lesson toward total power is to learn to be here, now.

Another element of satori is that even while you're in the here and now, you must learn the ability to project forward. What this means is you must be able to look where you are in your current path and be able to project forward to see where the path is leading. Now, this is different from living in the future in that you simply observe the future as if it were a movie you're watching. You don't allow it to have any impact on you now, other than changing the course of your path. You have no emotional attachment to the future, you only do this as a lesson. Each and every one of us will be faced with a series of choices throughout our lives that will determine the direction our life takes.

For example, years ago I was a heavy smoker. Now I have sixteen nieces and nephews with nine brothers and sisters, and even though my family is very large, we're very close. One day one of my young nephews asked me for a cigarette. It was in that single moment I realized that if I stayed on the path I was then on, one day I would have to explain to my own children not to smoke even though daddy did. I also realized that on my current path I could, by example, be responsible for a great number of family members that I loved becoming smokers, in that moment starting with my nephew. How about you?

What's happening in your life that's making you less than effective and taking you down a path that you don't want to go? Will the choice that you make to have one more drink of alcohol keep you moving down that path of physical self-destruction? What about your relationships? If you keep closing down or not communicating, do you think the current relationship will still be there in one year, five years, or ten years from now? How about your money? Could you ever reach financial independence doing things the way that you're doing them now?

"What you do today will determine how you feel tomorrow."

This process of projection works just as well in the short term. Before you have that next glass of wine project forward to the morning and see if you like how it feels. Before you open your mouth to prove to your mate that you're right, project forward and notice whether or not that's going to have you sleeping on the couch tonight. Before you gamble away that money, go forward a couple of hours and experience the emotion of not being able to pay your rent.

Remember there is no right or wrong, there are only consequences. Just be certain they are the consequences that you want.

Life is going to teach you lessons and the lessons are going to get harder and harder until you learn them, and you'll know that you've learned them when you finally change your actions.

To know if you're on the right path, if it's the effective path to be on, you must know where you are going. Do you remember the exercise you did in the beginning of this book about using your imagination to create your perfect day at work and your perfect day at play? Is your current path leading you closer to that day or further away? It's either one or the other. Projecting forward quickly and determining where you're going so you can come back to the present, making any necessary adjustments, is the most powerful way to notice where you're at in your life.

As I've said before, when a rocket blasts off on a mission to the moon it's constantly monitored and thousands of adjustments are made just to get it to its destination. No one gets angry that it's off course; in fact it's clearly understood that no matter how well the mission is planned, it's definitely going to get off course. Instead the adjustments are made in an unemotional, detached, and focused way during the mission. Do the same thing for your life. Realize that you're going to get off your path from time to time and expect to. Project forward quickly each time you notice the path going in a way that's less than fun and see if you like where it's going.

Chapter 42

The Four Steps to Total Enlightenment

To begin with let's define enlightenment and why you would want to live the enlightened life. The dictionary defines enlightenment as being in the light or knowing the universal truth of life. Can you imagine what kind of peace you'd experience if you knew the truth at all times? You'd be able to make intelligent decisions regarding your life. You'd have more power to create your life exactly the way you wanted to. Imagine knowing exactly what to do in any circumstance to create the highest amount of emotional, spiritual, financial, and physical abundance.

The first step is to **surrender and find your life perfect**. Surrender to yourself, to others, and to your present place in life. Surrender and find your life perfect. Enjoy every moment as the learning experience that it is. Live each moment for what it is and accept the responsibility to enjoy each moment. Love your life and have the faith that it's unfolding exactly the way that's perfect for you. You may not be able to understand why it is your life is happening the way that it is and yet just do it. Decide right now that your life is happening in immaculate universal order.

Many people meet this lesson with a certain amount of resistance. Very few people want to admit that their life is less than what they want it to be. They question the idea of being able to find every moment in their lives perfect. People ask about when someone dies, or about the starving children in the world, or the homeless. Finding your life perfect is not a way to ignore what's happening around you. Actually, just the opposite. It's a way to realize that everything happens for a purpose and it serves the master plan of the universe. Finding your life in any way less than perfect is a waste of your time. When someone dies, it doesn't necessarily mean that's the worst thing that could happen for them. In fact quite often it could have been the best thing that could have happened to them. When I see the starving people in this world it reminds me to sit up, take notice, and realize that if we don't do something right now, the entire planet is going to starve.

I believe that people who have nothing in an abundant universe tend to be people who do nothing. People who take personal action end up being the people who find the path to enlightenment, surrendering and enjoying whatever they receive. Expending any energy on wishing things were different uses up energy that could have been used in the process of attainment. Oftentimes when I hear people curse the universe for their circumstances, I wonder to myself, how would they respond if they believed the universe had planned it that way? Instead of getting angry or depressed because the world did you wrong, thank your universe, and surrender to the fact that you don't always know what's best for you.

When you learn to surrender and find your life perfect, you have mastered the first step in finding fulfillment in life.

The second step in finding enlightenment is to **forgive the past completely.** When you learn to truly forgive others you release the negative energy that will stop the universe from providing the blessing that it has to offer you.

Most people are carrying around so much emotional baggage that it's a wonder they have any energy left to carry on the responsibilities of today. Once you release the emotional baggage that you hold on to so dearly you will free your spiritual mind to grow. If you've ever had a garden, you know that you first dig up the soil and get it ready for planting. Once you plant your crops you must guard against the weeds that will grow and choke out what you've planted. It's important to remove all the weeds so they don't kill the good plants. Emotional baggage does the same thing to your mind. When you hold on to your problems or hold on to resentments these weeds will cloud your thinking and eventually will choke out everything that the universe has to provide for you. Who haven't you forgiven in your life? What emotional baggage are you carrying with you that stops you from getting the things that you want from life?

Forgiving is a freeing event to all that seek to truly forgive. Choose this moment to forgive the past completely, let it go and feel that freedom for life rush through your body and soul. The difference between a physical scar and an emotional or mental one is that an emotional and mental scar can be healed with no signs.

The people that hurt you really had no idea of the pain they were inflicting. If Sam punches Bob in the stomach and Sam feels the pain instead of Bob, I guarantee you that Sam is going to stop punching Bob. In fact no one would hurt anybody if they felt the pain they were inflicting on other people. When someone has caused you pain, when a lover has broken your heart, when your parents scarred you, forgive them. The past is to learn from, not to hold on to.

Remember that whoever hurt you did the very best they could with what they had at the time. Not forgiving them gives them the power to hurt you again and again. They will continue to hurt you until you are able to release your feelings. When you hold on to that resentment you give away your power. If you truly don't like the person that hurt you, then stop giving them the power to keep hurting you. The second step to total enlightenment is to completely forgive what has happened in the past.

The third step to total enlightenment is to **practice utilization versus toleration**. Utilize what comes up rather than tolerate what comes up. Some people believe that they're doing just great because they can handle whatever comes up in their lives. When putting up with circumstances in your life you must not only surrender, you must embrace the circumstances as perfection. Ask yourself what's great about what's happening right now. Ask how you can use these occurrences to go for more. Every moment of your life is filled with opportunities and lessons to be learned. Embrace all moments in your life, and utilize them to go for more instead of less.

Years ago I was a professional magician. At the time David Copperfield had already done seven TV specials and had cornered the market on magic performances on television. Rather than getting angry, I decided to utilize all of the talents of observation and understanding the human psyche that I had developed as a magician to become the leading authority in the world on hypnosis.

I now hypnotize more people and teach more people how to hypnotize themselves and others than almost anyone on the planet. Looking back on what might have seemed like a bad situation in a highly competitive magic market, I realized that the level of joy and confidence and contribution I'm feeling now never could have come about if I had experienced that as a bad situation. I realize now that the very best thing that could have happened to me is exactly what did. Trust life that the very best is happening to you. Have faith that you will understand the lesson when you are supposed to and not before. Trust that everything happens with a universal order to it. When you learn to take whatever happens in your life and utilize the circumstance for good, you'll have learned the ultimate lesson. There are no mistakes. Edison knew over a thousand ways not to invent the lightbulb. Columbus was looking for India. Post-it Notes started off as tape that wouldn't stick. There are no mistakes, only opportunities to learn and to utilize. Utilize your life and don't sell yourself short by just tolerating life.

The fourth step to total enlightenment is to **serve others**. Once you have mastered the art of utilization you'll have more abundance in every area of your life than you could ever imagine. The steel magnate Andrew Carnegie spent half his life making millions and half his life giving it away. Since during his life he was always in service to others it became easy to enlist their support and get them to work toward his master plan. Once you begin to finally live totally in the present moment, while being aware of where your path is going, and you've released all mental and emotional garbage from the past, you'll start creating passion, profit, and power in your life. Your heart will feel secure to open up to others. The love for others is the greatest gift that you can share with the universe.

"No man has ever risen to real stature until he has found that it is finer to serve somebody else than it is to serve himself."

—WOODROW WILSON

Once you've learned to utilize whatever comes up in your life, it will be as if the floodgates of abundance had burst open to shower you with the riches of success. You'll deal with your relationships in a way that will allow others to be the way they are and you will have no attachment to how other people respond to you. Since you will be without judgment, you'll accept that those around you are doing the very best they can with what they have. You'll move in a loving spirit that will enable you to seek the goodness of others while life provides you with the opportunity to help others. When you love others and give to them in a freely loving way, people will want to be around you and help you in all areas of your life.

As your interactions with others become more joyful more opportunities will open up to you. People will want to be near you and will want to give you more because they know that you will give freely back to them. When you focus on the serving of others, people will be inspired to support you on your path creating even more abundance.

> *"Only a life lived for others is worthwhile"*
> —ALBERT EINSTEIN

To recap, the four steps to total enlightenment are: Step 1, find your life perfect and deal with what emerges. Imagine and have faith that your life is unfolding exactly the way it's supposed to be even if you don't understand. Step 2, forgive the past completely. Do it for yourself and reap the harvest. Forgive and recapture the power that you've given away. Step 3, learn the art of utilization instead of toleration and cursing the universe for what is going on around you. Utilize what the universe is doing for you now and be aware that there's a grand plan for your life. Power comes from taking whatever you're getting and finding the value in it. When you've done the first three steps you'll have more love, more money, and more peace of mind than you can ever use alone. These three steps provide you with the resources to take the most important step and that is to serve others. Find joy in total contribution. The greatest gift you can give to the universe is to give back to the world what you have reaped.

When you have mastered enlightenment you will know that you know. You trust the universe and expect to have the necessary tools to deal with life in harmony. Enlightened people live in the light, they understand the truth. The simple mind-set of believing you have the answers will let your mind draw upon the universal storehouse of knowledge.

This is sometimes called "the collective awareness," as Napoleon Hill talked about in his very famous and effective book *Think and Grow Rich*.

He called it the mastermind. How do you think you would feel on a day-to-day basis if you were absolutely certain you had all the answers to all of life's challenges? When you reach that state in life, no matter what came up, you'd know exactly what to do and have the confidence to do it.

What you believe is true for you and nothing else. If you believe you're slow or have a tough time learning, you impede the learning process. You actually tell your brain to interrupt the electron connection that makes learning easy.

In my private sessions, I've taught people that used to believe that they had a learning disability, like dyslexia, to refuse to believe the programming the outside world forced upon them. I teach them how to reprogram their minds in ways that allow them to reach their true intellectual potential. Everything begins in thought. As Kahlil Gibran said in his famous book *The Prophet,* "As a man thinketh so he is."

What would happen if you believed the reverse? What if you believed you were a genius? Think you are a genius and you'll begin thinking the way a genius thinks. Every mind has the same potential at birth. Some people decide through the circumstances of their life that they're smart and they'll know the answers. Others decide that they're not smart and fulfill that program. Everything begins with thought. Right now say the words: "I am a genius." I know if you said it at all you probably smiled. I also know if you don't say them you're denying that potential in yourself. So say it again out loud: "I am a genius." It got easier to say that time, didn't it? In the Subconscious Reprogramming sessions one of the rules of the mind is that every time you respond in a certain way it gets easier to respond that way again. Learn to be happy with the simplest of things and the greatest of things will occur more often.

The next time you're having a tough day and you think your life is bad remember this Indian bricklayer who was working on a four-story building in India. One day his boss asked him to bring the bricks down from the fourth floor, so he carefully created a pulley system for a barrel to bring the bricks down. He tied the rope down to the ground so he could later go down and release the rope and let the barrel down with the bricks. After carefully loading the barrel with these heavy bricks, he went down to the bottom to release the rope. Having misjudged the weight of the barrel, the moment he untied the rope, the barrel began speeding down from the fourth floor. Not wanting to damage the barrel and destroy the bricks he held fast to the rope. Since the barrel of bricks was heavier than he was, as he was going up and the barrel was going down, the heavy barrel, loaded with bricks, hit him on his shoulder, breaking his collarbone. As he continued to fly up, at the top of his flight, his fingers jammed into the pulley, breaking all of them. By now he was in so much pain he could barely hold on, and yet he held on. Simultaneously, the barrel smashed into a thousand pieces, sending all the bricks flying. Without the bricks the barrel was lighter than the man and the man came flying down, holding on to the piece of rope, while the splintered barrel went flying up, shooting splinters into his backside. At the bottom of his flight the man hit the ground with a solid thud.

By now he was totally exhausted and he made the mistake of letting go of the rope, releasing the pieces of the barrel that had gone up to come falling back down, landing on his head, which is what put him in the hospital. So the next time you're having a tough day, realize you can handle it and learn the lessons as you go along.

Chapter 43

Subconscious Reprogramming for More Power

"It's not enough to learn, one must become."
—MARSHALL SYLVER

Now that you have learned many powerful and effective strategies for relating, it's time to integrate this material for maximum impact on your life. This chapter, like the two similar ones on Passion and Profit programming, is a synopsis of the material taught in this section. The material is written in a specific language syntax to have the greatest possible impact on your subconscious mind. The chapter can be used in one of two ways. One is to record it onto an audiocassette and then play it back as you relax. When you record it, make sure you allow for about two minutes at the front of the tape for you to breathe deep and relax. When you record it onto tape you will read the script in the second person instead of as it's written in the first person. "You will relax" instead of "I will relax." "You recognize that you are indeed worthy . . ." instead of "I recognize that I am indeed worthy . . ." In this way the tape you have created becomes your own personal Subconscious Reprogrammer.

Another method of reprogramming your mind with this is to use the reprogramming script as an affirmation exercise. You simply read the

reprogramming statements out loud to yourself every day exactly as they are written. This method is extremely effective because it forces you to focus your entire attention on the new programs. Often when we are listening we sometimes let our mind wander. By being an active participant in your positive reinforcement, these statements will help you stay more focused and hear what you're saying. Both methods are valuable. If you choose to use this method of reprogramming, then read the entire chapter out loud exactly as it is written.

Subconscious Reprogramming Script for POWER:

I recognize that self-mastery is the ability to control my thoughts, my habits, my disciplines physically, emotionally, and mentally. I take full responsibility for where I am right now. I recognize my current circumstances were created by me and I can choose to create them differently in any moment.

I recognize that my financial, emotional, and physical health are totally dependent upon my ability to take action. I know that power is for use. I've decided right now to step out of being a student and decide to be what I am studying.

I am indeed a person of power. I take immediate, productive, positive steps toward what I want. I know to expect positive results in advance and I play the game to its utmost. I realize that everything begins in thought and I choose my thoughts carefully, recognizing that I am, indeed, in control of my mind.

I recognize I can create my life on purpose. I know that I can now take charge of the fifteen hundred words per minute moving through my brain. I am not a prisoner of fate. I, indeed, control my mind and my mind takes charge of my destiny. As I think, so I am, and providence has a way of taking care of me once I've decided which direction my life will take.

I am indeed a worthy human being. People love me and I am a money and a people magnet. Each and every day I look for things to happen in ways that support me, and what I look for, I find. What I focus on expands.

I know that I can win the game and to win the game, I must

play, and I eagerly play the game of life. Each and every day that goes by, I'm getting healthier all the time. I am indeed a master of my own mind and my own personal programming.

I am careful about the words that I say when I use the expression "I" or "I am." I know that when I use words "I" or "I am," they immediately program me for the words that follow and I constantly talk to myself in ways that are self-empowering and self-nurturing by saying things like "I am unstoppable. Everything I touch turns to gold. I am a dynamic, creative, awesome human being."

I know that reality is created through validation and I seek out validation for the things that I want and I easily move over the things that do not support me. I realize how other people can program me, so that when people say things to me that are less than what I want, I make a mental note that it's their opinion and not what's true.

I recognize that I indeed have all the tools necessary to accomplish what I want financially, in my relationships, and in my life, and in both my physical and emotional body. I recognize that I must become good at planning and I plan each and every day in advance and set down priorities to accomplish the things that I want.

I am also disciplined and I recognize that in my life I'll have either discipline or regrets. I know that discipline is really just a mental habit and I choose to create mental habits that empower me and serve me and support me in getting what I want. My mind moves in the direction of its dominant thought. What I focus on expands and nothing has any power except the power that I give to it. I choose to give power to circumstances, people, and events that support me in getting what I want.

I recognize it takes twenty-one days to form a new habit and that a habit is something done often, hence easily. I recognize that the more excited and impassioned I get about making the changes that I want in my life, the easier it gets to make them. Each and every day that goes by, my new, positive, productive, powerful habits are happening easier for me.

I realize that as life goes by, I indeed choose in any given moment how I want to respond. I ask myself what questions, instead of why questions. Instead of asking myself "Why is this happening to me?" I ask myself, "What can I do right now that's positive and productive and moves me in the direction of what I want?"

I recognize sometimes I don't know I'm getting somewhere when I truly am and so therefore I'm persistent. I'm persistent in going for the things that I want, realizing when I'm doing something wrong, right can feel wrong to me. I choose to experiment with my life, to risk in new ways, to test new ways of doing, test new ways of being and thinking and doing to produce new results in my life.

I am excited about changing course the moment I realize I'm off course and I forgive myself quickly by saying things like "That's not like me, I'm a positive individual." "That's not like me, I lose weight easily and readily." "That's not like me, I always focus on going for more in my relationships and creating more love and abundance around me."

I now have a new and powerful method of changing my habits. I have now learned to act as if what I want is already true. I know that when I "act as if," I am confident. I send out to my subconscious mind the signal to find the elements of confidence stored there, and as I act as if I'm confident, the outside world reflects back to me that which I project. As each and every day goes by, I choose to act as if what I want is unfolding in the moment. As I now act as if all of my greatest desires are happening, I find the evidence around me to support that.

I realize that self-mastery is the ability to be passionate, and every day I choose to be passionate about my relationships, about my inspiration, about the accumulation of wealth. I possess an emotional intensity that's magnetic, charismatic, and draws people to me. I move with a definition of purpose. I'm so excited about what's happening in my life that I desire to share it with others, and because I do share it with them in a way that's inspirational, they desire to support me.

I understand that nothing has any power except the power that I give to it and there is a way for me to get what I want that's different from how I've been doing it and it works. I live by the strategy of the ultimate scorecard. I know that I'm always winning or losing and I choose to win. I know I'm either getting closer or further away in my relationships and I choose to ask myself the question: "How can I bring us closer?"

I realize either I did it or I didn't and I choose to let go of the gray area and be honest with myself. I know that I must be willing to do whatever it takes, more than willing to do what I'm willing to do, and I am willing to do whatever the task at hand requires. I realize that putting myself at stake is powerful and I choose to put myself at stake with the world, with myself, with all of the people I encounter, by committing to them and telling them exactly what I'm doing now and what I intend to do in the future.

I constantly ask myself: "What's positive and productive and moves me in the direction of what I want most?" I realize that everything I do either detracts or assists me in my successes. I know the only way I can truly do something ineffective is to do nothing, so every moment I choose to do something. By making my decisions quickly, by taking some immediate action, I know that I'll either step closer to what I want or learn a way that doesn't work, which takes me one step closer anyway.

I've learned to fail forward fast and I never see failure as failure, only as the lesson of one more way that doesn't work and one step closer to what does. I know that action and not thought is what gets me what I want. I take action easily and quickly. I know that in order to win I must be willing to lose. I know it's impossible to win a game that I don't play. I risk often. I risk easily and I risk at the highest levels, knowing that tomorrow never comes and that I alone am responsible for my success.

Anything I don't do right now isn't going to get done. I realize there's no time like the present. The quality of my life is the quality of my communication, both with myself and with others. I have now released the word "try" from my life, realizing that try implies failure and I'll either do it or I won't.

I've also released the word "can't" from my vocabulary, recognizing it's either I don't know how to or I don't want to. If I don't want to, I choose to release the thing that causes me stress and with it the tension. If it's that I don't know how to, today I make the choice to learn, to move one step closer to what I want by attaining the knowledge necessary.

I know that success is a habit and a discipline and I also release the word "but" from my vocabulary, recognizing it negates everything that comes before it.

I pay close attention to what I'm hoping for and instead of hoping, I start knowing my success is assured.

I know that if something happens is different from when it happens and that saying when it happens is expressing the positive expectancy that it will occur. Success leaves clues and even though it's simple, I know it's not easy. When I do what wealthy people do, I create wealth.

I make this day a game and I play to win, and I enjoy the game as much as the victory. I recognize that all success in life is dependent upon my preparation for the game. I realize it's not enough to win in the moment; I must constantly prepare myself for the game or play the game. Success in any area goes to the person who realizes for everything there is a season. I know that others who might have been born into more fortunate circumstances have nothing on me, that I have everything that they have.

I choose to realize that I can get what I want regardless of my current circumstances, that it only takes desire, drive, and dedication. And I am totally committed to being the very best at what I do. I know that someone has to be the best and it's going to be someone just like me, so I commit to being the best and striving toward excellence every day.

I let go of excuses and alibis and I put myself at stake. I realize that other people make excuses, not me. Other people complain about their circumstances, not me; I utilize them. I don't want to know the odds and I take full responsibility for my own success.

I always answer people when they ask how I'm doing with "fantastic" or "perfect" or "awesome." I know that when I say I'm fantastic or perfect or awesome, it programs into my mind the thought that this is how I am and my subconscious mind immediately goes to work to find the elements to support me in being that way. I know when I'm having a challenging day that I can say, "I'm getting better all the time." As I say that to myself, my mind seeks out the evidence that things are, indeed, getting better and, sure enough, they do. I know that small commitments lead to large commitments, that some is better than none, and better late than never.

I know that it doesn't get better than this, that here and now is the most effective place to be. I realize ineffective people spend the majority of their time in a time other than the present. Not me. I am committed to the here and the now and to enjoying every second of my life. Because I enjoy my life here and now, my life is full and rich and wide and it allows me the opportunity to get more. I let my credo be "Work hard and play hard" so I can get more pleasure from all of my life. I now focus my entire attention on where I am at this moment. I know if my mind is going to be somewhere else, I might as well go there, and instead I choose to focus my attention on the here and the now. All of these beneficial ideas and concepts make a deep and lasting impression upon my subconscious mind, never to be removed, to be recalled the moment I say or think the word "Power." (*Take a long deep breath right now and clench your hand into a fist and say the word "Power" out loud. Take another long deep breath right now and as you exhale say the word "Power" out loud.*)

I realize what might have been is not necessarily what would have been and what should have been is what isn't. To win the game of life, I know how to deal with what is, as well as with whatever emerges. I realize I don't really have a choice other than dealing with what emerges and I do so joyfully. I see my problems as challenges. I embrace stress and I recognize that the more stress I can endure, the greater the rewards in my life. I realize that in my life there are many puzzles, many challenges, and yet they do have solutions and I can win the game.

I realize the key to enjoying the game is to have as much fun playing as I have winning and I always savor the wanting as much as the having. I know that all I truly have to do is have fun and be happy. Since what I focus on expands, I focus on what's working. I let go of what's not fun. I focus on the good in others and I find more good.

I focus on the good in myself and that too expands. I surrender to the fact that things are the way they are and I use my energy to go for more. I realize that everything happens for a reason and that it serves me.

I recognize that anybody can win at an easy game. It's when I win at a game that was challenging that I become a true champion.

I know that everything counts. There is no time-out. I live impeccably. I play to win and I enjoy the game. I've nullified good and bad and I've let go of good luck and bad luck, realizing it's always been me that decided.

I know I don't have to fix anything to go for more. I can begin going for more right now. I know in order for things to change, I must change. I know the world is never going to change, it will always stay the same. Right now I take charge of my destiny and I change myself and go for more. I embrace change. I step out of my comfort zone and I do something differently right now. In my own mind, I think these words: "No risk, no goodies." Throughout my day, I smile and say it often, "No risk, no goodies." I risk today.

I ask for what I want from others. I risk and take a chance on myself. I risk today and ask for support from others. If I don't do it now, I'm not going to do it. I know that things only get done in the moment that I do them now. I also realize that if what I was setting out to do were easy, everybody would have already done it and there'd be no satisfaction. By virtue of the fact that I'm challenged in my pursuits, I know that I am taking a step in the direction of great attainment, of great victory, of a champion's win.

I realize that the moment I enjoy the journey as much as the destination, my life is fulfilling, enjoyable, and worthy of the celebration. I realize that power is the ability to take action now. It's the ability to live the majority of my life in satori, in the present.

I find myself projecting forward only as an observer, only to see what's there and to know whether or not I am on the right path. I surrender quickly and find my life perfect no matter what's occurring around me, recognizing that finding my life any less than perfect is a waste of my time. I am no fool. I choose to find my life perfect and surrender to the fact that it's unfolding as it should be and I'm happy with that.

I quickly forgive others and forgive my past, realizing the past is not the present, nor does it equal the future. In the present I make choices to enjoy my life, to live every moment as if it were my last. From this day forward, I choose to utilize the challenges that come up for me, not simply to tolerate them, but to actually embrace them and to use them to go for more.

I know that when I do this process of utilization, it allows me to

PASSION, PROFIT, & POWER   295

constantly create abundance in my relationships, in my wealth, and in my emotional and physical well-being. I choose to be abundant now by experiencing whatever comes up as perfect and going for more. I know that the greatest way to create more in my life is to serve others, and as I serve others, they're inspired to give more back to me, completing the never-ending circle of abundance and excitement in my life.

I realize that I indeed am a powerful, productive, intelligent human being certainly worthy of all the wonderful things this life has to give me. I now trust myself and I stay in the present moment. All I really have to do is be happy and I'm happiest with the simplest of things; so the greatest of things appear even more miraculous. Power is for use. Power is to take action now. Do it now. All of these beneficial ideas and concepts make a deep and lasting impression upon my subconscious mind, never to be removed, to be recalled the moment I say the word "Power." *(Take a long deep breath and breathe out now and say the word "Power" out loud. Take another long deep breath and as you exhale say the word "Power" out loud.)*

Appendix

MAKING YOUR OWN PERSONALIZED SUBCONSCIOUS REPROGRAMMING TAPES

"If you're going to run tapes in your mind you might as well do the recording on purpose."

—MARSHALL SYLVER

Now that you have read this book, you understand the ingredients for producing your own successful Subconscious Reprogramming audiocassettes.

Using a cassette is actually what we call Projected Subconscious Reprogramming. Even though it's your own voice, you record it in the second person by saying: "You easily and readily lose weight" as opposed to "I easily and readily lose weight." In this way it will be as if someone else is talking to you. To create your cassette, here is the specific formula.

Step No. 1: Write out the program you are working on. Be it weight loss or nonsmoking or prosperity or speaking clearly and with confidence, when you write out your program, make it about eight to ten minutes long. When you write on a regular piece of paper that will be about three pages.

Step No. 2: Leave two minutes of blank tape at the beginning of your recording to breathe deeply and relax. This will allow for any leader tape as well as give you ample opportunity to get settled in as you listen to the tape.

Step No. 3: Set your recording levels. Do a test. Record a few sentences and play it back. If it's at the proper volume, continue from there.

Step No. 4: Record your prewritten program. That's the program that you wrote in step 1 that was eight to ten minutes long regarding the area that you're working on right now.

Step No. 5: Give yourself a five count back to full awareness as follows. "On number 1, you feel relaxed and comfortable. On number 2, your body has a natural energy coursing through its veins. On number 3, you feel as if your body has been washed in a crystal-clear brook and you feel fantastic. On number 4, your eyes and mind are being washed in that brook and you are seeing and thinking more clearly. On number 5, open your eyes wide awake, fully aware."

Just a couple of things to think about as you make your own Subconscious Reprogramming audiocassettes. First of all, be good to yourself and be gentle on your own voice. The first time I heard my own voice, it didn't sound like me, and the first time you hear your own voice on audiocassette, it can be a little bit surprising. Trust me, you sound great.

Secondly, since you are creating this audiocassette so that you will focus on training your mind for success in a specific area, then besides the specific script that I have given you there are other elements that you can include that will make it more effective. The elements that you want to include are a plan of what you want and how you want to attain it. Be specific. It should also include a section visualizing where you want yourself to actually be. Project yourself into the future and experience it as if it were already a reality. This will excite your imagination and make it easier for you to "act as if." Finally, for support and reinforcement, listen to your tape for approximately twenty-one days. As you know by now, it takes about that long to form a new habit and to affix it in your subconscious mind.

As you progress, you're going to need to rerecord your cassette to keep up with those wonderful goals and plans that you are attaining.

Since I've also given you the rules of how your mind operates and how to structure mega-impactive subconscious suggestions, you now know how to create your own personal Subconscious Reprogramming tapes for any specific area you are working on to truly get what you want.

GOING FOR MORE: STEPS TO ADVANCED INTEGRATION

"What if you viewed your life as a seminar?"

So where do you go from here? You know how to create awesome relationships, you understand the strategies of the ultrawealthy, you now have the ability to live in the present. Even though I have only skimmed the surface there is more than enough here to massively enhance your life. Making your Subconscious Reprogramming tapes will have a dramatic impact on how much effect this material has on your life. This is really not a book, it is a way of life. I often ponder how much more enjoyment all of us would get from our lives if we viewed it as a seminar. At my seminars I put people through many exercises that are designed to teach them the lessons neccesary to increase the quality of their lives. Some of them make the attendees laugh and many make them cry. In the very least the processes make them think about new ways of responding and being. Since they are in the safe confines of the seminar room, no matter how challenging the confronting of their fears, they always know that they will be all right. In the end they'll eat the fire, walk on the broken glass or fire, smash the board, and make that breakthrough and walk away victorious.

I consider the musician and lyricist Kenny Loggins to be one of the most spiritually centered people on the planet. Not only has his music brought much joy to my life, it has also given me many spiritual insights for which I am eternally grateful. One of the most enlightening albums ever created is his *Leap of Faith* album. It is appropriately titled in that all of our greatest growths are preceded by a leap of faith, a jump into the unknown. In my own jumps I have discovered that it is easier to figure out where I'm going to land after I am in the air than before I launched myself. (There is a unique certainty in having to choose that makes you do so.) In a seminar you know that there is a way to win in the exercises that you do. You know that there is a lesson to be learned that will aid you on your path through the black forest to the castle. Some of the games or exercises have more impact for some than for others. That's fine: you take what you get and what you don't get you don't take.

"Don't dream it, be it."

—THE ROCKY HORROR PICTURE SHOW

The most dangerous thing is when the attendee of the seminar leaves and goes back to the seminar called life and doesn't realize they are one and the same. In that realm it can be easy to pretend that you're not the same (when in fact you are) and that there is no answer to the game or exercises that occur (when in fact there always is). There are certain things that will make the process of living in the light more enjoyable.

"On with the dance and let the joy be unconfined. That's my motto! Whether there is any dance to dance or joy to unconfine!"

—MARK TWAIN

The first step is to **use the advanced integration material**. Live the life. Be what you have read. Since it works, every victory will make it easier—each accomplishment will reinforce the last. Particularly do the verbal or recorded Subconscious Reprogramming every day for at least a week. It will only take you ten minutes and the results will be tremendous.

The second step is to **share the information with others**. This will reinforce the material by its use and help you to surround yourself with people who think the same way you do and support you in what you want. You will be serving them and also keeping yourself congruent.

The third step is to **go for more**. Learn more. Attend a seminar, read another book, advance your life so that the things you learned in the beginning become simpler. If what you were setting out to do were easy, everybody would already have done it and there'd be no satisfaction or reward.

"May all of your greatest desires be instantaneously fulfilled."

—PERSIAN CURSE

"May you live an interesting life."

—CHINESE CURSE

By virtue of the fact that you are challenged by your pursuits, you've already taken the first steps in achieving excellence. If all of your desires were fulfilled the moment that you wanted them, your life would be boring.

Make your journey the adventure. Full effort is full victory. I know that life is challenging, that's what makes it interesting. I also know that if you are on track seventy percent of the time, you are forty percent ahead. Stay on track, every step in the right direction is a win. Find pleasure in being your best. The odds are stacked in your favor. All the resources are right at your fingertips. It's now up to you to determine where you will go. Will this be a celebration of victory or an excuse, like the less effective people. I know you have what it takes and I'm proud to be associated with you. Live every day as if it is your last. Appreciate all the blessings you possess. Take care of others, so they have the energy to support you.

Thanks for letting me be a part of your life. Send me a letter and let me know about your success. Better yet, make plans now to come meet me in person at one of my seminars. You are indeed a loving, desirable, incredible human being, worthy of all the abundance this life has to offer. I leave you with one thought and that is to remember to **Celebrate Life!**

Maximum respect,
Marshall Sylver

SYLVER ENTERPRISES INC. AND
MIND POWER INC.

The mission statement of the companies of Marshall Sylver is to **Entertain, Energize, Educate, and Enlighten.** Through the hundreds of public and private seminars that are held on an annual basis hundreds of thousands of people are positively impacted to make a quantum leap in their own development. Sylver Enterprises sales and motivational seminars are on the cutting edge of subconscious persuasion and motivational technology. Mind Power Inc. television programs can be seen around the world and daily in the United States. Marshall Sylver's hypnosis production show can be frequently seen in Las Vegas, Nevada, as well as in corporate and public appearances worldwide. For information on seminars, shows, other books, and audio and video training materials, contact Sylver Enterprises for a free copy of their magazine newsletter, *The Power Press.* All correspondence and inquiries can be directed to:

Sylver Enterprises Inc.
4545 West Reno, Suite B-2
Las Vegas, NV 89118 U.S.A.
1-800-92-POWER   1-800-927-6937